Insights into the
Doctrine &
Covenants

THE CAPSTONE OF OUR RELIGION

Insights into the
Doctrine &
Covenants

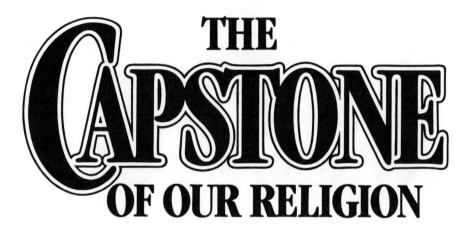

THE
CAPSTONE
OF OUR RELIGION

Edited by Robert L. Millet and Larry E. Dahl

Bookcraft
Salt Lake City, Utah

Library of Congress Catalog Card Number: 88-63457

ISBN 0-88494-684-3

First Printing, 1989

Printed in the United States of America

Contents

Preface

"The Book of Mormon is the 'keystone' of our religion," President Ezra Taft Benson has reminded us, "and *the Doctrine and Covenants is the capstone,* with continuing latter-day revelation. The Lord has placed His stamp of approval on both the keystone and the capstone." (Conference Report, April 1987, p. 105, italics added.) The Prophet Joseph Smith thus asked the telling question: "Take away the Book of Mormon and the revelations, and where is our religion?" He answered, "We have none." (*Teachings of the Prophet Joseph Smith,* p. 71.) Indeed, the Latter-day Saints are not only committed to the fact that God has spoken in ages past, but we glory in "all that He does now reveal," and cherish the belief "that He will yet reveal many great and important things pertaining to the Kingdom of God" (Articles of Faith 1:9).

The book of Doctrine and Covenants is a collection of sacred prophecies, revelations, visions, and inspired instructions given through Joseph Smith and his successors in the Presidency of the restored Church. These divine directives are given not only to members of the Church but to every living soul that shall inhabit the earth in this final dispensation of grace. Thus it is that the Lord's preface to the Doctrine and Covenants declares that "the voice of the Lord is unto all men, and there is none to escape." Thereby "the voice of warning shall be unto all people, by the mouths of my disciples, whom I have chosen in these last days." (D&C 1:2, 4.) The Prophet himself referred to the Doctrine and Covenants as "the foundation of the Church in these last days, and a benefit to the world, showing that the keys of the mysteries of the kingdom of our Savior are again entrusted to man" (see heading to D&C 70).

The essays in this book, *The Capstone of Our Religion: Inspiring Insights into the Doctrine and Covenants*, focus upon some of the salient doctrines and overarching messages contained in the Doctrine and Covenants. No effort has been made here to study that scripture sequentially or section by section, but rather attention has been focused upon major themes running through the whole of the sacred collection. Each of the individual contributors is responsible for his own conclusions, and the volume is a private endeavor and not a production of either Brigham Young University or The Church of Jesus Christ of Latter-day Saints. Although the writers and editors have sought to be in harmony with the teachings of the standard works and the leaders of the Church, the reader should not regard this work as a primary source for gospel understanding but should turn instead to the scriptures and the words of modern prophets for authoritative doctrinal statements.

The authors and editors are committed to the belief that God has spoken anew; that he has made known his mind and will and purposes through prophets and Apostles in this day and age; and that The Church of Jesus Christ of Latter-day Saints is the kingdom of God on earth, is in the line of its duty, and is, in the language of the revelation, "the only true and living church upon the face of the whole earth" (D&C 1:30). We make no apology for the fact that these articles have been written and this book compiled with a bias of belief. It is an expression of testimony, a statement of faith.

ROBERT L. MILLET
LARRY E. DAHL

How Our Doctrine and Covenants Came to Be

Richard O. Cowan

The Doctrine and Covenants is truly a unique book. It is "modern scripture" not only in the sense that it applies to our day, but also because it originated in the present dispensation. Belief in modern revelation is one of the most distinctive tenets of the Latter-day Saints' faith. In a world where there are so many problems and differing religious opinions, current guidance through a living prophet is vital.

The Bible shows how God sent one prophet after another and gave them revelation to guide his children on earth. "Surely the Lord God will do nothing," Amos testified, "but he revealeth his secret unto his servants the prophets" (Amos 3:7). Through the prophet Nephi the Lord promised continued revelation "that I may prove . . . that I am the same yesterday, today, and forever." He then added, "And because that I have spoken one word ye need not suppose that I cannot speak another; for my work is not yet finished; neither shall it be until

Richard O. Cowan is Professor of Church History and Doctrine at Brigham Young University.

the end of man, neither from that time henceforth and forever" (2 Nephi 29:9; compare Hebrews 13:8). The Bible specifically predicts latter-day revelation that would come through Elijah (Malachi 4:5–6), Elias (Matthew 17:11), an angel (Revelation 14:6–7), and even through Christ himself (Acts 3:19–21).

President Spencer W. Kimball testified that since the beginning of the present dispensation, revelation has come "in a never-ending stream" through the prophets whom the Lord has appointed. "Revelation continues," he emphasized, and "the vaults and files of the Church contain these revelations which come month to month and day to day."[1]

All such revelations should be regarded as scripture in a general sense (D&C 68:2–4). From this material the Church makes inspired selections to publish as official, or canonized, scripture. "All inspired sayings and writings are true . . . and should be accepted and believed by all who call themselves Saints," emphasized Elder Bruce R. McConkie. "But the revelations, visions, prophecies, and narrations selected and published for official use are thereby made binding upon the people in a particular and special sense. They become part of the standard works of the Church. They become the standards, the measuring rods, by which doctrine and procedure are determined."[2] Our canon of scripture (what has officially been included in the standard works) is not static; it is dynamic. The Doctrine and Covenants provides an excellent illustration of how this canon of scripture has responded to the needs of the Saints at various times. The content of this book of modern scripture has been expanded and even contracted, and individual revelations have not always been added in the first new edition after they were received.

The Articles and Covenants, 1830

The first step leading to our Doctrine and Covenants came just two months after the Church was organized. At its first conference, held in Fayette, New York, on 9 June 1830, the "Articles and Covenants [were] read by Joseph Smith, Jr. and received by [the] unanimous voice of the whole congregation."[3]

This first formally canonized portion of latter-day revelation consisted of what we now know as sections 20 and 22. The first of these revelations reviews the basic doctrines taught in the Book of Mormon and defines duties of priesthood offices and how ordinances are to be performed; hence it is sometimes called "the constitution of the Church." Section 22 is a brief revelation emphasizing the need for baptism by proper authority. In Joseph Smith's day churches customarily issued statements setting forth basic doctrinal beliefs, procedures, and "platforms"—standards of conduct for the benefit of members or prospective converts. The Lord provided such a statement for his restored Church by revelation in the material accepted as the Articles and Covenants. Early Latter-day Saint missionaries frequently quoted from this document as they taught the restored gospel.

At first, the Prophet did not record his revelations immediately. But the Lord instructed him in July 1830 to "continue in calling upon God in my name, and writing the things which shall be given thee" (D&C 24:5). Joseph Smith complied with this instruction. "As early as the summer of 1830, the Prophet, acting under divine commandment, was engaged in copying and arranging the revelations received up to that time, evidently with a view to their publication in book form."[4] Thus within a few months of the Church's organization, the processes were well under way which would result the following year in the decision to publish the first book of modern revelations.

The Book of Commandments, 1831

No year produced more Doctrine and Covenants revelations than did 1831. Some thirty-seven sections, more than one-fourth of the total, were received during that one year alone. These revelations were copied by hand for the use of the early Saints, but there was a growing demand for them to be more widely available. Therefore an important conference beginning 1 November 1831 approved the first publication of the revelations commonly referred to as the Book of Commandments or Covenants and Commandments. Arrangements were made for the book to be printed on a press which was publishing a Latter-day Saint newspaper in Independence, Missouri.

By the summer of 1833 the project of publishing the revelations was nearing completion. Five large "forms," or sheets, each containing thirty-two pages, hence a total of 160 pages in all, had been printed. On 20 July however, an anti-Mormon mob broke into the log home of editor William W. Phelps and destroyed the press. Through the quick and courageous action of Church members who happened to be at the scene, several hundred of the large unbound sheets were rescued. The Saints cherished the copies of the revelations that they had saved and bound them in various ways.

The revelations published in the Book of Commandments roughly parallel the first sixty-four sections of our present Doctrine and Covenants. Hence they included not only the instructions on Church organization (now section 20), but also important information on qualifications for Church service (section 4), the Atonement (sections 18 and 19), the pre-earthly existence and fall (section 29), the "Law of the Church" (section 42), the last days (section 45), gifts of the Spirit (section 46), and the establishment of Zion (sections 58, 63, and 64, etc.).

We do not know, however, how many other revelations might have been included if the work had not been disrupted. The Book of Commandments text ended with the phrase "the rebellious are not of the blood of Ephraim" in what is now the middle of the thirty-sixth verse in section 64; the remaining seven and one-half verses were added in the next edition. It is likely that section 68 would have been included, since this revelation was given at the time of the November 1831 conference and specifically included "items in addition to the covenants and commandments" (D&C 68:13). These items included instructions concerning the duties of bishops, parents, and members. What is now known as section 133, with its emphasis on preparing for the last days, was definitely to be included. In May of 1833 the Saints' newspaper, the *Evening and Morning Star,* published this revelation, explaining that the *Star* had earlier printed the preface (section 1) and so was now publishing the appendix (section 133) to the book of revelations which would be issued within the year. During the previous ten months the *Star* had carried section 68 and five other revelations—sections 65 (a prayer for the Kingdom to roll forth), 72 (the calling of a second bishop), 76 ("The Vision" of the degrees of glory), 83 (responsibility to support family members), and part of 88 ("The Olive Leaf")—suggesting the possibility that they too might have been included.

Not all of the revelations received in that day were canonized by being included in these officially published compilations. Those charged with selecting which revelations to include sought inspiration for their task. At a council meeting in 1832, the Prophet appointed W.W. Phelps, Oliver Cowdery, and John Whitmer to review the revelations "and select for printing such as shall be deemed by them proper, as dictated by the Spirit."[5] At least seventy-three published revelations have been found which have never been added to the Doctrine and Covenants. Many of these were published in the *History of the Church*. For example, in 1835 the Lord declared: "Behold I am well pleased with my servant Isaac Morley, and my servant Edward Partridge, because of the integrity of their hearts in laboring in my vineyard, for the salvation of the souls of men. Verily I say unto you, their sins are forgiven them."[6] Another revelation three years later instructed: "Verily thus saith the Lord, let my servant Brigham Young . . . provide for his family" before leaving on his mission.[7] In 1840 Elder Orson Hyde was shown by vision that he should labor in some of the leading cities of the world, including Jerusalem.[8]

During 1829–1833 the Prophet received, on the average, twenty revelations per year that are now in the Doctrine and Covenants. During the decade 1834–1844, by contrast, he received only an average of three Doctrine and Covenants revelations per year. If uncanonized revelations are added, the difference is not so great. An analysis of the content of these revelations suggests that most of those included in the canon contain essential information on gospel doctrine or Church organization, revealed primarily during the early years of the Restoration, while those not included tend to be of a more personal nature and were received typically during the latest years of the Prophet's ministry.

Years	D&C Revelations	Other Revelations
1829–33	20	3
1834–44	3	6

Not all of Joseph Smith's revelations were published in the next possible edition of the Doctrine and Covenants. This was especially true of the more personal revelations received later in his life.

Years	In Next Edition	In Later Edition	Not yet in D&C
1823–31	82%	8%	10%
1831–35	68%	7%	25%
1835–44	7%	27%	66%

Of the seventy-one known revelations received through the time of section 64, 82 percent were included in the Book of Commandments, and an additional 8 percent were published in later editions of the Doctrine and Covenants. By contrast, of the seventy-seven revelations received during the last nine years of the Prophet's life, only 7 percent were selected for the 1844 edition of the Doctrine and Covenants, and 27 percent more were included later on.

The Doctrine and Covenants, 1835

Additional significant revelations were received after the selection for the Book of Commandments had been made. These included instructions on the history and nature of priesthood (now section 84), the Word of Wisdom (section 89), God's glory (section 93), and Church organization (section 107).

Not long after the destruction of the press in 1833, steps were being taken to publish an even larger compilation of latter-day revelations. On 19 April 1834, Oliver Cowdery and Sidney Rigdon were appointed to work together "in arranging the Book of Covenants."[9] Note that the collected revelations were then being called the "Book of Covenants." On 24 September of that year, a Church council expanded this committee to include the complete First Presidency—Joseph Smith, Oliver Cowdery (who was the associate president with Joseph), Sidney Rigdon, and Frederick G. Williams (who were the First and Second Counselors). Their assignment was to "arrange the items of doctrine of Jesus Christ, for the government of his church of the Latter Day Saints. . . . These items are to be taken from the Bible, Book of Mormon, and the revelations which have been given to said church up to this date, or shall be until such arrangement is made."[10]

By the summer of 1835 the committee had completed its work, and a special solemn assembly convened on 17 August to accept the new book of scripture. The volume would bear a new title, Doctrine and Covenants. This title reflected the two rather distinct parts of the book. In addition to the collected revelations, it also included the seven Lectures on Faith prepared for use in the School of the Elders during the 1834–1835 season. These lectures emphasized the importance of knowing God's attributes and being willing to sacrifice in order to have a more powerful faith in him. They were placed in the first part of the book; the heading of this section explained that they were "On the *doctrine* of the Church of the Latter Day Saints." The revelations were placed in "Part second: *Covenants* and Commandments."[11] Hence the title of the whole volume was drawn from the key word in the title of each of these two parts.

The Prophet had been personally involved in preparing the lectures for publication: "During the month of January [1835], I was engaged . . . in preparing the lectures on theology for publication in the book of Doctrine and Covenants."[12] Nevertheless, an important distinction was made at the time between these school lectures on one hand, and God's revelations on the other. The preface to the 1835 edition explained:

> The first part of the book will be found to contain a series of lectures as delivered before a theological class in this place, and in consequence of their embracing the important doctrine of salvation, we have arranged them in the following work.

The second part contains items or principles for the regulation of the Church, as taken from the revelations which have been given since its organization, as well as from former ones.[13]

Elder John Smith made the same distinction. Speaking for the Kirtland high council at the 17 August 1835 assembly, he bore record that "the revelations in said book were true, and that the lectures were judiciously arranged and compiled, and were profitable for doctrine." This distinction would be the key to a later decision to no longer publish the Lectures on Faith in the same volume with the revelations. After Elder Smith's remarks, the high council and the entire congregation unanimously accepted the new book as "the doctrine and covenants of their faith."[14]

The 1835 edition added forty-five new revelations. Some of these may have been intended for inclusion in the Book of Commandments, while others had been received since the destruction of the press in Missouri. Other important changes were made in this "covenants" section; revelations had been called chapters in the Book of Commandments, while now they were known as sections. Formerly they had been divided in fairly short verses, while now they were arranged into very long paragraph-length verses. The arrangement in the Book of Commandments had been essentially chronological, while the 1835 Doctrine and Covenants grouped the revelations in an entirely different way. Section 1, the Lord's preface, was followed by four revelations on Church government (now sections 20, 107, 84, and 102). They were followed by what we now know as sections 86 and 88. The next fourteen sections were key revelations drawn from the Book of Commandments. The remainder of the book contained other revelations, some in chronological order and others not.

After the conference had accepted the Lectures on Faith and the revelations, two other documents, not specifically identified as revelations, were then presented. W.W. Phelps read an "article on Marriage" and Oliver Cowdery read an "article on 'Governments and Laws in General' " (now section 134). These too were approved and ordered published in the Doctrine and Covenants.[15]

Since the very existence of the Doctrine and Covenants is dependent on latter-day revelation, it is surprising to find certain individuals objecting to the new edition. Some believed the Book of Commandments had been complete and perfect, so they felt no need for the expanded Doctrine and Covenants. Lyman Wight, for example, described the Book of Commandments as celestial, while he regarded the Doctrine and Covenants as only telestial.[16] Then others, such as David Whitmer, denied that the Prophet had any right to alter or supplement the revelations published in the earlier book. Elder B.H. Roberts, on the other hand, later explained that "some of the early revelations first published in the 'Book of Commandments,' in 1833, were revised by the Prophet himself in the way of correcting errors made by the scribes and publishers; and some additional clauses were inserted to throw increased light upon the subjects treated in the revelations, and paragraphs added, to make the principles or instructions apply to officers not in the Church at the time some of the earlier revelations were given."[17] What are now verses 65–67 in section 20 are an example of such an addition; they refer to priesthood offices which had been restored following the time of the original revelation.

The 1844 Edition

A new edition of the Doctrine and Covenants, published shortly after the Prophet's martyrdom in 1844, added eight more sections. These included revealed direction on tithing (now section 119) as well as on temple ordinances (sections 124, 127, and 128), and an appraisal of Joseph Smith's contributions (section 135). Publications of the Doctrine and Covenants for the next thirty years would maintain the same content and arrangement as this 1844 edition.

Major Expansion, 1876

The next significant new edition of the Doctrine and Covenants appeared in 1876. A total of twenty-five revelations given through Joseph Smith from thirty-three to fifty-three years earlier were now added to the scriptural canon. (The Reorganized

Church of Jesus Christ of Latter Day Saints in Independence, Missouri, has continued to add sections to its Doctrine and Covenants, but has never included these twenty-five revelations given through Joseph Smith in its scriptures.)

One of Joseph Smith's revelations added in the 1876 edition was section 87, the "Prophecy on War." This had earlier been published in the original edition of the Pearl of Great Price, printed in Britain in 1851. This precedent of transferring material from the Pearl of Great Price to the Doctrine and Covenants would be followed a century later.

Other revelations given through Joseph Smith which were added at this time included Moroni's prophecy concerning Elijah (now section 2), restoration of the Aaronic Priesthood by John the Baptist (section 13), questions and answers on the Book of Revelation (section 77), the dedicatory prayer for the Kirtland Temple and the restoration of keys (sections 109–110), communications in Liberty Jail (sections 121–23), and other important items of instruction (sections 130–132). An 1847 revelation through Brigham Young for the Pioneers (section 136) was also added in 1876.

The revelations were restored to essentially a chronological order, and the present shorter verse divisions were introduced. These features made the new book much easier to study and reference. Preparation of this volume was the assignment of Elder Orson Pratt. The Historian's Office journal records:

> Elder Orson Pratt has been engaged, at times, for several days, in recopying and arranging the order in which the revelations are to be inserted in the edition of the Book of Doctrine and Covenants, now in the hands of the printer. By the counsel of President B. Young, Elder Pratt has divided the various revelations into verses and arranged them for printing, according to the order of date in which they were revealed.[18]

For the first time, a section earlier included in the Doctrine and Covenants was deleted. President Brigham Young asserted that the 1835 statement on marriage had been written by Oliver Cowdery who insisted that it be included in the Doctrine and Covenants contrary to the repeated counsel of Joseph Smith.

The Prophet was away preaching in Michigan when the assembly in Kirtland approved the 1835 edition.[19] This statement was deleted from the Doctrine and Covenants because it had now been superseded by a revelation from God on the subject of marriage (section 132).

Interestingly, this is a change in the Doctrine and Covenants canon which appeared in another language before it appeared in English. The first German edition was issued in 1876, but it was based on the shorter 1844 canon rather than on the expanded version which appeared in English later that year (1876). Nevertheless, the German edition became the first to drop the 1835 article on marriage. In another case, translations falsely anticipated changes which never came in English. In 1882 President John Taylor received a revelation calling George Teasdale and Heber J. Grant to fill vacancies in the Council of the Twelve. The next year he received another revelation concerning the organization of local seventies quorums. These revelations were published widely in Church periodicals. Beginning in 1888, Swedish, German, and Danish versions of the Doctrine and Covenants, published in Salt Lake City, carried these documents as sections 137–139. However, they never were added to the official canon in English. President Heber J. Grant did not choose to include them in the new English edition of 1921 and instructed that all editions of the scriptures contain the same material. Hence the German edition published in 1923 dropped these John Taylor revelations, setting the pattern for a similar cut in subsequent Swedish and Danish editions.

The Manifesto

An important addition to the Doctrine and Covenants was made just after the turn of the century. As early as the spring of 1889 President Wilford Woodruff was disapproving plural marriages. The general conference of October 1890 accepted the Official Declaration, or Manifesto, in which President Woodruff publicly advised the Latter-day Saints to "refrain from contracting any marriage forbidden by the law."[20] This affirmation was published and circulated widely. Nevertheless, during the opening years of the present century a member of the panel considering Elder Reed Smoot's right to retain his seat in the United States Senate asked why the revelation authorizing polygamy was contained in the Doctrine and Covenants, while the declaration suspending it was not.[21] The Manifesto was included in the Doctrine and Covenants beginning with the 1908 printing. In England, a page bearing the Manifesto was glued into copies of the book which had been printed there two years earlier.[22]

The 1921 Edition

In 1920 a committee drawn from the Quorum of the Twelve was appointed to prepare a new edition of the Book of Mormon for publication. The following year their assignment was extended to include the Doctrine and Covenants and The Pearl of Great Price. The committee's chairman was Elder George F. Richards. Elder James E. Talmage, one of the committee members, played a key role in much of the detail work. Major refinements would include easier-to-read double-column pages and improved section headings. The committee also considered the possibility of adding more revelations to the canon, but did not do so.[23] Their major change was the deletion of the *Lectures on Faith*, which had been published with the revelations since 1835. The introduction in the 1921 edition explained that this material was "never presented to nor accepted by the Church as being otherwise than theological lectures or lessons."[24]

As early as 1879, Elder Orson Pratt had suggested the possibility of dropping the *Lectures on Faith* in order to make room for other material in the volume. President John Taylor indicated, however, that Church leaders did not feel ready to make that change, at least at that time.[25] Even though the portion of the volume labeled as doctrine in 1835 was gone, the full title Doctrine and Covenants continued. This title is still descriptive of what the volume contains, because the revelations certainly set forth the doctrines as well as the covenants which God has revealed.

Doctrine and Covenants Selections, 1930

In 1930 the Church published a volume containing extracts from the Doctrine and Covenants. Entitled *Latter-day Revelation*, this collection presented forty-one of the sections in whole or in part. It was only about one-third as long as the regular edition of the Doctrine and Covenants. The book's preface explained that many early revelations dealt only with individual callings or with conditions which existed only at a particular time. "Except as illustrative instances of the Lord's way of directly communicating with His prophets, many of these revelations, once of present and pressing significance, became relatively of reduced importance with the passing of the conditions that had brought them forth."[26] Under the direction of the First Presidency, Elder James E. Talmage had the responsibility of making the selection, and much of his time on weekends during the later months of 1930 was devoted to this project. "The purpose of this undertaking," Elder Talmage wrote, "is to make the strictly doctrinal parts of the Doctrine and Covenants of easy access and to reduce its bulk," thereby making it more suitable for use by missionaries, investigators, and Church members in general.[27] The publication of these selections did not represent a change in the Doctrine and Covenants canon itself, but did have an impact on the publication of the revelations in several non-English languages. The Spanish translation of *Latter-day Revelation* appeared in 1933, for example, and it remained the only version of the Doctrine and Covenants available in that language until the full text was finally translated fifteen years later.

Our Present Edition, 1981

For the first time in over a century, the 1981 edition added numbered sections to the Doctrine and Covenants. Section 137 includes the Prophet Joseph Smith's 1836 vision of the celestial kingdom in which he learned that those who died without hearing the gospel on earth will have an opportunity to inherit that kingdom. Section 138 records President Joseph F. Smith's 1918 vision of how the Savior inaugurated gospel preaching in the spirit world. As the introduction to the new edition points out, both revelations set forth "the fundamentals of salvation for the dead." These two revelations were added to the Doctrine and Covenants at a time of unprecedented temple building and activity, illustrating how the scriptural canon may be enlarged to meet or reflect a particular need at a given time. These two sections had been added to the Pearl of Great Price in 1976, but they were transferred to the Doctrine and Covenants with this new edition. Hence they followed the precedent established a century earlier by section 87.

Another far-reaching addition in 1981 was the inclusion of Official Declaration–2, announcing President Spencer W. Kimball's 1978 revelation extending the blessings of the priesthood to all races. This revelation was received at a time of worldwide Church growth. Just as sections 137 and 138 showed how those who had died without the opportunity may still accept the gospel, Official Declaration–2 established that the full blessings of the gospel can be enjoyed by all who are living on the earth. As was the case with Official Declaration–1, or the Manifesto, Official Declaration–2 is not an actual record of the revelation itself, but rather it is an inspired announcement that the revelation had been received. This may explain why these two documents have the unique status of "Official Declarations" rather than appearing as numbered sections in the Doctrine and Covenants.

There is another significant, yet often overlooked, addition in connection with Official Declaration–1. A year after the Manifesto had been issued, President Wilford Woodruff related the revelation which had led to the suspension of plural marriages and assured the Saints that the Lord would never allow the Prophet to lead the Church astray. Excerpts from President Woodruff's remarks are now found on pages 292–93 in the new editions of the Doctrine and Covenants.

Expanded historical notes and more specific content summaries enhance the section headings in the new edition. An easier-to-follow cross-referencing system also makes the new volume of scripture more useful as an aid to gospel study. When the assignment to prepare this new edition had first been given, President Spencer W. Kimball gave those involved in the project the charge " 'to assist in improving doctrinal scholarship throughout the Church.' " Every effort has been been made "to put into the hands of the members of the Church the tools that will enable them better to study and understand the Lord's revelations through his prophets."[28]

Publication of the 1981 edition of the "Triple Combination" came two years after the appearance of the Latter-day Saint edition of the King James Bible. This volume had included an extensive new Bible dictionary based not only on the most recent scholarship, but, more important, on latter-day revelation; it also included a six-hundred-page Topical Guide. Reflecting on the significance of issuing these new editions of scripture, Elder Boyd K. Packer declared: "As the generations roll on, this will be regarded, in the perspective of history, as the crowning achievement in the administration of President Spencer W. Kimball." Elder Packer also added this prophetic remark: "With the passing of years, these scriptures will produce successive generations of faithful Christians who know the Lord Jesus Christ and are disposed to obey his will. . . . They will develop a gospel scholarship beyond that which their forebears could achieve. They will have the testimony that Jesus is the Christ and be competent to proclaim Him and to defend Him."[29]

Notes

1. In Conference Report, Apr. 1977, p. 115.

2. "A New Commandment," *Ensign*, Aug. 1976, p. 7.

3. Donald Q. Cannon and Lyndon W. Cook, eds., *Far West Record* (Salt Lake City: Deseret Book Co., 1983), p. 1.

4. Doctrine and Covenants, 1921, p. iii.

5. Cannon and Cook, eds., *Far West Record,* p. 46.

6. *History of the Church of Jesus Christ of Latter-day Saints,* 7 vols., ed. B.H. Roberts (Salt Lake City: Deseret Book Co., 1957), 2:302–3.

7. Ibid., 3:23.

8. Ibid., 4:375–76.

9. Ibid., 2:51.

10. Doctrine and Covenants, 1835, p. 255.

11. Doctrine and Covenants, 1835, pp. 5, 75, italics included.

12. *History of the Church,* 2:180.

13. Doctrine and Covenants, 1835, iii–iv; *History of the Church,* 2:250–51. See also Larry E. Dahl, ''Authorship and History of the Lectures on Faith,'' in a symposium on the Lectures on Faith, Religious Studies Center, Brigham Young University, March 1988.

14. *History of the Church,* 2:244–46.

15. Ibid., 2:246–47.

16. Ibid., 2:481.

17. Ibid., 1:173, note.

18. Historian's Office Journal (7 July 1874–14 Nov. 1875), p. 70, located in the Historical Department of the Church.

19. Lyndon W. Cook, *The Revelations of the Prophet Joseph Smith* (Salt Lake City: Deseret Book Co., 1985), pp. 295, 348–49.

20. D&C, Official Declaration 1.

21. Smoot hearings, 1:107.

22. Robert J. Woodford, ''The Historical Development of the Doctrine and Covenants,'' Ph.D. Dissertation, Brigham Young University, 1974, pp. 92–93.

23. George F. Richards, journal, 29 July 1921, cited in Woodford, ''Historical Development,'' p. 95.

24. Doctrine and Covenants, 1921, v.

25. Woodford, ''Historical Development,'' pp. 83–87.

26. *Latter-day Revelation* (Salt Lake City: Church of Jesus Christ of Latter-day Saints, 1930), iv.

27. Journal of James E. Talmage, 28 June 1930.

28. Bruce T. Harper, ''The Church Publishes a New Triple Combination,'' *Ensign,* Oct. 1981, p. 9.

29. In Conference Report, Oct. 1982, p. 75.

2

The Doctrine and Covenants and the Book of Mormon

John M. Madsen

The Book of Mormon and the Doctrine and Covenants are inseparable, powerful witnesses of the divinity of Christ and his great latter-day work. These two volumes of scripture bear witness of each other and fulfill, at least in part, the promise of the Lord to Enoch when he said, "And righteousness will I send down out of heaven; and truth will I send forth out of the earth, to bear testimony of mine Only Begotten; his resurrection from the dead; yea, and also the resurrection of all men; and righteousness and truth will I cause to sweep the earth as with a flood, to gather out mine elect from the four quarters of the earth" (Moses 7:62).

President Ezra Taft Benson explains:

The Book of Mormon has come forth out of the earth, filled with truth, serving as the very "keystone of our religion." . . . God has also sent down righteousness from

John M. Madsen is Associate Professor of Ancient Scripture at Brigham Young University.

heaven. The Father Himself appeared with His Son to the Prophet Joseph Smith. The angel Moroni, John the Baptist, Peter, James, and numerous other angels were directed by heaven to restore the necessary powers to the kingdom. Further, the Prophet Joseph Smith received revelation after revelation from the heavens during those first critical years of the Church's growth. These revelations have been preserved for us in the Doctrine and Covenants.[1]

What is the relationship between the Book of Mormon and the Doctrine and Covenants? How does the Lord feel about the Book of Mormon? What does the Lord say about the Book of Mormon in the revelations contained in the Doctrine and Covenants?

Revelations Relating to the Book of Mormon

Section 2 of the Doctrine and Covenants is a precious extract from the words of the angel Moroni to Joseph Smith on the evening of 21 September 1823. One cannot help but wonder who was more excited about what was occurring and what was soon to unfold—Moroni or the young prophet? Joseph reports:

> He called me by name, and said unto me that he was a messenger sent from the presence of God to me, and . . . that God had a *work* for me to do; and that my name should be had for good and evil among all nations, kindreds, and tongues, or that it should be both good and evil spoken of among all people.
> He said there was *a book* deposited, written upon gold plates, giving an account of the former inhabitants of this continent, and . . . the fulness of the everlasting Gospel was contained in it, as delivered by the Savior to the ancient inhabitants [Joseph, also must have been not only overwhelmed but overjoyed, for the Savior had promised, on the occasion of the First Vision, that "the fullness of the Gospel should at some future time be made known unto me." *History of the Church* 4:536];
> Also, that there were two stones in silver bows—and these stones, fastened to a breastplate, constituted what is called the Urim and Thummin—deposited with the plates . . . and that God had prepared them for the purpose of *translating the book*. (Joseph Smith—History 1:33–35.)

After delivering his glorious message regarding the book to come forth, the angel Moroni began quoting prophecies of the Old and New Testaments, the first of which was from the third and fourth chapters of Malachi. Joseph noted, however, that the angel quoted the fourth chapter of Malachi with "a little variation from the way it reads in our Bibles" (Joseph Smith—History 1:36). These quotations from Malachi by the angel Moroni are included in the Doctrine and Covenants as section 2. This incident illustrates the close relationship between the coming forth of the Book of Mormon and many of the revelations contained in the Doctrine and Covenants.

As a direct consequence of the book which was to come forth containing the fulness of the everlasting gospel, the Prophet Joseph Smith would receive "instruction and intelligence" during the next four years from the angel Moroni and other heavenly messengers, "respecting what the Lord was going to do, and how and in what manner his kingdom was to be conducted in the last days" (Joseph Smith—History 1:54).

On 22 September 1827 Joseph Smith finally obtained the plates and soon began the work of translation. In July of 1828, two additional revelations, sections 3 and 10, were received in connection with the translation of the Book of Mormon. They have to do with the 116 pages of manuscript which had been entrusted to Martin Harris that he might "carry the writings home and show them."[2]

Of these events the Prophet recorded: "Notwithstanding, . . . the great restrictions which he had been laid under, and the solemnity of the covenant which he made with me, he [Martin Harris] did show them to others, and by strategem they got them away from him, and they never have been recovered unto this day."[3]

None can know the depths of the suffering, the sorrow, the torment through which Joseph passed, realizing that he had "set at naught the counsels of God" (D&C 3:7). The 116 pages of manuscript translated from the first part of the plates were lost, the Urim and Thummim were taken from the Prophet, and the work of translation ceased. After what must have seemed a terribly long time, Joseph Smith was again given the Urim and Thummim, by means of which he received the revelation we know as section 3 of the Doctrine and Covenants. He records, "After I had obtained the above revelation [D&C 3], both the plates and the Urim and Thummim were taken from me again; but in a few days they were returned to me, when I inquired of the Lord, and the Lord said thus unto me [D&C 10]."[4]

In March of 1829, Martin Harris, deeply repentant over his folly in losing the 116 pages, again journeyed to Harmony, Pennsylvania. He was desirous of the privilege of seeing the plates for himself. The Prophet inquired of the Lord, and another revelation was received which would be included in the Doctrine and Covenants as section 5.

In April of 1829 yet another revelation was given to the Prophet Joseph Smith as a direct consequence of the coming forth of the Book of Mormon. Oliver Cowdery, having heard about the work in which Joseph was engaged, journeyed to Harmony, Pennsylvania, and immediately became involved in the work of translation, assisting Joseph as a scribe. Of these events, the Prophet Joseph wrote, "I commenced to translate the Book of Mormon, and he [Oliver Cowdery] began to write for me, which having continued for some time, I inquired of the Lord through the Urim and Thummim, and obtained the following [D&C 6]."[5] Also in April 1829, two other revelations were received as a direct result of the coming forth of the Book of Mormon. These revelations, known as sections 8 and 9, came to Joseph Smith by means of the Urim and Thummim. Joseph explained: "Whilst continuing the work of translation, during the month of April, Oliver Cowdery became exceedingly anxious to have the power to translate bestowed upon him, and in relation to this desire the following revelations [D&C 8–9] were obtained:"[6]

Section 13 of the Doctrine and Covenants probably illustrates as well as any other the connection between the Book of Mormon and the Doctrine and Covenants. Said Joseph:

> We still continued the work of translation, when, in the ensuing month (May, 1829), we on a certain day went into the woods to pray and inquire of the Lord respecting baptism for the remission of sins, that we found mentioned in the translation of the plates. While we were thus employed, praying and calling upon the Lord, a messenger

from heaven descended in a cloud of light, and having laid his hands upon us, he ordained us, saying:

"Upon you my fellow servants, in the name of Messiah, I confer the Priesthood of Aaron, which holds the keys of the ministering of angels, and of the gospel of repentance, and of baptism by immersion for the remission of sins; and this shall never be taken again from the earth until the sons of Levi do offer again an offering unto the Lord in righteousness." (Joseph Smith—History 1:68–69.)

These words spoken by the heavenly messenger who identified himself as "John, the same that is called John the Baptist in the New Testament," have since become section 13 of the Doctrine and Covenants. This heavenly messenger further explained to Joseph and Oliver on this occasion that he acted under the direction of Peter, James, and John, who held the keys of the Priesthood of Melchizedek, which priesthood, he said, "would in due time be conferred on [Joseph and Oliver] (Joseph Smith —History 1:72). Thus did the coming forth of the Book of Mormon not only result in revelation after revelation but was the catalyst for the restoration of sacred keys and powers preparatory to the reestablishment of the church and kingdom of God in these latter days.

Soon after these events took place, Hyrum Smith arrived in Harmony, Pennsylvania, to learn from his brother about the work in which Joseph was engaged. Of his visit Joseph said, "my brother Hyrum Smith came to us to inquire concerning these things, when at his earnest request, I inquired of the Lord through the Urim and Thummim, and received for him the following [D&C 11]."[7] Still another revelation was received in May 1829, this time in behalf of a Mr. Joseph Knight, Sen., of Colesville, Broome County, New York. He had "kindly and considerately brought us a quantity of provisions, in order that we might not be interrupted in the work of translation by the want of such necessaries of life. . . . Being very anxious to know his duty as to this work, I inquired of the Lord for him, and obtained the following: [D&C 12]."[8]

The preface to section 14 of the Doctrine and Covenants also clearly illustrates the intimate relationship between the coming forth of the Book of Mormon and the Doctrine and

Covenants. "The Whitmer family had become greatly interested in the translating of the Book of Mormon. The Prophet established his residence at the home of Peter Whitmer, Sen., where he dwelt until the work of translation was carried to completion and the copyright on the forthcoming book secured. Three of the Whitmer sons, each having received a testimony as to the genuineness of the work, became deeply concerned over the matter of their individual duty. This revelation [section 14] and the next two following (sections 15 and 16) were given in answer to an inquiry through the Urim and Thummim. David Whitmer later became one of the Three Witnesses to the Book of Mormon." Section 17 contains information about the promised witnesses.

Section 19 of the Doctrine and Covenants was given in March 1830 and was received through the Prophet Joseph Smith for Martin Harris. While the Book of Mormon is not expressly mentioned in this revelation, there is an obvious relationship between this revelation and the coming forth of the Book of Mormon. It seems that Martin Harris had come to the Prophet still deeply troubled about his standing before the Lord and concerned about the debt he had contracted to print the Book of Mormon. In the revelation the Lord addresses both matters. Joseph Fielding Smith refers to this revelation as "one of the great revelations given in this dispensation, there are few of greater import than this. This doctrine of the atonement of the Lord, as directly applying to the individual, and his exposition of 'Eternal Punishment' as here set forth, give to members of the Church light which was not previously known."[9] Following the completion of the work of translation, in July of 1829, arrangements were made for the printing and publication of the Book of Mormon. It took from the fall of 1829 until the spring of 1830, but the book was finally ready for sale and distribution by 26 March 1830.

The Lord's Testimony of the Book of Mormon

With the close relationship between the coming forth of the Book of Mormon and the receipt of revelation upon revelation clearly in mind, let us now examine what the Lord has said about the Book of Mormon in the revelations contained in the Doctrine and Covenants.

A little over a year and a half after the completion of the translation and publication of the Book of Mormon and the organization of the Church, the Lord revealed his "preface" to the book that was to contain his revelations to his people in this the dispensation of the fulness of times. In this revealed preface the Lord declared that the Book of Mormon was translated by the power of God. He testified that "after having received the record of the Nephites, yea, even my servant Joseph Smith, Jun.," was to have "power to translate through the mercy of God, by the power of God, the Book of Mormon" (D&C 1:29). Section 3, concerning the lost 116 pages, also affirms that the translation of the Book of Mormon came by the power of God, and underscores the importance of the Book of Mormon in the "works, and the designs, and the purposes of God" (D&C 3:1).

The Lord intended for the Book of Mormon to be translated and published to all the world. The mighty "works" and "designs" and "purposes" of the Lord in bringing forth this sacred record were not to be frustrated by careless or wicked men. Joseph was sorely and severely chastened for setting "at naught the counsels of God" (D&C 3:7). Twice it had been made known unto him that he must not permit Martin Harris to "carry the writings home and show them."[10] After receiving this divine rebuke, Joseph was told that, on condition of his repenting of "that which thou hast done," he was "still chosen" and "again called to the work" of translation and bringing forth the Book of Mormon (D&C 3:10). If he did not repent, Joseph was told, he would "become as other men, and have no more gift" to translate (D&C 3:11). Then came the following declaration: "When thou [Joseph] deliveredst up that which God had given thee sight and power to translate, thou deliveredst up that which was sacred" (D&C 3:12). There can be no question as to the sacred nature of these records and the power by which Joseph Smith was enabled to translate them.

The Lord made clear to the Prophet, and to all, some of his purposes for bringing forth the Book of Mormon. He said:

Inasmuch as the knowledge of a Savior has come unto the world, through the testimony of the Jews, even so shall the knowledge of a Savior come unto my people—

And to the Nephites, and the Jacobites, and the Josephites, and the Zoramites, through the testimony of their fathers—

And this testimony shall come to the knowledge of the Lamanites, and the Lemuelites, and the Ishmaelites, who dwindled in unbelief . . .

And for this very purpose are these plates preserved, which contain these records—that the promises of the Lord might be fulfilled, which he made to his people;

And that the Lamanites might come to the knowledge of their fathers, and that they might know the promises of the Lord, and that they may believe the gospel and rely upon the merits of Jesus Christ, and be glorified through faith in his name, and that through their repentance they might be saved. Amen. (D&C 3:16–20.)

In section 4 the Lord uses the phrase, "A marvelous work is about to come forth among the children of men" (v. 1). This same phrase, with slight variation, is used in several of the early revelations. This phrase seems to have special significance, and it is only used in the revelations prior to the publication of the Book of Mormon and the organization of the church and kingdom of God in the earth. Perhaps an examination of the meaning of this phrase will more clearly reveal how important the Book of Mormon is to the Lord and the accomplishment of his purposes. The revelations where this phrase is used are Doctrine and Covenants 4:1; 6:1; 11:1; 12:1; 14:1. In Doctrine and Covenants 6:9 the Lord instructs Oliver Cowdery that he is to "assist to bring forth my work." Oliver Cowdery was assisting Joseph Smith in the translation of the Book of Mormon, which contained the fulness of the everlasting gospel. With this record in hand, the Lord would send his servants forth to work "a marvelous work among the children of men, unto the convincing of many of their sins, that they may come unto repentance, and that they may come unto the kingdom of my Father" (D&C 18:44).

In section 5 of the Doctrine and Covenants the Lord has much to say about the Book of Mormon and its importance in

the accomplishment of his purposes. Martin Harris desired to
see the plates. Joseph inquired of the Lord and was told that he
was not to show the plates except to those persons whom the
Lord would designate (see D&C 5:1–3). The Lord reminded
Joseph that "you [Joseph] have a gift to translate the plates;
and this is the first gift that I have bestowed upon you; and I
have commanded that you should pretend to no other gift until
my purpose is fulfilled in this; for I will grant unto you no other
gift until it [the translation and publication of the Book of Mor-
mon] is finished" (D&C 5:4). Once again the Lord made it clear
to his servant Joseph Smith that the Book of Mormon had to be
translated and made available before his great latter-day work
was to proceed.

Also in section 5, in verses 5–16, the Lord explained why the
Book of Mormon is so important in the accomplishment of his
great latter-day work. In these verses he repeatedly speaks of
"my word" and "my words." It seems in this particular revelation the Lord was referring to his "word" or "words" that were
contained in the Book of Mormon, which was to come forth.
The verses might then be read as follows:

> Verily I say unto you, that woe shall come unto the in-
> habitants of the earth if they will not hearken unto my
> words [that are contained in the Book of Mormon];
>
> For hereafter you shall be ordained and go forth and
> deliver my words [contained in the Book of Mormon]
> unto the children of men.
>
> Behold, if they will not believe my words [contained in
> the Book of Mormon], they would not believe you, my
> servant Joseph, if it were possible that you should show
> them all these things which I have committed unto you.
>
> Oh, this unbelieving and stiffnecked generation—mine
> anger is kindled against them.
>
> Behold, verily I say unto you, I have reserved those
> things which I have entrusted unto you, my servant
> Joseph, for a wise purpose in me, and it shall be made
> known unto future generations;
>
> But this generation shall have my word [contained in
> the Book of Mormon] through you. (D&C 5:5–10.)

The Book of Mormon exposes the hearts of men. If they accept the words of Christ contained in the Book of Mormon they

will come to know that Joseph Smith is a true prophet. If they will not believe the words of the Book of Mormon, seeing the plates and other tangible objects will not convince them. The Book of Mormon is a powerful testimony that Joseph Smith is a prophet of God. And to a generation which is to receive the word of God through Joseph Smith, that testimony is critical. Multiplying the evidence, the Lord promised additional witnesses.

> And in addition to your testimony, the testimony of three of my servants, whom I shall call and ordain, unto whom I will show these things, and they shall go forth with my words [contained in the Book of Mormon] that are given through you [Joseph Smith, Jun].
>
> Yea, they shall know of a surety that these things are true, for from heaven will I declare it unto them. I will give them power that they may behold and view these things as they are;
>
> And to none else will I grant this power, to receive this same testimony among this generation, in this the beginning of the rising up and the coming forth of my church out of the wilderness—clear as the moon, and fair as the sun, and terrible as an army with banners.
>
> And the testimony of three witnesses will I send forth of my word [contained in the Book of Mormon]. And behold, whosoever believeth on my words [contained in the Book of Mormon], them will I visit with the manifestation of my Spirit; and they shall be born of me, even of water and of the Spirit. (D&C 5:11–16.)

These few verses of scripture illustrate as plainly as any other the great truth declared by the prophet Joseph that "the Book of Mormon [is] . . . the keystone of our religion."[11] A witness of the divinity and truthfulness of the Book of Mormon confirms that Jesus is the Christ, that Joseph Smith is his prophet, and that The Church of Jesus Christ of Latter-day Saints as organized by the Prophet Joseph, is true. With such a witness of the Spirit, courageous souls from all the nations of the earth where the message of the Restoration has been proclaimed have eagerly submitted to the ordinance of baptism under the hands of authorized servants of the Lord. They have been born of water and of the Spirit. The Lord solemnly declares in D&C

5:18–20 that the testimony of the Three Witnesses as to the truthfulness of the word of the Lord contained in the Book of Mormon would "go forth unto the condemnation of this generation if they harden their hearts against them;" for he assures us, "my word [contained in the Book of Mormon] shall be verified."

In section 6 of the Doctrine and Covenants, the Lord makes another reference to the Book of Mormon and reveals something more of his feelings concerning it. Oliver Cowdery was informed among many other things that if his desires were "good," he would be privileged to assist Joseph Smith in translating. He was also told of other records which have been "kept back because of the wickedness of the people" (v. 26). Thus the Book of Mormon is a translation of only a portion of the sacred records that will eventually come to light. (See 2 Nephi 27, 3 Nephi 26, and Ether 4:4–7.) The words of the Lord in D&C 6:28–31 must have been sobering to Joseph and Oliver, for the Lord suggests that "if they [the world] reject my words [contained in the Book of Mormon] and this part of my gospel and ministry, blessed are ye for they can do no more unto you than unto me. And even if they do unto you even as they have done unto me, blessed are ye, for you shall dwell with me in glory. But if they reject not my words [contained in the Book of Mormon], which shall be established by the testimony which shall be given, blessed are they."

The Lord, in section 8, makes reference to the Book of Mormon in response to Oliver Cowdery's desire to translate. He assures Oliver that he shall receive "a knowledge concerning the engravings of old records, which are ancient, which contain those parts of my scripture of which has been spoken by the manifestation of my Spirit" (D&C 8:1). Once again the Lord bears his witness as to the divine source of the "scripture" contained on the plates.

In the opening verse of section 10, the Lord places the responsibility for the loss of the 116 pages of manuscript squarely upon the Prophet Joseph Smith. Though he had lost the writings and his gift to translate, this gift to translate was again restored. Joseph was admonished to be faithful to this trust and "continue on unto the finishing of the remainder of the work of translation as you have begun" (D&C 10:1–4). The Lord then told Joseph that he should "not translate again those words" which had gone forth out of his hands (D&C 10:30). In the instructions that follow we gain insight into the Lord's feelings about the contents of that portion of the records which were yet to be translated and published as the Book of Mormon.

The Lord said:

> The account which is engraven upon the plates of Nephi is more particular concerning the things which, in my wisdom, I would bring to the knowledge of the people . . .
>
> Behold, there are many things engraven upon the plates of Nephi which do throw greater views upon my gospel; therefore, it is wisdom in me that you should translate this first part of the engravings of Nephi, and send forth in this work.
>
> And, behold, all the remainder of this work does contain all those parts of my gospel which my holy prophets, yea, and also my disciples, desired in their prayers should come forth unto this people.
>
> And I said unto them, that it should be granted unto them according to their faith in their prayers;
>
> Yea, and this was their faith—that my gospel, which I gave unto them that they might preach in their days, might come unto their brethren the Lamanites, and also all that had become Lamanites because of their dissensions.
>
> Now, this is not all—their faith in their prayers was that this gospel should be made known also, if it were possible that other nations should possess this land;
>
> And thus they did leave a blessing upon this land in their prayers, that whosoever should believe in this gospel in this land might have eternal life;
>
> Yea, that it might be free unto all of whatsoever nation, kindred, tongue, or people they may be. . . .
>
> And for this cause have I said: if this generation harden not their hearts, I will establish my church among them.
>
> Yea, and I will also bring to light my gospel which was ministered unto them, and behold, they shall not deny that which you have received, but they shall build it up

and shall bring to light the true points of my doctrine, yea, and the only doctrine which is in me.

And this I do that I may establish my gospel, that there may not be so much contention; yea, Satan doth stir up the hearts of the people to contention concerning the points of my doctrine, and in these things they do err, for they do wrest the scriptures and do not understand them. . . .

Yea, if they will come, they may, and partake of the waters of life freely.

Behold, this is my doctrine—whosoever repenteth and cometh unto me [by accepting the "words," contained in the Book of Mormon], the same is my church. (D&C 10:40, 45–51, 53, 62–63, 66–67.)

In response to prayers of faith, ancient prophets were assured that the words of the Lord would be preserved and come forth in the latter days, and they prophesied that it would be so (see 1 Nephi 13:34–35; Mormon 8:23–26; 2 Nephi 3:12–14). Through these great promises and prophecies recorded centuries before the coming forth of this "standard" and "keystone" in the arch of the Lord's latter-day work, we can see somewhat more vividly the power and intensity behind the words of the Lord to Joseph Smith when he said "the works, and the designs, and the purposes of God cannot be frustrated, neither can they come to naught. . . . Remember, remember that it is not the work of God that is frustrated, but the work of men" (D&C 3:1, 3), and "the devil has sought to lay a cunning plan, that he may destroy this work . . . Verily, I say unto you, that I will not suffer that Satan shall accomplish his evil design in this thing" (D&C 10:12, 14).

In section 17 of the Doctrine and Covenants we gain further insight into the Lord's feelings about the Book of Mormon. To Oliver Cowdery, David Whitmer, and Martin Harris, who desired to see the plates, the Lord said:

Behold, I say unto you, that you must rely upon my word [again, I think this phrase has reference primarily to the words of the Lord contained in the Book of Mormon] which if you do with full purpose of heart, you shall have a view of the plates, and also of the breastplate, the sword

of Laban, the Urim and Thummim, which were given to
the brother of Jared upon the mount, when he talked with
the Lord face to face, and the miraculous directors which
were given to Lehi while in the wilderness, on the borders
of the Red Sea.

And it is by your faith that you shall obtain a view of
them, even by that faith which was had by the prophets
of old.

And after that you have obtained faith, and have seen
them with your eyes, you shall testify of them, by the
power of God. (D&C 17:1–3.)

Even as the three men were promised a view of the plates
and of the other instruments entrusted to the Prophet Joseph
Smith, it is my faith that all who "rely upon" the Lord's words
as contained in the Book of Mormon, "with full purpose of
heart" and who endure faithfully, "even by that faith which
was had by the prophets of old," shall likewise one day "obtain
a view" of the plates and of all "those things" which were entrusted to the Prophet Joseph Smith (see D&C 5:9). Following
this promise made to the Three Witnesses, the Lord explains
that they are to testify that they have seen the plates, "even as
my servant Joseph Smith, Jun., has seen them; for it is by my
power that he has seen them, and it is because he had faith"
(D&C 17:5). The words that follow represent a most powerful,
direct witness as to the divinity and truthfulness of the Book of
Mormon. The Lord himself testifies, "And he [Joseph Smith]
has translated the book, even that part which I have commanded him, and as your Lord and your God liveth it is true"
(D&C 17:6). Who can read or hear this testimony and ever
wonder how the Lord feels about the Book of Mormon? It is a
serious thing to hear or to read these words, for these words are
sufficient to condemn us if we should ever reject the Book of
Mormon or be unfaithful to the cause of Christ and his kingdom. The Lord concludes this revelation with the following
promise to the Three Witnesses: "If you do these last commandments of mine, ["obtain a view" of the plates, and "testify of them by the power of God"] . . . the gates of hell shall
not prevail against you; for my grace is sufficient for you, and
you shall be lifted up at the last day. And I, Jesus Christ, your

Lord and your God, have spoken it unto you, that I might bring about my righteous purposes unto the children of men.'' (D&C 17:8–9.) Once again, the Lord indicates that the Book of Mormon must come forth, in order for him to accomplish his great latter-day work.

In section 18, through the Prophet Joseph Smith to his scribe, Oliver Cowdery, the Lord said:

> Behold, I have manifested unto you, by my Spirit in many instances, that the things which you have written are true; wherefore you know that they are true.
>
> And if you know that they are true, behold, I give unto you a commandment, that you rely upon the things which are written.
>
> For in them are all things written concerning the foundation of my church, my gospel, and my rock.
>
> Wherefore, if you shall build up my church, upon the foundation of my gospel and my rock [as contained in the Book of Mormon], the gates of hell shall not prevail against you.
>
> Behold, the world is ripening in iniquity; and it must needs be that the children of men are stirred up unto repentance [by the teachings contained in the Book of Mormon], both the Gentiles and also the house of Israel. (D&C 18:2–6.)

The Lord does not only bear witness to the truthfulness of the Book of Mormon. He declares that the doctrines contained in it are to serve as the very "foundation" of his church and the great latter-day work of stirring the Gentiles and the house of Israel to repentance in a world that is ripening in iniquity.

The work of translation having been completed and the arrangements for printing and publication of the Book of Mormon having been made, the Lord instructed Martin Harris to pay the printing costs. And again the Lord affirmed the content and purpose of the book.

> And again, I command thee that thou shalt not covet thine own property, but impart it freely to the printing of the Book of Mormon, which contains the truth and the word of God—
>
> Which is my word to the Gentile, that soon it may go to the Jew, of whom the Lamanites are a remnant, that

they may believe the gospel, and look not for a Messiah to come who has already come (D&C 19:26–27; see also 2 Nephi 25:15–20).

The most extensive discussion of the Book of Mormon in the Doctrine and Covenants is found in section 20. In this revelation the Lord names the precise date, namely 6 April 1830, on which his Church was to be organized in this last dispensation. It appears significant that the revelation to formally organize the Church was not given until the Book of Mormon was translated, printed, and available for distribution.

After specifying the day on which the Church was to be organized and confirming that Joseph Smith and Oliver Cowdery were duly called of God and authorized to organize and give leadership to his Church, the Lord declares the following with regard to the Book of Mormon:

> God ministered unto him [Joseph Smith, Jun.] by an holy angel . . .
> And gave unto him commandments which inspired him;
> And gave him power from on high, by the means which were before prepared, to translate the Book of Mormon;
> Which contains a record of a fallen people, and the fulness of the gospel of Jesus Christ to the Gentiles and to the Jews also;
> Which was given by inspiration [or revelation] and is confirmed to others by the ministering of angels, and is declared unto the world by them [the Three Witnesses]
> Proving to the world that the holy scriptures [the Bible] are true, and that God does inspire men and call them to his holy work in this age and generation, as well as in generations of old;
> Thereby showing that he is the same God yesterday, today, and forever. Amen.
> Therefore, having so great witnesses [Joseph Smith, Jun., the Three Witnesses, the Eight Witnesses and now the millions of souls who have received a witness of the Spirit as to its divinity], by them shall the world be judged, even as many as shall hereafter come to a knowledge of this work [the Book of Mormon].

> And those who receive it [the Book of Mormon] in faith, and work righteousness, shall receive a crown of eternal life;
>
> But those who harden their hearts in unbelief, and reject it [the Book of Mormon], it shall turn to their own condemnation—
>
> For the Lord God has spoken it; and we, the elders of the church, have heard and bear witness to the words of the glorious Majesty on high, to whom be glory forever and ever. Amen. (D&C 20:6–16.)

The Lord then gives an extensive summary of the doctrines of salvation found in the Bible and suggests that the Book of Mormon "proves to the world" that the doctrines contained in the holy scriptures are indeed true. The revelation continues:

> By these things we know that there is a God in heaven, who is infinite and eternal from everlasting to everlasting the same unchangeable God, the framer of heaven and earth, and all things which are in them;
>
> And that he created man, male and female, after his own image and in his own likeness, created he them;
>
> And gave unto them commandments that they should love and serve him, the only living and true God, and that he should be the only being whom they should worship.
>
> But by the transgression of these holy laws man became sensual and devilish, and became fallen man.
>
> Wherefore, the Almighty God gave his Only Begotten Son, *as it is written in those scriptures which have been given of him* [the Bible and the Book of Mormon—the Doctrine and Covenants and the Pearl of Great Price had not yet been published]
>
> He suffered temptations but gave no heed unto them.
>
> He was crucified, died, and rose again the third day;
>
> And ascended into heaven, to sit down on the right hand of the Father, to reign with almighty power according to the will of the Father;
>
> That as many as would believe and be baptized in his holy name, and endure in faith to the end, should be saved—
>
> Not only those who believed after he came in the meridian of time, in the flesh, but all those from the beginning, even as many as were before he came, who believed

in the words of the holy prophets, who spake as they were inspired by the gift of the Holy Ghost, who truly testified of him in all things, should have eternal life,

As well as those who should come after, who should believe in the gifts and callings of God by the Holy Ghost, which beareth record of the Father and of the Son;

Which Father, Son, and Holy Ghost are one God, infinite and eternal, without end. Amen.

And we know that all men must repent and believe on the name of Jesus Christ, and worship the Father in his name, and endure in faith on his name to the end, or they cannot be saved in the kingdom of God.

And we know that justification through the grace of our Lord and Savior Jesus Christ is just and true;

And we know also, that sanctification through the grace of our Lord and Savior Jesus Christ is just and true, to all those who love and serve God with all their mights, minds, and strength.

But there is a possibility that man may fall from grace and depart from the living God;

Therefore, let the church take heed and pray always, lest they fall into temptation;

Yea, and even let those who are sanctified take heed also.

And we know that these things are true and according to the revelations of John, neither adding to, nor diminishing from the prophecy of his book [the Book of Revelation], the holy scriptures [the Bible], or the revelations of God [the Doctrine and Covenants and all other scripture that shall come forth in the latter days] which shall come hereafter by the gift and power of the Holy Ghost, the voice of God, or the ministering of angels.

And the Lord God has spoken it; and honor, power and glory be rendered to his holy name, both now and ever. Amen. (D&C 20:17–36, emphasis added.)

In Doctrine and Covenants 27 the Lord added yet another powerful witness of the divinity of the Book of Mormon. He said:

. . . wherefore, marvel not, for the hour cometh that I will drink of the fruit of the vine with you on the earth, and with Moroni, whom I have sent unto you to reveal the Book of Mormon, containing the fulness of my everlasting gospel, to whom I have committed the keys of the record of the stick of Ephraim (D&C 27:5).

The Book of Mormon is identified here as "the record of the stick of Ephraim," and Moroni is designated as the one holding "the keys" of this sacred record (see Ezekiel 37:19).[12]

In Doctrine and Covenants 42, a revelation known as "the Law of the Church," the Lord confirms again that the Book of Mormon contains "the fulness of the gospel" (v. 12; see also 20:9; 27:5; 135:3). The Lord had promised young Joseph Smith in the First Vision that the fulness of the gospel would be made known unto him at some future time. Soon, the angel Moroni had confirmed that "the fulness of the everlasting gospel" as "delivered by the Savior to the ancient inhabitants" of the American continent was contained in "the book" that lay buried in the nearby hill called Cumorah (see D&C 39:5–6; 76:40–42; 3 Nephi 27:13–21).[13]

It is the gospel, even the fulness thereof, that leads humble souls to Christ and his Church and kingdom. All those who have entered into the safe "fold" of "the good shepherd" may then partake of all other ordinances necessary for exaltation in the celestial kingdom.

Another significant reference to the Book of Mormon is found in section 84 of the Doctrine and Covenants. To the Saints in 1832 the Lord said:

> And your minds in times past have been darkened because of unbelief, and because you have treated lightly the things you have received—
> Which vanity and unbelief have brought the whole church under condemnation.
> And this condemnation resteth upon the children of Zion, even all.
> And they shall remain under this condemnation until they repent and remember the new covenant, even the Book of Mormon and the former commandments which I have given them, not only to say, but to do according to that which I have written—
> That they may bring forth fruit meet for their Father's kingdom; otherwise there remaineth a scourge and a judgment to be poured out upon the children of Zion. (D&C 84:54–58.)

On several occasions President Ezra Taft Benson has challenged members of the Church to free themselves from that same condemnation pronounced upon the early Latter-day Saints. In April of 1986 he explained:

> Some of the early missionaries, on returning home, were reproved by the Lord in section 84 of the Doctrine and Covenants because they had treated lightly the Book of Mormon. As a result, their minds had been darkened. The Lord said that this kind of treatment of the Book of Mormon brought the whole Church under condemnation, even all the children of Zion. And then the Lord said, "And they shall remain under condemnation until they repent and remember the new covenant, even the Book of Mormon." [see verses 54–57]. Are we still under that condemnation?
>
> And now grave consequences hang on our response to the Book of Mormon. "Those who receive it," saith the Lord, "in faith, and work righteousness, shall receive a crown of eternal life;
>
> "But those who harden their hearts in unbelief, and reject it, it shall turn to their own condemnation—For the Lord God has spoken it." (D&C 20:14–16.)
>
> Is the Book of Mormon true? Yes.
>
> Whom is it for? Us.
>
> What is its purpose? To bring men to Christ.
>
> How does it do this? By testifying of Christ and revealing His enemies.
>
> How are we to use it? We are to get a testimony of it, we are to teach from it, we are to hold it up as a standard and "hiss it forth."
>
> Have we been doing this? Not as we should, nor as we must.
>
> Do eternal consequences rest upon our response to this book? Yes, either to our blessing or our condemnation.
>
> Every Latter-day Saint should make the study of this book a lifetime pursuit. Otherwise he is placing his soul in jeopardy and neglecting that which could give spiritual and intellectual unity to his whole life.[14]

In section 135 are to be found these further references to the Book of Mormon. These sobering and powerful words were written by Elder John Taylor of the Council of the Twelve, who witnessed the martyrdom of Joseph and Hyrum Smith.

> To seal the testimony of this book [the Doctrine and Covenants] and the Book of Mormon, we announce the

martyrdom of Joseph Smith the Prophet, and Hyrum Smith the Patriarch. . . .

Joseph Smith, the Prophet and Seer of the Lord, has done more, save Jesus only, for the salvation of men in this world, than any other man that ever lived in it. In the short space of twenty years, he has brought forth the Book of Mormon, which he translated by the gift and power of God, and has been the means of publishing it on two continents; has sent the fulness of the everlasting gospel, which it contained, to the four quarters of the earth; has brought forth the revelations and command-ments which compose this book of Doctrine and Cove-nants, and many other wise documents and instructions for the benefit of the children of men; gathered many thousands of the Latter-day Saints, founded a great city, and left a fame and name that cannot be slain. He lived great, and he died great in the eyes of God and his peo-ple; and like most of the Lord's anointed in ancient times, has sealed his mission and his works with his own blood; and so has his brother Hyrum. In life they were not divided, and in death they were not separated! (D&C 135:1, 3.)

Clearly the Book of Mormon was central to the mission of Joseph Smith, the prophet of the Restoration.

Finally, in Doctrine and Covenants 136, there is a strongly implied reference to the Book of Mormon. To Brigham Young the Lord said, "I did call upon [Joseph Smith] by mine angels, my ministering servants, and by mine own voice out of the heavens, to bring forth my work; which foundation he did lay, and was faithful; and I took him to myself" (D&C 136:37–38). Surely, that foundation involves the Book of Mormon. Earlier the Lord explained that in the things which were written by the hand of Oliver Cowdery as dictated by the Prophet Joseph were "all things written concerning the foundation of my church, my gospel, and my rock" (D&C 18:4). Is not the Lord again saying that which he has said so many times and in so many ways: that the foundation for his great latter-day work is the Book of Mor-mon? And could it not be said that the single work ac-complished by the Prophet Joseph Smith, that would do more "for the salvation of men in this world" (D&C 135:3), was the translation and publication of the Book of Mormon? Is it not the Book of Mormon that was to convince the Jew and the Gentile that Jesus is the Christ, the Eternal God, manifesting himself unto all nations?

Conclusion

The Doctrine and Covenants has much to say about the Book of Mormon. They are true companion volumes of the word of the Lord. President Ezra Taft Benson has explained the important relationship of these two sacred books:

> Excluding the witnesses to the Book of Mormon, the Doctrine and Covenants is by far the greatest external witness and evidence which we have from the Lord that the Book of Mormon is true. . . .
> The Doctrine and Covenants is the binding link between the Book of Mormon and the continuing work of the Restoration through the Prophet Joseph Smith and his successors. . . .
> The Book of Mormon brings men to Christ. The Doctrine and Covenants brings men to Christ's kingdom. . . .
> The Book of Mormon is the 'keystone' of our religion, and the Doctrine and Covenants is the capstone, with continuing latter-day revelation. The Lord has placed His stamp of approval on both the keystone and the capstone.[15]

Notes

1. In Conference Report, Oct. 1986, p. 102.

2. *History of The Church of Jesus Christ of Latter-day Saints,* 7 vols., ed. B. H. Roberts (Salt Lake City: Deseret Book Co., 1957), 1:21.

3. Ibid.

4. Ibid., 1:23.

5. Ibid., 1:32–33.

6. Ibid., 1:36.

7. Ibid., 1:44–45.

8. Ibid., 1:47–48.

9. Joseph Fielding Smith, *Church History and Modern Revelation,* 2 vols. (Salt Lake City: Deseret Book Co., 1953), 1:85.

10. *History of the Church,* 1:21.

11. Ibid., 4:461.

12. See Joseph Fielding Smith, *Answers to Gospel Questions,* 5 vols. (Salt Lake City: Deseret Book Co., 1957–66), 3:197–98; see Keith Meservy, "Ezekiel's Sticks," *Ensign*, February 1987, pp. 4–13 for more information about the "stick" of Ephraim.

13. See Bruce R. McConkie, *Mormon Doctrine*, 2nd ed. (Salt Lake City: Bookcraft, 1966), pp. 331–34, concerning "the gospel."

14. See *A Witness and a Warning* (Salt Lake City: Deseret Book Co., 1988), pp. 6–8.

15. In Conference Report, Apr. 1987, p. 105.

3

Learning the Spirit of Revelation

Robert L. Millet

"S alvation cannot come without revelation," Joseph Smith taught. "It is in vain for anyone to minister without it."[1] It should thus come as no surprise to Latter-day Saints to learn that when the time had fully arrived for the promised restitution of all things; when the glorious day of restoration had dawned, it was necessary for God to make known through Joseph Smith a myriad of pertinent truths. Not the least of these was the nature and scope of revelation itself—from whence it comes, the manner in which it is to be received, and how it is to be understood. Thus numerous passages in the Doctrine and Covenants describe, some almost as a passing comment, what people must do to qualify for the gifts and guidance of that member of the Godhead known as the Revelator. "It remained for Joseph Smith to announce to a disbelieving world," one Latter-day

Robert L. Millet is Associate Professor and Chairman of the Department of Ancient Scripture at Brigham Young University.

Saint has written, "that that same God who spoke so freely in times past not only could, but had spoken again, and that the promise of James that any who sought the wisdom of heaven in faith still had claim upon it."[2]

The Light of Christ and the Holy Ghost

The Lord pulled back the veil, tore away the theological cobwebs of centuries of darkness and apostasy, and revealed to Joseph the Seer the nature and kind of being we worship. "The Father has a body of flesh and bones as tangible as man's," he explained; "the Son also; but the Holy Ghost has not a body of flesh and bones, but is a personage of spirit. Were it not so, the Holy Ghost could not dwell in us" (D&C 130:22). The Prophet thus made clear that our God is an exalted man, a man of holiness, a resurrected, immortal being in whose image man is in reality created.[3] The *corporeal* or physical nature of the Almighty was thus made known once again through the one called and chosen in premortality to reveal God to man in the final dispensation of time.

Some of the revelations in the Doctrine and Covenants also do much toward explaining the *divine* nature of God. It is appropriately stated that God is omnipotent: he has all power. He is omniscient: he has all knowledge. It is in the Doctrine and Covenants we learn that through his influence, that divine glory and power which emanates from him to fill the immensity of space, he is omnipresent: he is everywhere present at once. Inasmuch as God is a physical being he cannot occupy more than one space at a time, but through his glory (called in the scriptures the Light of Christ or the Spirit of Jesus Christ) he is able to be in and through and round about all things.

> He that ascended up on high, as also he descended below all things, in that he comprehended all things, that he might be in all and through all things, the light of truth;
> Which truth shineth. This is the light of Christ. As also he is in the sun, and the light of the sun, and the power thereof by which it was made.

As also he is in the moon, and is the light of the moon, and the power thereof by which it was made;

As also the light of the stars, and the power thereof by which they were made;

And the earth also, and the power thereof, even the earth upon which you stand.

And the light which shineth, which giveth you light, is through him who enlighteneth your eyes, which is the same light that quickeneth your understandings;

Which light proceedeth forth from the presence of God to fill the immensity of space—

The light which is in all things, which giveth life to all things, which is the law by which all things are governed, even the power of God who sitteth upon his throne, who is in the bosom of eternity, who is in the midst of all things. (D&C 88:6–13.)

This is a most remarkable revelation. Through it we become privy to the fact that the Light of Christ is the governing principle in nature, the power by which the cosmos is held in check and by which order and organization exist. Elder Parley P. Pratt wrote that the Light of Christ, "in its less refined existence," is "the physical light which reflects from the sun, moon, and stars." In its higher degrees, it serves as the means "by which we reason, discern, judge, compare, comprehend and remember the subjects within our reach. Its inspiration constitutes instinct in animal life, reason in man, vision in the Prophets, and is continually flowing from the Godhead throughout all his creations."[4] According to Elder Bruce R. McConkie, the Light of Christ "defies description and is beyond mortal comprehension. . . . It has neither shape nor form nor personality. It is not an entity nor a person nor a personage. It has no agency, does not act independently, and exists not to act but to be acted upon. It is variously described as light and life and law and truth and power. . . . It is the power of God who sitteth upon his throne. It may be that it is also priesthood and faith and omnipotence, for these too are the power of God."[5]

The Light of Christ is given to every man and woman at birth as a natural endowment; it is described as that spirit which "giveth light to every man that cometh into the world" (D&C 84:46; compare John 1:9; Moroni 7:16). It is a director, a moral monitor which is "innate, inborn, and intuitional in nature. Call it conscience, if you will; say that it is a divine inheritance from a Divine Parent; identify it as a spark of divinity sent by Deity to fire the soul with the flames of righteousness; . . . it has many names. But what counts is that it is real."[6] The revelations further attest that "every one that hearkeneth to the voice of the Spirit [the Light of Christ] cometh unto God, even the Father. And the Father teacheth him of the covenant which he has renewed and confirmed upon you . . . for the sake of the whole world." (D&C 84:47–48.) That is to say, if men and women in the world will respond to the quiet promptings and subtle whisperings of the Light of Christ within them, they will be led, either in this life or the next, to that higher light of the Holy Ghost found only in the covenant gospel through membership in the Lord's Church. President Joseph F. Smith explained that this light "strives with the children of men, and will continue to strive with them, until it brings them to a knowledge of the truth and the possession of the greater light and testimony of the Holy Ghost."[7] Elder McConkie has thus described the influence of the Light of Christ and the ministry of the Holy Ghost as follows:

> The light of Christ (also called the Spirit of Christ and the Spirit of the Lord) is a light, a power, and an influence that . . . is everywhere present and accounts for the omnipresence of God. It is the agency of God's power and the law by which all things are governed. It is also the agency used by the Holy Ghost to manifest truth and dispense spiritual gifts to many people at one and the same time. For instance, it is as though the Holy Ghost, who is a personage of spirit, was broadcasting all truth throughout the whole universe all the time, using the light of Christ as the agency by which the message is delivered. But only those who attune their souls to the Holy Spirit receive the available revelation. It is in this way that the person of the Holy Ghost makes his influence felt in the heart of every righteous person at one and the same time.[8]

Revelation for the Church

The Restored Church was less than six months old when difficulties regarding revelation were encountered. "Brother

Hiram Page had in his possession a certain stone,'' Joseph Smith recorded, "by which he had obtained certain 'revelations' concerning the upbuilding of Zion, the order of the Church, etc., all of which were entirely at variance with the order of God's house, as laid down in the New Testament, as well as in our late revelations.''[9] In describing this incident in Church history, Newel Knight observed that "even Oliver Cowdery and the Whitmer family had given heed to them. . . . Joseph was perplexed and scarcely knew how to meet this new exigency. That night I occupied the same room he did,'' Brother Knight continued, "and the greater part of the night was spent in prayer and supplication. After much labor with these brethren, they were convinced of their error, and confessed the same, renouncing [Page's] revelations as not being of God.''[10] It was because of Page's claims to revelation for the Church that the Lord spoke through Joseph Smith to Oliver Cowdery, giving what we now know as section 28 of the Doctrine and Covenants.

> Behold, I say unto thee, Oliver, that it shall be given unto thee that thou shalt be heard by the church in all things whatsoever thou shalt teach them by the Comforter, concerning the revelations and commandments which I have given.
> But, behold, verily, verily, I say unto thee, no one shall be appointed to receive commandments and revelations in this church excepting my servant Joseph Smith, Jun., for he receiveth them even as Moses. (D&C 28:1–2.)

Some five months later another episode provoked a similar oracle from the Lord. A Mrs. Hubble, presumably a recent convert to the Church, "professed to be a prophetess of the Lord and professed to have many revelations, and knew the Book of Mormon was true, and that she would become a teacher in the Church of Christ. She appeared to be very sanctimonious and deceived some who were not able to detect her in her hypocrisy: others however had the spirit of discernment, and her follies and abominations were made manifest.''[11] Again in reply the Lord spoke of Joseph Smith as "him whom I have appointed unto you to receive commandments and revelations from my hand. And this ye shall know assuredly—'' the Savior reemphasized, "that there is none other appointed unto you to receive commandments and revelations until he be taken, if he abide in me." And then, in summarizing the course the Saints were to follow in that day and forevermore, the Master said: "And this shall be a law unto you, that ye receive not the teachings of any that shall come before you as revelations or commandments; and this I give unto you that you may not be deceived, that you may know they are not of me" (D&C 43:2–3, 5–6).

The principle is clear and the doctrine certain: only the President of the Church—the Prophet, Seer, and Revelator for the Church—has the right to receive divine direction for the whole Church, for this is the person the Lord will inspire "to move the cause of Zion in mighty power for good" (D&C 21:7). "He alone," explained President J. Reuben Clark, Jr., "has the right to receive revelations for the Church, either new or amendatory, or to give authoritative interpretations of scriptures that shall be binding on the Church, or change in any way the existing doctrines of the Church. He is God's sole mouthpiece on earth for The Church of Jesus Christ of Latter-day Saints, the only true Church. He alone may declare the mind and will of God to His people."[12] This principle and practice ensure orthodoxy in the Church and kingdom of God, an institution guided and led by Him whose house is a house of order.

Receiving Personal Revelation

"No man can receive the Holy Ghost," the Prophet explained, "without receiving revelations," for "the Holy Ghost is a revelator."[13] President Joseph F. Smith likewise taught that "every individual in the Church has just as much right to enjoy the spirit of revelation and the understanding from God which that spirit of revelation gives him, for his own good, as the bishop has to enable him to preside over his ward."[14] We thus find numerous instances in the Doctrine and Covenants—particularly in the early revelations to the Church—detailing such matters as how and in what manner God may choose to communicate with his people.

An important insight pertaining to the spirit of revelation came to Oliver Cowdery in April of 1829. Oliver, who desired to translate and thus do more than act as scribe to the Prophet in their work with the gold plates, was told: "Oliver Cowdery, verily, verily, I say unto you, that assuredly as the Lord liveth, who is your God and your Redeemer, even so surely shall you receive a knowledge of whatsoever things you shall ask in faith, with an honest heart. . . . Yea, behold, I will tell you in your mind and in your heart, by the Holy Ghost, which shall come upon you and which shall dwell in your heart. Now, behold, this is the spirit of revelation; behold, this is the spirit by which Moses brought the children of Israel through the Red Sea on dry ground." (D&C 8:1–3.)[15] We note with much interest that revelation is to be given to the heart as well as to the mind, that the divine communication is to involve the feelings as well as the natural cognitive processes of man. In commenting upon these verses, Joseph F. McConkie has written:

> We observe that neither [Oliver] nor Joseph was to experience any suspension of their natural faculties in the process of obtaining revelation. Quite to the contrary, their hearts and minds were to be the very media through which the revelation came. Prophets are not hollow shells through which the voice of the Lord echoes, nor are they mechanical recording devices; prophets are men of passion, feeling, and intellect. One does not suspend agency, mind, or spirit in the service of God. It is . . . with heart, might, mind and strength that we have been asked to serve, and in nothing is this more apparent than the receiving of revelation. There is no mindless worship or service in the kingdom of heaven.[16]

In a sense, the mind and the heart serve as a system of witnesses, a means whereby one may not be deceived or misled to trust his eternal salvation to either the rational processes alone or to the feelings, or emotions, alone.

As to the workings of the Spirit of God, and as to the matter of things coming into the mind, let us here observe that almost always a revelation from God will be rational, will make sense, will be in harmony with the commonly accepted standards and ideals set down by God and prophets and the laws of the land. "In the Church," Elder Boyd K. Packer has pointed out, "we are not exempt from common sense. You can know to begin with that you won't be prompted from any righteous source to steal, to lie, to cheat, to join anyone in any kind of moral transgression."[17] Yes, God did command Abraham to sacrifice Isaac, and Nephi to slay Laban, but these were rare exceptions, and both Abraham and Nephi were prophets and seers: they knew the voice of the Lord implicitly and thus could converse with the Spirit, which had come to be a constant companion. The Lord will not reveal to an individual member of the Church anything that is out of harmony with law and order and good judgment, or in conflict with the order of the Church and the position of the leaders of the Church. Further, God will never call upon his people to perform an action which is unnatural or indecorous in the eyes of God and man.[18]

Enos, the son of Jacob, explained concerning his own spiritual odyssey: "I went to hunt beasts in the forests; and the words which I had often heard my father speak concerning eternal life, and the joy of the saints, sunk deep into my heart. And my soul hungered." After crying unto God "all the day long" in "mighty prayer," Enos declared that "there came a voice unto me, saying: Enos, thy sins are forgiven thee, and thou shalt be blessed." After Enos had learned that the remission of sins had come because of his faith in Jesus the Christ, after he had begun to feel a desire for the welfare of the Nephites, and after he had continued his struggle in the Spirit, he recounted, "Behold, the voice of the Lord came into my mind again, saying: I will visit thy brethren according to their diligence in keeping my commandments." (Enos 1:3–4, 10.) Joseph Smith also spoke of the manner in which the Spirit may act upon the mind: "A person may profit by noticing the first intimation of the spirit of revelation; for instance, when you feel pure intelligence flowing into you, it may give you sudden strokes of ideas, so that by noticing it, you may find it fulfilled the same day or soon; (i.e.) those things that were presented unto your minds by the Spirit of God, will come to pass; and thus by learning the Spirit of God and understanding it, you may grow into the principle of revelation, until you become perfect in Christ Jesus."[19]

The nature of the occasion, as well as the readiness and need of the recipient, dictates how a message from God may be communicated. Certain situations require a message which pierces to the very soul, others where that voice, although still and small, makes "the bones to quake" while it makes manifest the mind of the Lord (D&C 85:6; see also Helaman 5:30; 3 Nephi 11:3). In speaking of how God makes known his will through the heart of man, Elder Packer said: "These delicate, refined spiritual communications are not seen with our eyes nor heard with our ears. And even though it is described as a voice, it is a voice that one feels more than he hears."[20] President Ezra Taft Benson similarly taught: "We hear the words of the Lord most often by a feeling. If we are humble and sensitive, the Lord will prompt us through our feelings. That is why spiritual promptings move us on occasion to great joy, sometimes to tears. . . . The Holy Ghost causes our feelings to be more tender. We feel more charitable and compassionate. We are calmer. We have a greater capacity to love. People want to be around us because our very countenances radiate the influence of the Spirit."[21] Thus it is that Nephi explained to his errant brothers that in spite of the visible manifestations they had received from a benevolent God, they had remained unmoved and unchanged, incorrigible because they were "past feeling" (1 Nephi 17:45). Thus it is that the Lord explained to Oliver Cowdery that after he had studied and pondered and drawn conclusions on his own, he would come to feel those things which were right and from God (see D&C 9:8).

One of the precious but often overlooked aspects of revelation through our feelings is peace. In one sense, to be at peace is to have received a meaningful revelation, to have the inner awareness that God is pleased with one's life and that the course charted by the individual is in harmony with the divine will (see D&C 59:23). In another sense, peace is a means by which the Lord responds to petitions and answers prayers. "Blessed art thou," the Lord said to Oliver Cowdery, "for what thou hast done; for thou hast inquired of me [concerning the truthfulness of the Restoration], and behold, as often as thou hast inquired thou hast received instruction of my Spirit. . . . Behold, thou knowest that thou hast inquired of me and I did enlighten thy mind; and now I tell thee these things that thou mayest know that thou hast been enlightened by the Spirit of truth." The Savior then continued with his instructions and an invitation: "Verily, verily, I say unto you, if you desire a further witness, cast your mind upon the night that you cried unto me in your heart, that you might know concerning the truth of these things." This is a reference to the occasion when, while residing in the Smith home, Oliver had inquired of the Lord concerning the truthfulness of the family's claims concerning Joseph Smith, Jr., and the coming forth of the Book of Mormon. "Did I not speak peace to your mind concerning the matter?" the Lord asked. "What greater witness can you have than from God?" (D&C 6:14–15, 22–23.)

The responses to the humble petitions to God by his children are many and varied, as are the ways in which those answers are given. The Doctrine and Covenants identifies and illustrates a number of ways revelation comes: personal appearance of the Lord (see D&C 110:1–10); personal appearance of other heavenly messengers (see D&C 110:11–15; 128:20); vision (D&C 76; 137; 138); the voice of God (see D&C 128:21); through the Urim and Thummim (see D&C 3, 6, 11, 14); and the Holy Ghost speaking to our minds and hearts (see D&C 8:2–3; 9:7–9). It would be a mistake for the Latter-day Saints to suppose that answers and confirmations come only in one way—as a burning in the bosom, for example. The Lord desires to communicate with his children and will choose the means which will most clearly and persuasively convey his holy words and his perfect will to those who seek him diligently. "If thou shalt ask," he stated as early as 1831, "thou shalt receive revelation upon revelation, knowledge upon knowledge, that thou mayest know the mysteries and peaceable things—that which bringeth joy, that which bringeth life eternal" (D&C 42:61).

Teaching and Learning by the Spirit: A Form of Revelation

In a revelation called "the law of the Church," the Lord established the divine standard under which teachers of the gospel are to operate. "And the Spirit shall be given unto you by the prayer of faith; and if ye receive not the Spirit ye shall not teach" (D&C 42:14). This statement appears to be both a command and a prophecy. That is, the gospel teacher is told to seek for and to live worthy of the guidance and confirming power of that Spirit, which causes lessons to go down into the heart and burn like fire. In addition, the Lord affirms that which every teacher knows only too well—that if the Spirit of the Lord does not accompany the presentation of the message, then true spiritual communication, edification, and lasting learning will not take place.

Indeed, the teacher is under obligation to teach the gospel "by the Spirit, even the Comforter which was sent forth to teach the truth." In the language of our Lord, "he that is ordained of me and sent forth to preach the word of truth by the Comforter, in the Spirit of truth, doth he preach it by the Spirit of truth or some other way? And if it be by some other way it is not of God. And again, he that receiveth the word of truth, doth he receive it by the Spirit of truth or some other way? If it be some other way it is not of God." (D&C 50:14, 17–20.) In offering commentary upon these verses, particularly upon the manner in which someone might seek to convey the word of truth in some other way, Elder Bruce R. McConkie observed:

> If you teach the word of truth—now note, you're saying what is true, every thing you say is accurate and right—by some other way than the Spirit, it is not of God. Now what is the other way to teach than by the Spirit? Well, obviously, it is by the power of the intellect.
>
> Suppose I came here tonight and delivered a great message on teaching, and I did it by the power of the intellect without any of the Spirit of God attending. Suppose that every word that I said was true, no error whatever, but it was an intellectual presentation. This revelation says: "If it be by some other way it is not of God" (D&C 50:18).
>
> That is, God did not present the message through me because I used the power of the intellect instead of the power of the Spirit. Intellectual things—reason and logic —can do some good, and they can prepare the way, and they can get the mind ready to receive the spirit under cer-

tain circumstances. But conversion comes and the truth sinks into the hearts of people only when it is taught by the power of the Spirit.[22]

One of the early messages of this dispensation is that adequate preparation must precede the power which accompanies a gospel presentation. Hyrum Smith was instructed in May of 1829: "Behold, this is your work, to keep my commandments, yea, with all your might, mind and strength." And then the Master Teacher spoke of the prerequisites for spiritual power: "Seek not to declare my word, but first seek to obtain my word, and then shall your tongue be loosed; then, if you desire, you shall have my Spirit and my word, yea, the power of God unto the convincing of men. But now hold your peace; study my word which hath gone forth among the children of men [e.g., the Bible], and also study my word which shall come forth among the children of men, or that which is now translating [the Book of Mormon]." (D&C 11:20–22.)

This directive is certainly in harmony with what we find in the Book of Mormon. Of the sons of Mosiah the Nephite record attests that "they had waxed strong in the knowledge of the truth; for they were men of a sound understanding and they had searched the scripture diligently, that they might know the word of God. But this is not all; they had given themselves to much prayer, and fasting; therefore they had the spirit of prophecy, and the spirit of revelation, and when they taught, they taught with power and authority of God." (Alma 17:2–3.) In stressing that the study of scripture is directly associated with the receipt of revelation, Elder McConkie explained to the regional representatives of the Church in 1982:

> Our tendency—it is an almost universal practice among most church leaders—is to get so involved with the operation of the institutional church that we never gain faith like the ancients, simply because we do not involve ourselves in the basic gospel matters that were the center of their lives.
>
> We are so wound up in programs and statistics and trends, in properties, lands, and mammon, and in achieving goals that will highlight the excellence of our work, that we "have omitted the weightier matters of the law."

And as Jesus would have said: "These [weightier things] ought ye to have done, and not to leave the other undone" (Matthew 23:23).

Let us be reminded of the great basic verities upon which all church programs and all church organization rest.

We are not saved by church programs as such, by church organizations alone, or even by the Church itself. It is the gospel that saves. The gospel is "the power of God unto salvation" (Romans 1:16). . . .

May I suggest, based on personal experience, that faith comes and revelations are received as a direct result of scriptural study.

Paul says "faith cometh by hearing" the word of God (Romans 10:17). Joseph Smith taught that to gain faith men must have a knowledge of the nature and kind of being God is; they must have a correct idea of his character, perfections, and attributes; and they must so live as to gain the assurance that their conduct is in harmony with the divine will.

Faith is thus born of scriptural study. Those who study, ponder, and pray about the scriptures, seeking to understand their deep and hidden meanings, receive from time to time great outpourings of light and knowledge from the Holy Spirit. This is what happened to Joseph Smith and Sidney Rigdon when they received the vision of the degrees of glory.

However talented men may be in administrative matters; however eloquent they may be in expressing their views; however learned they may be in worldly things—they will be denied the sweet whisperings of the Spirit that might have been theirs unless they pay the price of studying, pondering, and praying about the scriptures.[23]

As we note from the above comment, the revelations specify the curriculum of the gospel teacher—that which is to be taught. "And again, the elders, priests, and teachers of this church shall teach the principles of my gospel, which are in the Bible and the Book of Mormon, in which is the fulness of the gospel. And they shall observe the covenants and church articles[24] to do them, and these shall be their teachings, as they shall be directed by the Spirit." (D&C 42:12–13). In our standard works—which now include the Doctrine and Covenants and the Pearl of Great Price—when supplemented with the words of modern prophets and Apostles, we have a standard which directs all that we should teach in the Church. These books of holy writ constitute the canon of scripture, the rule of faith and doctrine against which truth and error are to be measured. Those who teach the message of the Restoration are to say "none other things than that which the prophets and apostles have written, and that which is taught them by the Comforter through prayer of faith" (D&C 52:9; compare verse 36; 80:4). In what is a marvelous recommendation for gospel teachers to see to it that they teach from the standard works,[25] Elder McConkie has also written that "those who preach by the power of the Holy Ghost use the scriptures as their basic source of knowledge and doctrine. They begin with what the Lord has before revealed to other inspired men. But it is the practice of the Lord to give added knowledge to those upon whose hearts the true meanings and intents of the scriptures have been impressed. Many great doctrinal revelations come to those who preach from the scriptures."[26]

Trying the Spirits

"Believe not every spirit," John the Beloved taught, "but try the spirits whether they are of God: because many false prophets are gone out into the world" (1 John 4:1). For those interested in spiritual things; for those intent on knowing the will of the Lord and doing it, such is an essential exercise, for "nothing is a greater injury to the children of men than to be under the influence of a false spirit when they think they have the Spirit of God."[27] It is but fitting, then, to attend to some of the instructions delivered through Joseph Smith to enable the Saints of the Most High to stay on that strait and narrow course which leads to life eternal.

In the early days of the Church, "a custom of admitting only members and earnest investigators to the sacrament meetings and other assemblies of the Church had become somewhat general" (Preface to D&C 46). In March of 1831 the Lord instructed the Saints:

> And again I say unto you, concerning your confirma-
> tion meetings, that if there be any that are not of the
> church, that are earnestly seeking after the kingdom, ye
> shall not cast them out.
>
> But ye are commanded in all things to ask of God,
> who giveth liberally; and that which the Spirit testifies
> unto you even so I would that ye should do in all holiness
> of heart, walking uprightly before me, considering the end
> of your salvation, doing all things with prayer and thanks-
> giving, that ye may not be seduced by evil spirits, or doc-
> trines of devils, or the commandments of men; for some
> are of men, and others of devils.
>
> Wherefore, beware lest ye are deceived; and *that ye
> may not be deceived seek ye earnestly the best gifts,*
> always remembering for what they are given;
>
> For verily I say unto you, they are given for the bene-
> fit of those who love me and keep all my commandments,
> and him that seeketh so to do; that all may be benefited
> that seek or that ask of me, that ask and not for a sign
> that they may consume it upon their lusts.
>
> And again, verily I say unto you, I would that ye
> should always remember, and always retain in your minds
> what those gifts are, that are given unto the church. (D&C
> 46:6–10, italics added.)

The revelation then enumerates the various gifts of the Spirit,
including the knowledge that Jesus is the Christ, as well as the
gift to believe on the faith of those who know; the differences of
administration and the diversities of operations, the gifts of
wisdom and of knowledge, faith to heal as well as to be healed,
prophecy, discernment, tongues, and the interpretation of
tongues. (See D&C 46:13–25; compare 1 Corinthians 12;
Moroni 10.)

The gifts of the Spirit of God are given to the Saints to enable them to discern and perceive those manifestations, beliefs,
voices, and persons which claim heaven as the source of their
authority but in reality represent the views and vagaries of men
or the damning doctrines of demons. Because of the Restoration, because keys and powers and priesthoods and authorities
have been delivered to man once again, and because the power
to confer and enjoy the gifts and manifestations of the Holy
Ghost is among us, every man and woman who qualifies is able

to speak in the name of God the Lord, even the Savior of the world (see D&C 1:20). Every person possessing the testimony of Jesus becomes a prophet (see Revelation 19:10) and is thereby able to discern and dispel that which is not of the Light. Further, since "the spirits of the prophets are subject to the prophets" (1 Corinthians 14:32), it is appropriate and right and orderly that "unto the bishop of the church, and unto such as God shall appoint and ordain to watch over the church and to be elders unto the church, are to have it given unto them to discern all those gifts lest there shall be any among you professing and yet be not of God" (D&C 46:27). "Not every spirit, or vision, or singing, is of God," the Prophet taught. "The devil is an orator; he is powerful. . . . The gift of discerning spirits will be given to the Presiding Elder. Pray for him that he may have this gift."[28] And thus it is that the revelations speak emphatically of the President of the Church, the presiding officer in the earthly kingdom, as he who is to "preside over the whole church, and to be like unto Moses—Behold, here is wisdom; yea, to be a seer, a revelator, a translator, and a prophet, having all the gifts of God which he [God] bestows upon the head of the church" (D&C 107:91–92).

The challenge of discerning when a teaching or a manifestation or revelation is from God was a significant challenge for the early Latter-day Saints, just as it is for us today. On the occasion when the first high priests of this dispensation were called and ordained (in June of 1831), some unusual spiritual displays were evident. A revelation given through Joseph Smith indicated a central guide, a standard, a pattern by which the Saints should judge that which is of God from that which is not. "And again," the Lord said, "I will give unto you a pattern in all things, that ye may not be deceived; for Satan is abroad in the land, and he goeth forth deceiving the nations—"

> Wherefore he that prayeth, whose spirit is contrite, the same is accepted of me if he obey mine ordinances.
> He that speaketh, whose spirit is contrite, whose language is meek and edifieth, the same is of God if he obey mine ordinances.
> And again, he that trembleth under my power shall be made strong, and shall bring forth fruits of praise and

wisdom, according to the revelations and truths which I have given you.

And again, he that is overcome and bringeth not forth fruits, even according to this pattern, is not of me.

Wherefore, by this pattern ye shall know the spirits in all cases under the whole heavens. (D&C 52:14–19.)

Only those who obey the ordinances of God, his laws, commandments, and statutes, including the rites and ceremonies, necessary for salvation (e.g., baptism and confirmation at the hands of an authorized servant of God), are accepted of him. In the true and saving sense, only those who have entered in at the strait gate bring forth fruits and works which originate with God and thus are to be received as his. "The whole world lieth in sin," the Savior explained, "and groaneth under darkness and under the bondage of sin. And by this you may know they are under the bondage of sin, because they come not unto me." (D&C 84:49–50.) More specifically, the Lord had remarked to Sidney Rigdon just after he had joined the Church that "there are none that doeth good except those who are ready to receive the fulness of my gospel, which I have sent forth unto this generation" (D&C 35:12). The Light of Christ and the influence of the Holy Ghost[29] are available to all men and women; the people of the earth may thereby be led into all truth, the fulness of which is to be found in the "only true and living Church upon the face of the whole earth" (D&C 1:30). But the gift of the Holy Ghost and the gifts of the Holy Ghost are reserved for baptized members, those who have truly come unto Christ and forsake the ways of the world.

Conclusion

"We believe all that God has revealed, all that He does now reveal, and we believe that He will yet reveal many great and important things pertaining to the Kingdom of God" (Articles of Faith 1:9). This statement of belief is as true of individuals as it is of the institutional Church. There are great and important things yet to be made known to those Latter-day Saints who search, ponder, and pray. The Lord is no respecter of persons. He does not simply bless office holders, nor does he only endow with knowledge from on high those called to direct the destiny of the Church. "God hath not revealed anything to Joseph," the Prophet himself observed, "but what he will make known unto the Twelve, and even the least Saint may know all things as fast as he is able to bear them."[30] In the words of a modern Apostle, "we are entitled to revelation. I say that every member of the Church, independent and irrespective of any position that he may hold, is entitled to get revelation from the Holy Ghost; he is entitled to entertain angels; he is entitled to view the visions of eternity; and if we would like to go the full measure, he is entitled to see God the same way that any prophet in literal and actual reality has seen the face of Deity."[31]

Some time after Joseph Smith's death, he appeared to Brigham Young and gave specific and pointed instructions as to why the members of the Church must labor to acquire and keep the Spirit of the Lord. "Tell the people to be humble and faithful," Joseph Smith counseled his successor, "and be sure to keep the Spirit of the Lord and it will lead them right.

> Be careful and not turn away the small still voice; it will teach them what to do and where to go; it will yield the fruits of the kingdom. Tell the brethren to keep their hearts open to conviction, so that when the Holy Ghost comes to them, their hearts will be ready to receive it. They can tell the Spirit of the Lord from all other spirits; it will whisper peace and joy to their souls; it will take malice, hatred, strife and all evil from their hearts; and their whole desire will be to do good, bring forth righteousness and build up the kingdom of God. Tell the brethren if they will follow the Spirit of the Lord, they will go right. Be sure to tell the people to keep the Spirit of the Lord; and if they will, they will find themselves just as they were organized by our Father in Heaven before they came into the world. Our Father in Heaven organized the human family, but they are all disorganized and in great confusion."

"Joseph then showed me the pattern," President Young continued, "how they were in the beginning. This I cannot describe, but I saw it, and saw where the Priesthood had been taken from the earth and how it must be joined together, so that there would be a perfect chain from Father Adam to his latest posterity. Joseph again said, 'Tell the people to be sure to keep the Spirit of the Lord and follow it, and it will lead them just right.' "[32]

Growing into and learning the spirit of revelation is a central duty as well as a consummate privilege of those who belong to The Church of Jesus Christ of Latter-day Saints. God has spoken. He speaks now. He will yet speak. There is a crying need in this generation for more and better-attuned listening ears. And there is much need to understand how and in what manner the Lord communicates with his people. The Doctrine and Covenants is a marvelous collection of revelations—many and varied in type and kind, but sure and certain evidences of the reality that God is the same yesterday, today, and forever; that he who is infinite is ever ready to reveal himself and his will to those of us who are so very finite; that he is "merciful and gracious unto those who fear him," and delights to honor those who serve him "in righteousness and in truth." In his own words, "To them will I reveal all mysteries, yea, all the hidden mysteries of my kingdom from days of old, and for ages to come, will I make known unto them the good pleasure of my will concerning all things pertaining to my kingdom. Yea, even the wonders of eternity shall they know, and things to come will I show them, even the things of many generations." (D&C 76:5, 7–8.)

This is the Lord's work and must be undertaken according to his holy will and in harmony with his grand and glorious purposes. "This latter-day work is spiritual," President Ezra Taft Benson has taught. "It takes spirituality to comprehend it, to love it, and to discern it. Therefore, we should seek the Spirit in all we do. That is our challenge."[33]

Notes

1. *Teachings of the Prophet Joseph Smith,* comp. Joseph Fielding Smith (Salt Lake City: Deseret Book Co., 1976), p. 160.

2. Joseph Fielding McConkie, "The Principle of Revelation," in *Studies in Scripture, Volume 1: The Doctrine and Covenants,* eds.

Robert L. Millet and Kent P. Jackson (Sandy, UT.: Randall Book Co., 1984), p. 81.

3. For prophetic statements as to the corporeality of God prior to this statement in section 130, see *The Words of Joseph Smith,* eds. Andrew F. Ehat and Lyndon W. Cook (Provo, Utah: Religious Studies Center, Brigham Young University, 1980), pp. 60, 64. For a detailed discussion of Joseph Smith's teachings regarding God's physical nature, see Robert L. Millet, "The Supreme Power Over All Things: The Doctrine of the Godhead in the Lectures on Faith," a Symposium on the Lectures on Faith, Religious Studies Center, Brigham Young University, March 1988.

4. Parley P. Pratt, *Key to the Science of Theology*, 9th ed. (Salt Lake City: Deseret Book Co., 1965), p. 47.

5. Bruce R. McConkie, *A New Witness for the Articles of Faith* (Salt Lake City: Deseret Book Co., 1985), p. 257.

6. McConkie, *New Witness for the Articles of Faith,* p. 45.

7. Joseph F. Smith, *Gospel Doctrine* (Salt Lake City: Deseret Book Co., 1971), pp. 67–68.

8. McConkie, *New Witness for the Articles of Faith,* p. 70.

9. *History of The Church of Jesus Christ of Latter-day Saints,* 7 vols., ed. B. H. Roberts (Salt Lake City: Deseret Book Co., 1957), 1:109–10.

10. From Newel Knight Journal in LDS Church Archives; cited in Lyndon W. Cook, *The Revelations of the Prophet Joseph Smith* (Salt Lake City: Deseret Book Co., 1985), pp. 39–40.

11. From *An Early Latter Day Saint History: The Book of John Whitmer, Kept by Commandment,* eds. F. Mark McKiernan and Roger D. Launius (Independence, Missouri: Herald Publishing House, 1980), p. 42, spelling corrected. Joseph Smith's record of this event is given as follows: "Soon after the foregoing revelation [D&C 42] was received, a woman came making great pretensions of revealing commandments, laws and other curious matters." (*History of the Church,* 1:154.)

12. From "When Are the Writings and Sermons of Church Leaders Entitled to the Claim of Being Scripture?" address delivered to Seminary and Institute teachers at Brigham Young University, 7 July 1954, in *J. Reuben Clark: Selected Papers,* ed. David H. Yarn, Jr. (Provo, UT.: Brigham Young University Press, 1984), p. 101. It is true that all of the elders of the Church, when moved upon by the

power of the Holy Ghost, have the right to speak forth scripture—the will, mind, word, and voice of the Lord (see D&C 68:1–4). Yet, as Paul taught, "the spirits of the prophets are subject to the prophets" (1 Corinthians 14:32), and thus there is a head, a single prophet responsible for scripture being delivered or clarified or expanded for the entire Church.

13. *Teachings of the Prophet Joseph Smith,* p. 328.

14. In Conference Report, Apr. 1912, pp. 9–10; compare *Teachings of the Prophet Joseph Smith,* p. 111.

15. Moses was the head of a dispensation and thus a prophet's prophet. Of him the Lord Jehovah explained to Aaron and Miriam: "If there be a prophet among you, I the Lord will make myself known unto him in a vision, and will speak unto him in a dream. My servant Moses is not so, who is faithful in all mine house. With him will I speak mouth to mouth, even apparently, and not in dark speeches; and the similitude of the Lord shall he behold." (Numbers 12:6–8; compare Exodus 33:11.) But the above verse indicates that Moses— like all prophets, and, for that matter, all men and women—walked most often and most surely by the kindly light and whisperings of the Spirit.

16. From "The Principle of Revelation," p. 83.

17. In Conference Report, Oct. 1979, p. 29.

18. See *Teachings of the Prophet Joseph Smith*, pp. 156–57, 209, 214. See also Marion G. Romney, in Conference Report, Apr. 1942, pp. 17–18.

19. *Teachings of the Prophet Joseph Smith*, p. 151.

20. From "The Candle of the Lord," in *That All May Be Edified* (Salt Lake City: Bookcraft, 1982), p. 335; compare Conference Report, Oct. 1979, p. 28; see also 1 Nephi 17:45.

21. Boyd K. Packer, *Come Unto Christ* (Salt Lake City: Deseret Book Co., 1983), p. 20.

22. *"The Foolishness of Teaching,"* address delivered to Church Educational System personnel (Salt Lake City: The Church of Jesus Christ of Latter-day Saints, 1981), p. 9.

23. From "Holy Writ: Published Anew," an address delivered at a seminar for Regional Representatives, 2 April 1982.

24. The "articles and covenants" were specifically what we have today as sections 20 and 22 of the Doctrine and Covenants. See

Richard O. Cowan, "How Our Doctrine and Covenants Came to Be," in this volume.

25. In 1938 President J. Reuben Clark, Jr. stressed to Church educators that "your chief interest, your essential and all but sole duty, is to teach the Gospel of the Lord Jesus Christ as that has been revealed in these latter days. You are to teach this Gospel using as your sources and authorities the Standard Works of the Church, and the words of those whom God has called to lead his people in these last days. You are not, whether high or low, to intrude into your work your own peculiar philosophy, no matter what its source or how pleasing or rational its seems to you to be. To do so would be to have as many different churches as we have seminaries — and that is chaos." ("The Charted Course of the Church in Education," address delivered on 8 August 1938; in *J. Reuben Clark: Selected Papers,* p. 253.)

26. Bruce R. McConkie, *The Promised Messiah* (Salt Lake City: Deseret Book Co., 1978), pp. 515–16, italics added.

27. *Teachings of the Prophet Joseph Smith,* p. 205.

28. Ibid., p. 162.

29. Joseph Smith made a distinction between the Holy Ghost (i.e., the influence of the Holy Ghost) and the gift of the Holy Ghost. The former is the means, for example, by which an interested investigator of the faith comes to know the truth of the message of the Restoration (see Moroni 10:4–5). The latter — the gift of the Holy Ghost — comes only after baptism by proper authority at the hands of a legal administrator. See Smith, *Teachings of the Prophet Joseph Smith,* p. 199.

30. Ibid., p. 149.

31. From Bruce R. McConkie, "How to Get Personal Revelation," address delivered at a devotional assembly at Brigham Young University, 11 October 1966.

32. *Journal History,* 23 Feb. 1847.

33. Packer, *Come Unto Christ,* p. 23.

4

The Joseph Smith Translation and the Doctrine and Covenants: Historical and Doctrinal Companions

Robert J. Matthews

Throughout the forty years I have studied the Joseph Smith Translation, I have not been in a hurry, nor have I felt that I had a message for the Church. It has been a personal interest, and I have not felt a call to set anybody right.

During the years I was studying the manuscript, the effect it might have on others hardly crossed my mind. Few would have wanted the Joseph Smith Translation to draw much attention. But we have wider vision today, and we understand more about the background and the unity of the scriptures. We have made

Robert J. Matthews is Dean of Religious Education and Professor of Ancient Scripture at Brigham Young University. This article is adapted from an address delivered to the Ninth Annual Church Educational System Religious Educators Symposium, held at Brigham Young University 14–16 August 1985. It is used by permission of The Church of Jesus Christ of Latter-day Saints.

progress in the past decade, not only in the availability of the scriptures, but also in our understanding of them. The Joseph Smith Translation is not just a better Bible; it was the channel, or the means, of doctrinal restoration in the infancy of this Church.

The Prophet Joseph Smith Is the Appointed Channel for Revelation of the Word of God

I have spent a large segment of my life in thinking about the Joseph Smith Translation because of my love for the Prophet Joseph Smith. I am not a Bible scholar. I do not know the ancient languages, nor can I read an ancient manuscript. I am very interested in textual criticism and the history of the Bible, and to be able to study the ancient text would be important to me, but I have only the mother tongue of faith, and I consider Joseph Smith's views to be more important and to contain greater fundamental truth than all that the world of secular scholarship can produce. Joseph Smith taught by the spirit of revelation, and by that spirit he translated the Bible. The Lord says, in Doctrine and Covenants 5:10, "This generation shall have my word through" Joseph Smith. Therefore, I say we ought not to expect to get it in some other way. Our faith and our hopes for salvation are anchored in the Restoration far more than in any ancient book or manuscript.

Some Personal History

In the summer of 1944, when I was eighteen years of age, I was sitting one evening with my father and mother in our home listening to a radio address by Elder Joseph Fielding Smith on station KSL. He quoted John 1:18, "No man hath seen God at any time." He said that it was a mistranslation, and that this passage was corrected by revelation to Joseph Smith as follows: "No man hath seen God at any time, except he [God] hath borne record of the Son; for except it is through him no man can be saved" (JST, John 1:19). I had never before heard of Joseph Smith's translation of the Bible, but something forcibly struck me when Elder Smith said that it had been corrected by the Lord in a revelation.[1] I have never lost the feeling. It awakened in me an intense desire to know more. I did not say anything to my parents about the experience; I just knew that I had been touched inside.

Copies of the Joseph Smith Translation were scarce in my hometown, Evanston, Wyoming. I could find only one—an 1867 first edition, and the book of Revelation had been cut out of that. Few people knew anything about it. Two or three people tried to dissuade me, saying the Reorganized Church of Jesus Christ of Latter Day Saints had altered it. They also said that Joseph Smith had not finished it anyway and that the Church did not accept it.

I found no one (even at Brigham Young University) who seemed to sense that the Joseph Smith Translation was mainstream activity of the Prophet resulting in much of the doctrinal restoration in this dispensation. It was regarded only as a sideline of the Prophet's work. I finally obtained a copy of my own from N. B. Lundwall in 1947. From then until 1950 I made a word-for-word comparison of the Joseph Smith Translation with the King James Version. I was fascinated by it, but I knew absolutely nothing about its background.

I was anxious to see the original manuscript that the RLDS church possessed. I also learned that there was a partial copy known as the Bernhisel Manuscript, which was had by our Church. But both documents were unavailable for research at that time. Largely through the efforts of Reed C. Durham and the goodness of President Joseph Fielding Smith, the Bernhisel copy became available in about 1965. I tried for fifteen years to see the original manuscript in the RLDS archives; in 1968 they finally let me see it, read it, copy it, and take a few photographs.

No one is completely independent in researching a subject so large and complex, and I am indebted to President William E. Berrett, then the administrator of seminaries and institutes of religion, and to Richard P. Howard, historian of the RLDS church, and to several others, including President Joseph Fielding Smith and Elder Bruce R. McConkie. Just about everyone I have known has helped me in some way.

Multiple Contribution of Original Documents

The main reason I wanted to see the original manuscript was to determine whether the printed editions of the Joseph Smith Translation were published correctly. My interest was entirely in the text of the Bible. I was little interested in who the scribes were, how long it took to write it down, or where or when the work was done. The original manuscript was a great help in determining the accuracy of the printed text, and I am happy to report that my studies led me to the conclusion that the RLDS church has printed the Joseph Smith Translation in very close harmony with the manuscript, although there have been some corrections in spelling and grammar.

The search would have ended at that point had it not been that the manuscript had much more to say in addition to giving the biblical text. It took some time before I realized what else the original manuscript had to offer. To begin with, there were four manuscripts. One document covered chapters 1 through 24 of Genesis. Another manuscript, with a slightly different and enlarged text, started over with Genesis 1 and covered not only the twenty-four chapters, but continued on all the way through the entire Old Testament.

There was also a manuscript for Matthew, starting with chapter 1 and going consecutively through chapter 26. Then a second manuscript, with a slightly enlarged text, started over with Matthew, chapter 1, and continued on all the way through the New Testament. These manuscripts were dated in various places. Also, the handwriting changed from time to time as different scribes were employed, and the spelling changed with each scribe.

Even more significant was that it became evident there were initial drafts and there were more polished, more extensive revisions. The manuscripts give us an idea of how the translation was done and of how revelation comes. It was clear that the Prophet Joseph had to struggle, meditate, and ask for light. The translation was not just a process of pouring information from one vessel to another. Nor was it a matter of inserting doctrine already understood. The manuscripts suggest that the Prophet received inspiration line upon line, here a little and there a little.

It was a learning experience for him. I could see that understanding of spiritual things is progressive, and it comes as one is able to bear it.

Eventually I noticed that changes in handwriting and the dates on the manuscripts correspond with facts in Church history and sections in the Doctrine and Covenants. Oliver Cowdery, John Whitmer, and Sidney Rigdon move in and out of the manuscripts the same way they move in and out of the pages of Church history. Their lives are interwoven in the fabric and the writing of the Joseph Smith Translation. Richard Howard had already written a little on this subject, but it had more meaning when I could see it first hand. It gave me a particular thrill to hold in my hands the very pages that the Prophet and others had held in their hands and upon which they had written.

The Joseph Smith Translation and the Doctrine and Covenants are Inseparable in Both Doctrine and History

Many of the pages contain the dates on which the Prophet was translating a particular passage or series of chapters. Historically, such information is useful. It is even more exciting for its doctrinal implications. It became apparent that some of the revelations in the Doctrine and Covenants carry the same date as (or one of near proximity to) the date when a chapter in the Bible was translated. Sometimes the subject matter was similar, and often the wording of the Joseph Smith Translation is very close to the wording in the Doctrine and Covenants. This similarity called attention to the fact that the Joseph Smith Translation and the Doctrine and Covenants were close together in the daily activity of the Prophet's life. Sections 29, 76, 77, 91, and others are examples of such closeness, where the translation of a Bible passage and a section in the Doctrine and Covenants have the same root.

What adds more to the discovery is that the listed dates show clearly that some doctrines were revealed and recorded in the Joseph Smith Translation before these same doctrines appeared in the Doctrine and Covenants. This is the case with the age of accountability for children (eight years old). We generally look to Doctrine and Covenants 68:25–28, dated November 1831, for this information. But the Joseph Smith Translation, Genesis 17:11, which was given to Abraham, also mentions that children become accountable at eight years of age. If we knew only the printed page, these would appear simply as similar doctrines, but the dating on the manuscript shows the Joseph Smith Translation passage to have been written at least as early as April, eight months before the date for Doctrine and Covenants 68. This fact alone has to influence our view of Church history and our understanding of how the doctrinal restoration occurred; it certainly gives the Joseph Smith Translation greater prominence.

Some have thought that the Prophet simply went through the Bible, making it conform to Mormon doctrine — Mormonizing the Bible, they often call it. But the historical sequence shows this is not so. Translating the Bible was the process by which the revelation of these doctrines was given to Joseph Smith. How much Mormon doctrine was there in 1830 to copy from? Most of it was revealed later. If Elder McConkie had written *Mormon Doctrine* in 1830, it would have been very thin.

These examples persuade us that the Joseph Smith Translation is as much at home in a symposium on the Doctrine and Covenants as it would be in a Bible symposium. We are not talking about a few isolated passages, but about dozens of sections and verses, dealing with such basic cornerstones of doctrine as the age of accountability, the building of Zion, the patriarchal orders of Enoch and Melchizedek, the degrees of glory, premortal existence, priesthood, marriage, and the second coming of the Savior.

We see by these examples that there is an advantage in working with original sources. There is much to be learned by getting behind the printed page. We would never have been able to see the many relationships between the Joseph Smith Translation and the Doctrine and Covenants without the manuscript of the Joseph Smith Translation. In brief, we have been able to discern that the early sections of the Doctrine and Covenants deal with the translation and publication of the Book of Mormon and that many later sections relate directly to the translation and publication of parts of the Bible.

Becoming Literary Archaeologists

Every revelation that has been received was given at some specific place and time in some specific situation. But the past becomes covered with tradition and blurred with time, very similar to the way vegetation and drifting sands eventually cover rocks and structures. Time passes, leaders pass on, and new personalities come into prominence. As a consequence, we often do not know what lies just below the surface of the ground or behind a printed page, and so there often arises a misunderstanding, or perhaps no understanding at all. To know how it really was, we sometimes have to become literary archaeologists and dig down to original or prepublication sources. Then we see things we had not known, or we see them in a different light than ever before, no matter how many times we have trodden the path—whether it be a path through the field or through the printed pages of a book.

No matter how well a person knows the surface or how many times he has traveled over the ground, he will not know what lies even just under the surface—what form of art or architecture, or what message that past can tell—until he or someone else removes the surface accumulation and examines the facts of an earlier day. It is the same way with the Doctrine and Covenants and the Joseph Smith Translation. Many passages of the Doctrine and Covenants cannot be understood unless one knows the background; and in some cases the background can be discerned only by the manuscripts of the Joseph Smith Translation.

The Joseph Smith Translation Is Not Supported by the Present Work of Bible Scholars

Time and space will not permit an extensive examination of all the implications and evidences that the Book of Mormon, the Joseph Smith Translation, and the Doctrine and Covenants have in common. Remember that the Book of Mormon declares in 1 Nephi 13:24 that the Bible, when first written, was clear and plain, and that it is a witness for Jesus Christ. It also declares that many plain and precious things have been taken out of the Bible; these missing parts, however, will be restored again (see 1 Nephi 13:20–41).

The question is frequently asked of me, "Is the Joseph Smith Translation supported by modern non-Latter-day Saint scholarship and manuscript discoveries?" The answer is a resounding no, accompanied by a qualified yes. For example, you are all aware that Matthew 5:22 in the King James Version speaks out against hating one's brother "without a cause." The Book of Mormon, the Joseph Smith Translation, and modern scholarship all agree that the words "without a cause" should not be in that sentence. We ought not to hate our brother, even if there is a cause. Another example is the word "conversation," as found in various places in Peter and Paul's writings. This word is translated "behavior" or "conduct" by modern scholars. The Joseph Smith Translation does the same. So there is some small correlation in the meaning of words.

In the main, however, for the great messages in the Joseph Smith Translation about the Creation, premortal existence, the Fall, Adam, Eve, Satan, Enoch, Noah, and Melchizedek, there is little manuscript or scholarly support from the world of biblical studies.

Many plain and precious things are gone from the secondary biblical manuscripts, and there are no original manuscripts of the Bible available today by which to reclaim the loss. If these great doctrines were available by mere scholarship, there would have been no need for the Prophet Joseph Smith to restore them. We are living in an apostate world. The saving truths and the power of the gospel are not to be found in the teachings of the world. Through the restoration of the priesthood, the covenant, and the work of the Prophet Joseph Smith we have come to know the plan of salvation. The Restoration could not be brought about by putting new wine in old bottles nor a new patch on an old garment, but by a new restoration in a new dispensation, standing independent. As observed earlier in this discussion, the Lord declared that "this generation shall have my word through" Joseph Smith (D&C 5:10). This is in keeping with the saying that the Lord has chosen the "weak things" (or despised things) to "break down the mighty and strong" (D&C 1:19). It is through the prophets, priesthood, and revelation that the truth of the gospel has been revealed.

The World Lacks an Adequate Bible Manuscript

The modern problem with the Bible is not a matter of languages; it stems from a lack of an adequate Bible manuscript. There are plenty of scholars right here at Brigham Young University and at other places who can translate Greek, Hebrew, and Aramaic, but there is not available a complete and accurate manuscript from which to translate. All the known biblical documents are secondary sources. There are no originals. As you can see, working with secondary sources is not as good as working with originals.

Let me illustrate the problem with biblical documents in a way I know you will understand. Frequently, in the barbershop I see some young man just ahead of me with an abundance of hair. As he gets out of the chair and I get in, I say to the barber, "Make me look like him." There is always a laugh, and the reply is usually the same: "It's too late. Too much is gone, and it has been gone too long."

That is the way it is with the great manuscripts of the Bible. Wonderful though they may be, there is no way that a translator today could ever render the words to read like the originals, or like the plates of brass, or the Book of Mormon, or the Joseph Smith Translation, when it comes to bearing a strong witness of Jesus Christ and the plan of salvation. Those plain and precious doctrines are gone, but the Lord raised up another Prophet, and they are had again by those who believe in the words of Joseph Smith—but not by anyone else. Remember, "this generation shall have my word through" him.

A Doctrinal Restoration Had to Occur

According to 1 Nephi 13:25–29, a corruption of the Bible has taken place. This corruption was a deliberate act with willful intent to deceive, and it occurred before the Bible went forth among the nations, at least by the second century A.D. This altered Bible was weakened doctrinally. In order for this weakening to occur so early and so effectively, it had to be an inside job. Some person or persons close to the center, with access to originals or near-originals, must have altered the text. Subsequent copies were then made from the altered text, and it is these that have made their way among all nations. It may seem strange to us that officials in the New Testament Church would alter the Bible, yet we have had similar behavior even by Church historians in this dispensation. For example, John Whitmer confiscated the entire Church history manuscript, and Martin Harris lost 116 pages of valuable manuscript, which has never yet returned. We should not think that corruptions inside and early were impossible in the New Testament Church; they have occurred within our own.

I do not like to accuse anyone. I do not know who took out those precious parts of the Bible. I know only that the evidence shows the material is gone. It reminds me of a group of people camping in the hills. While they were away from camp, something came and tore down the tent, ate the bacon, and caused considerable havoc. When the campers returned and saw the damage, they said, "A bear has been here." They did not see the bear, but the evidence called for something of that caliber. One thing was certain to them; no chipmunk did all that damage. And so it is here; the evidence calls for certain conclusions.

Because of the removal of the plain and precious doctrines from the Bible record, many people lost their way; and in a couple of centuries the wayward, wandering church staged a Nicene council, which produced a philosophical creed reflecting the apostate condition of that church. Every doctrinal problem and question raised by that council and creed has been answered by the doctrines restored through the Book of Mormon, the

Joseph Smith Translation, the Doctrine and Covenants, and the Pearl of Great Price.

One of the great contributions of the Joseph Smith Translation is that it repeatedly clarifies biblical situations. It gives not only history, but also statements of purpose and explanation. On many individual matters about which the King James Version tells only what happened, the Joseph Smith Translation generally also tells why it happened.

The Joseph Smith Translation and the Brass Plates

As you know, Lehi, in 2 Nephi 2, gives a remarkable discourse wherein he tells how Satan came to be the devil in the premortal world. Lehi tells us that Adam and Eve would have had no children if there had been no Fall, and all things would have remained in their original state. Also, he says that the Messiah would come by reason of the Fall. Lehi says he learned all this marvelous doctrine from reading the plates of brass. As you know, absolutely none of these things is contained in the King James Version nor in any other Bible known to the modern world; however, all of these things: (1) Satan's history, (2) Adam's transgression, (3) the fact that man, the animals, and the earth would all have remained in their original state, (4) the fact that there would have been no children without the Fall, and (5) the role of the Messiah are found in the third, fourth, fifth, and sixth chapters of Joseph Smith's translation of Genesis. What is the point? Simply this: it is very clear that the contents of the Joseph Smith Translation, having received the touch of restoration through the hand of the prophet of God, resemble the doctrinal content of the brass plates more fully than do those of any other Bible. This is particularly so in Genesis and Isaiah but is also in other places.

We have not begun to appreciate the value of the Joseph Smith Translation, nor have we used it as a textual source the way we could. We seem to be too timid, perhaps a little too reluctant, maybe even a little embarrassed when we confront the academic world with a Bible based on revelation from God through a prophet and not certified by a manuscript from Babylon.

If the Prophet Joseph Smith were a famous athlete, actor, or race car driver, his opinions would be sought regarding all kinds of things not even close to his expertise—what breakfast cereal would he prefer? which shampoo or shaving cream? and which mouthwash is most effective? When it comes to gospel truth, revelation, and scripture, Joseph Smith is the greatest prophet in twenty centuries or more, yet we ignore his contributions in the subject of his greater expertise.

The Joseph Smith Translation and the Concept of Zion

Both the Old and the New Testaments tell about Zion and a New Jerusalem to be built in the last days. The Book of Mormon specifies even more particularly that this New Jerusalem will be built on the American continent and not in Asia. The Joseph Smith Translation also makes a special contribution to our understanding of Zion and the New Jerusalem.

In December 1830 the translation had reached Genesis, chapter 5, of the King James Version, where the great patriarch Enoch is mentioned. The Prophet Joseph Smith and Sidney Rigdon were living in Fayette, New York. The fifth chapter of Genesis in the King James Version contains only a few skinny comments about Enoch, saying that he is the son of Jared and was a good man, and implying that he was translated. The King James Version says nothing about Enoch's having a city or a people, nothing about Enoch's Zion. You can read everything the Bible has to offer about Enoch in less than thirty seconds. While the Prophet Joseph was translating these meager passages about Enoch in Genesis 5, he received a marvelous and extensive revelation about Enoch and his ministry; his teaching; his prophetic call; and his city and their laws, happiness, unity, and harmony. He learned that they were of one heart and one mind and that there were no poor among them. The length of the material about Enoch in the Joseph Smith Translation is eighteen times as long as in any other Bible.

This remarkable new information about Enoch and his people includes a statement that Enoch's city will come down from heaven and be joined with the city of New Jerusalem that is to be built on the earth by the Saints in the last days (see JST, Genesis 7:70–72 or Moses 7:62–64). The information about Enoch and his city is one of the most extensive and valuable contributions of the Joseph Smith Translation. Enoch, as you know, is a big man in Mormonism, but he is almost obliterated from the Bible and nearly forgotten in present-day Judaism, Catholicism, and Protestantism. Almost everything we know about Enoch we learn from the Joseph Smith Translation. The same is true about Melchizedek. He has been nearly lost to the Bible, yet he is large on the horizon of this dispensation. Almost all we know about Melchizedek we learn from the Joseph Smith Translation.

Soon after the revelation about Enoch was received and recorded, the Lord instructed Joseph Smith to cease translating temporarily and to move the headquarters of the Church to Ohio; there they would receive the "law" (see D&C 42) by which they would be governed. Let us look at the sequence: the Enoch material was received in December 1830; the command to cease translating and move is recorded in Doctrine and Covenants 37 (also received in December); the promise of the "law" is recorded in Doctrine and Covenants 38 (received in January); and the reception of the law comes in Doctrine and Covenants 42 (received in February). The next twenty sections or so, from Doctrine and Covenants 42–64 (all received within the next ten months), deal with the law of consecration, the founding of the New Jerusalem and Zion, and the economic system sometimes called the United Order.

The revelation about Enoch given in the Joseph Smith Translation was a pattern or a backdrop which introduced the idea of Enoch's Zion to the young Church. Then the Lord poured forth many specific revelations to the Prophet, showing him how to build a similar society, or Zion, or New Jerusalem, preparatory to the Second Coming and the return of Enoch's city.

It would be helpful to us, when studying the Doctrine and Covenants, if we read the Enoch material just before reading sections 37–64. It is chronologically accurate, and it helps recreate the setting in which these sections of the Doctrine and Covenants were received.

The revelation about Enoch was received in December 1830 just before section 37 was received. It is not therefore surprising that Enoch is mentioned again in sections 38 and 45. The whole concept of a latter-day Zion, of which Enoch's city was the prototype, was the principal topic of divine discussion at that period of time.

It Starts with the Joseph Smith Translation

The train of thought we have just pursued with Enoch and Zion is also demonstrated on other doctrinal topics. The Joseph Smith Translation is often used to introduce a doctrinal subject that is later enlarged upon in subsequent revelations printed in the Doctrine and Covenants. It is helpful to study all the sources on a given subject because each has some unique offering. It is also advantageous to study the chronological sequence, because then the progress of the information unfolds naturally, and the doctrine is easier to understand, since that is the way it was revealed in the first place.

Consider, for example, the book of Revelation. We start with the King James Version. Then we compare the corrections, clarifications, and additions given in the Joseph Smith Translation. That helps considerably. Then we read Doctrine and Covenants 77, which was revealed in connection with the Joseph Smith Translation. This section carries the doctrinal enlargement even further. Lastly, we read Doctrine and Covenants 88, which is still a further extension.

Another example of this type of relationship concerns the degrees of glory. We begin first with the Bible and the Book of Mormon, both of which make it unmistakably clear that all persons will be resurrected with a physical body (see 1 Corinthians 15:21–22; Alma 40:21, 23), never to die again. The Prophet was translating John 5:29 when he received the great vision of the three degrees of glory, Doctrine and Covenants 76. Later he received Doctrine and Covenants 88. Each revelation in its sequence is built upon the knowledge given earlier; each has given some new and additional concept not contained in the earlier. Can you see? Revelation is received line upon line—here a little and there a little. As far as a considerable portion of the Doctrine and Covenants is concerned, many of these revelations started with the Joseph Smith Translation.

Much of the background of the Joseph Smith Translation has already been adequately discussed in various books that have been published, and in the *Ensign*, so it does not seem necessary to recount those preliminary historical details in this discussion today. It seems more appropriate to talk about relationships, applications, causes, and consequences—what all this means to you and me and to our families and our students. I have tried to show that the translation of the Bible was a major, mainstream activity in the prophetic life of Joseph Smith, and that the Joseph Smith Translation is a major document, one not to be ignored, not only for biblical study, but also for the study of the Doctrine and Covenants, Pearl of Great Price, and LDS Church history. If I have not made that point clear at this stage, then I do not think anything else I could say will do it.

Why Has There Been Limited Use of the Joseph Smith Translation in the Church?

People often ask, "If the Joseph Smith Translation is as important as you say it is, why haven't we been using it in the Church all these years?" There are probably several reasons, but at least one is that maybe we weren't ready. For example, we have not used the Book of Mormon as we should have. We are getting better at it, but it was not until 1936 that there were even formal courses in Book of Mormon at Brigham Young University, and it was not until 1962 that it was a required subject. In like manner, I think neither we nor the world were ready to take on the consequences of having a Bible that is so far ahead of other Bibles and so far in advance of the scholarly world. We have used portions of it, such as the Book of Moses and the twenty-fourth chapter of Matthew in the Pearl of Great Price, and now we have much more of it in the footnotes and aids in the LDS edition of the Bible. Also, the fact that the RLDS church has possession of the manuscripts and has copyrighted the printed editions has been a limiting factor. Until recently we had no access to these manuscripts to corroborate the text.

How Did the Notion Arise That the RLDS Altered the Joseph Smith Translation?

A second question, which has often arisen, is: "Did the RLDS church alter the Joseph Smith Translation in their printing of it?" This has been a very common misunderstanding and an oft-repeated accusation.

I think I can explain how that mistaken notion got started, and when we work our way through it we need no longer be hampered by it. You remember that the manuscripts of the Joseph Smith Translation consist of preliminary drafts and later drafts. These represent different stages of the revision. Earlier manuscripts have fewer revisions than the later ones. Earlier manuscripts naturally do not reflect the later corrections.

In the early days of the Church, excerpts from the Joseph Smith Translation were published in the *Evening and Morning Star* and the *Times and Seasons,* and portions were used in the *Lectures on Faith.* Also, short excerpts were copied for personal use by various individuals, such as John Whitmer, Edward Partridge, Newell K. Whitney, and others. These were all done using early, preliminary drafts as the source. After Joseph Smith was killed, the entire manuscript was retained by Sister Emma Smith, and eventually it was given to the RLDS church in 1866. It was not available to the LDS church in Utah.

In 1851, when the Moses and Matthew material in the Pearl of Great Price was first published by Elder Franklin D. Richards in Liverpool, England, the source of the documents was the early printings from the Church newspapers. These, in turn, were based on the original, preliminary documents representing the early stages of the translation. When the RLDS church printed the Joseph Smith Translation in 1867, it used the later manuscripts containing the final revisions and corrections by the Prophet Joseph Smith. Hence, when LDS people, using the *Evening and Morning Star,* their private copies, and the Pearl of Great Price as their standard, compared their text with the RLDS printed text, they naturally concluded that the RLDS had made many alterations. I think that the mistaken notion came about because of a lack of understanding about the nature and condition of the original manuscripts. Had the Bernhisel copy been more widely known, it could have been of service because, incomplete and scant as it is, it yet reflects the later text and thus certifies the progressive nature of the manuscripts.

It would be well if we could free ourselves of the idea that the RLDS changed the text. We could then put our energies into studying the material, being thereby lifted spiritually. I should add that since their original printings, the Pearl of Great Price and the *Lectures on Faith* have been updated. They now reflect the later revision and agree with the Joseph Smith Translation. This was done by Elder Orson Pratt in 1878.

Testimony

I have an assurance that Joseph Smith is a prophet, that he restored the true gospel of Jesus Christ, and that he restored lost doctrines and lost scripture by revelation. We are engaged in the building of Zion on the earth today under the direction of living prophets and Apostles, who are inspired by the Holy Ghost. The Bible and the latter-day scriptures, including the Joseph Smith Translation, are the voice of God to the world in our day, and we grow in spirituality when we become acquainted with them and study them. Jesus is our only Savior. Joseph Smith is his prophet. The Brethren today are his true successors. We are building Zion today. The work of God is done by revelation. What I have written is true.

Notes

1. Joseph Fielding Smith, *The Restoration of All Things* (Salt Lake City: Deseret News Press, 1944), p. 57.

5

The Law of Consecration

Bruce A. Van Orden

The law of consecration as outlined in the Doctrine and Covenants and as undertaken by covenant in the House of the Lord does not consist merely of an economic law. To consecrate is "to set apart (a person or thing) as sacred to the Deity; to dedicate solemnly to some sacred or religious purpose, and so give the object itself a character of holiness; to make sacred or holy and so fit for a religious use."[1] President Spencer W. Kimball explained well the more total application of the law of consecration in the restored Church: "Consecration is the giving of one's time, talents, and means to care for those in need— whether spiritually or temporally—and in building the Lord's kingdom. . . . We consecrate when we give of ourselves."[2]

Hence, in order to understand and live the law of consecration, we must learn the basic principle that all that we have

---

Bruce A. Van Orden is Assistant Professor of Church History and Doctrine at Brigham Young University.

comes from the Lord (see Psalm 24:1) and that he expects us to use all he has given us—our time, our talents, and our means—for the benefit of our fellow beings, for the building up of the Kingdom of God, and for the establishment of Zion. As King Benjamin lovingly tells us,

> Are we not all beggars? Do we not all depend upon the same Being, even God, for all the substance which we have, for both food and raiment, and for gold, and for silver, and for all the riches which we have of every kind? . . .
>
> And now, if God, who has created you, on whom you are dependent for your lives and for all that ye have and are, doth grant unto you whatsoever ye ask that is right, in faith, believing that ye shall receive, O then, how ye ought to impart of the substance that ye have one to another. (Mosiah 4:19, 21.)

Over one half of the discussion in the Doctrine and Covenants on the law of consecration focuses on the economic aspects of the law—the consecrating of one's personal property and money to the Lord and his Church. Many principles of consecration contained in the Doctrine and Covenants, however, pertain to the consecrating of a person's time and talents as well. To understand the fulness of the meaning of the law of consecration, as with any other complex principle of the gospel, we are required to search the scriptures in numerous different chapters (or sections). No single chapter will suffice.

The Law of the Church

The law of consecration, economically speaking, has been a fundamental law of the Church since 1831 and has never been rescinded. It may be that there is no single "pure" method of administering this law that will be precisely reinstituted later on. Rather, there have been numerous specific programs established and modified throughout the history of the Church. Each in its time has been the official Church program. "Thus, it need not be imagined that the Latter-day Saints cannot truly live the law of consecration nor truly please God in their economic lives unless or until they reinstitute some particular aspect or phase of early Mormon consecration."[3]

One of the first hints to the Latter-day Saints that they would be granted valued inheritances from the Lord and that they must abide a certain law to receive these blessings came in the form of a revelation to Joseph Smith at the third general conference of the Church held in Fayette, New York, 2 January 1831. "I . . . deign to give unto you greater riches," the revelation promised, "even a land of promise, . . . the land of your inheritance, if you seek it with all your hearts." This inheritance from the Lord would be received by covenant and a "law" pertaining to the same would be received when the Saints reached Ohio (D&C 38:18–19, 32). This same revelation also foretold much of the law of consecration with these admonitions: "And let every man esteem his brother as himself, and practise virtue and holiness before me." Further, "I say unto you, be one; and if ye are not one ye are not mine." (D&C 38:24, 27.) "And [the leaders of the Church] shall look to the poor and the needy, and administer to their relief that they shall not suffer" (D&C 38:35). These same principles have been part and parcel of the law and mission of the restored Church ever since that third general conference.

Before the Prophet left for Kirtland, Ohio, he sent John Whitmer ahead to preside over the approximately 150 new converts in that area. Elder Whitmer discovered that a few of them had nobly joined together into what they called "the Family" and were attempting to have "all things common" as indicated in Acts 4:32. Unfortunately, some members of the Family took advantage of others, Whitmer observed, and because of dissension the group was fast "going to destruction."[4] Further revelation from God was obviously needed.

Revelation was not long in coming following the arrival of Joseph Smith in Kirtland in early February of 1831. Immediately the Prophet noticed "some strange notions and false spirits had crept in among [the Saints]. With a little caution and some wisdom," the Prophet Joseph related, "I soon assisted the brethren and sisters to overcome them. . . . The false spirits were easily discerned and rejected by the light of revelation."[5]

On 4 February the Prophet received a revelation calling Edward Partridge to be "a bishop unto the church" and instructing him "to spend all his time in the labors of the church"

(D&C 41:9). Five days later, in the presence of twelve elders who met together in mighty prayer, Joseph received another revelation (D&C 42) "embracing the law of the Church."[6] While not all of the "law" deals with economics or caring for the poor, Doctrine and Covenants 42:30–42 contains the underlying principles of the law of consecration and is generally considered the basic source whenever discussing this law. The words *consecration* or *consecrate* appear seven times in these verses.

The Lord in this revelation commanded members of the Church to consecrate their properties for the care of the poor and for the purpose of purchasing lands for the Church, particularly for the building up of the New Jerusalem. Members were to enter into this principle by covenant. The Saints were enjoined to not be proud in their hearts, to keep their clothing plain, to create beauty by the work of their own hands, to do all things in cleanliness, and to avoid idleness. These principles of the law of consecration have remained constant throughout the history of the Church. Only some of the practices and programs have changed, and these according to need and historical realities. In those early days of 1831, the Saints were asked to consecrate all of their property and substance by deed over to Bishop Partridge, who in turn gave every man a stewardship "as much as is sufficient for himself and family" (D&C 42:32). Further explanatory revelations followed which elucidated specific points regarding the economic application of the law (D&C 51, 57, 64, 70, 72, 78, 82, 85, 92, 94, 96, and 104).

This early economic system of consecration was conceived and practiced almost entirely in agrarian terms. In the early 1830s, before the Industrial Revolution hit America, access to land more than anything else signified social standing and was considered crucial to survival. But there were relatively few who joined the Church in 1831 or in the next few years who possessed much land. Those who did were called upon heavily to undergird the plan. Most did not own any land at all; converts were by and large poor. Redistribution of property thus resulted in a leveling down rather than a leveling up of the stewards' living standard. A combination of poor communication (across hundreds of miles from Ohio to Missouri and between branches in the United States), selfishness and obstinance among some members, lack of resources among most converts, and heavy outside persecution resulted in general frustration with and lack of fulfillment of early attempts to live the economic side of the law of consecration.

The United Order

A historical misunderstanding arose in the church regarding this early economic application of the law of consecration. Most Saints have thought that the united order was widely practiced in Ohio and Missouri. Indeed, the phrases *order, united order,* and *order of Enoch* frequently appear in the Doctrine and Covenants, thus adding credence to this assumption. In actuality, these are substitute phrases for "united firm," the original words in the revelations for an organization which was disbanded 23 April 1834 (see D&C 104). The wording was changed so that enemies of the Church and angry creditors would not use the printed revelations against the Church. Members of the united firm were also given coded names in several editions of the Doctrine and Covenants for the same reason.

The united firm was a business partnership between a handful of Church leaders, no more than twelve at any one time, to consolidate the financial resources and organizational and professional talents of these men to generate profits to be used for the personal living expenses as well as the economic needs of the Church. For example, it included each member of the First Presidency; landowning Church leaders Martin Harris, John Johnson, and Frederick G. Williams; storekeepers Newel K. Whitney and A. Sidney Gilbert; and printer-editor William W. Phelps. The main reason for the tremendous indebtedness accrued by the united firm was the destruction of the Church printing press and the closure of Sidney Gilbert's store by mobs in Independence, Missouri, in July 1833. It is important for modern students of the Doctrine and Covenants to realize that the important revelations that seem to speak of a united order (D&C 78, 82, 92, 96, and 104) in actuality give directions about the united firm.[7]

Indebtedness continued to plague the Church in Ohio and Missouri. Leaders were hard pressed to provide for the needs of the poor, to say nothing of caring for the normal operations of the Church. The Panic of 1837, a nationwide economic depression, also took a severe toll on Church resources. A terrible apostasy occurred in 1837–38 which left in its wake the loss of a member of the First Presidency, each of the three witnesses to the Book of Mormon, six members of the original Quorum of the Twelve Apostles, and close to a third of the total membership of the Church.[8]

After Joseph Smith's departure from Kirtland in January 1838, most loyal Saints in northern Ohio made every effort to leave for western Missouri, where a stake of Zion had been appointed. The high council in Kirtland devised a plan to transport in a body the "poorest of the poor" to Missouri by steamboat.[9] The actions of Church leaders, primarily from the Seventies Quorum, in directing approximately five hundred members of the Church as a body to Missouri clearly reflected the best of the revealed principles of the law of consecration.

Missouri: A New Development

The economic practices of the law of consecration officially changed in 1838. In a revelation to the Prophet in Far West, Missouri, on 8 July 1838, the Lord provided an answer to Joseph's plea, "O Lord! show unto thy servant how much thou requirest of the properties of thy people for a tithing."[10] Henceforth, the Saints would be required to "pay one-tenth of all their interest annually." This surplus would be consecrated "for the building of mine house, and for the laying of the foundation of Zion and for the priesthood, and for the debts of the Presidency of my Church." (D&C 119:2, 4.)

The law of tithing, while considered by some commentators in the past as an "inferior" law to the law of consecration, seems to have been merely a new phase of consecration.

Indeed, many hailed it as a markedly improved economic plan for obtaining donations and contributions. Admittedly, this program did not provide for the bishop to redistribute the wealth of the members, nor to allocate specific inheritances or personal stewardships. Yet, significantly, the equalizing effect of the 1838 plan on the members was identical to earlier programs. An honest consecration of all of one's surplus in addition to an annual consecration of one's net profits would achieve significant member equality.[11]

Some version of tithe paying has remained in the Church since 1838. Local bishops have always received tithes and other offerings from the members, whether in kind—in commodities or animals—or in cash. Often tithing was "consecrated" to the Church in the form of tithing labor—offering one day in ten to work on a sacred project, such as on the Nauvoo Temple. Today, in our late twentieth-century economy, paying a full and honest tithing in cash of all we earn has proven to be an efficient and productive means of both living the economic side of the law of consecration and also providing the Church with needed operating funds. Gratefully, as we live this sacred law, we can place total trust in the Council of the Disposition of Tithes composed of the First Presidency, the Council of the Twelve, and the Presiding Bishopric (see D&C 120).

In late 1838 Joseph Smith was incarcerated in the Richmond and Liberty jails in Missouri. In his absence from direct Church leadership, others, particularly Apostles Brigham Young, Heber C. Kimball, and John Taylor, successfully directed the relocation of the Saints and the care of the poor among them. This was surely applying the true law of consecration. From his cell in Liberty Jail, the Prophet encouraged exiled Saints to love and assist each other and to make sacrifices to help the less fortunate. "For a man to consecrate . . . ," he wrote, "is nothing more nor less than to feed the hungry, clothe the naked, visit the widow and the fatherless, the sick, and the afflicted, and do all he can to administer to their relief in their afflictions, and for him and his house to serve the Lord."[12]

Consecration in Nauvoo and the Great Basin

Following the Saints' gathering to Nauvoo, Illinois, new innovations pertaining to the law of consecration were introduced through the Prophet Joseph Smith. Several new bishops were called, wards in the city were established, and these bishops were charged with the care of the poor within their ward boundaries. The Church became officially incorporated and the Prophet became sole Trustee-in-Trust for the Church, thus giving the Church and its authorized leader legal powers to hold and sell property. Beginning in 1842, Joseph Smith introduced to trusted associates a sacred ritual, the Endowment of the Holy Priesthood. When the Nauvoo Temple was sufficiently completed in late 1845, which was after the death of the Prophet, the Apostles administered the endowment to the faithful Saints. Total commitment in all things was expected. Complete surrender to the Lord's will was required.

Brigham Young, who succeeded Joseph Smith as President of the Church and prophet of the Lord, was consistently faithful to the memory of his predecessor and to following the precepts of the law of consecration. He invoked the law in all of its aspects in numerous ways, such as establishment of home industries and manufacturing, self-sufficiency programs, two periods of spiritual "reformation," a cooperative movement, the boycotting of "Gentile" retail establishments, and finally in the 1870s a united order movement in the various Mormon colonies throughout the Intermountain West. President Young, if nothing else, was willing to innovate and experiment and never look back. If something failed, he tried something else. Eventually many programs associated with the greater law of consecration succeeded and laid the foundation for future successful activities.[13] Perhaps the greatest achievement of the hundreds of noteworthy accomplishments of Brigham Young was establishing the Kingdom of God upon the earth on a firm footing in the form of a far-flung commonwealth.

Welfare Services: A Modern Application

With the dispersion outward of the Saints in the 1920s and the arrival of the Great Depression in the 1930s, the Church established a more formal and elaborate program to apply the principles of the law of consecration. Known first as the Church security plan, later the welfare plan, and presently as Welfare Services, this program has steadily grown into hundreds of projects, farms, ranches, canneries, and storehouses. This plan, both in theory and practice, has become the envy of millions of people in public, private, and religious enterprises. In 1936 President Heber J. Grant summed up the multiplicity of goals, both moral and practical, of the Church's welfare system:

> Our primary purpose [in organizing the Church Security Plan] was to set up . . . a system under which the curse of idleness would be done away with, the evils of a dole abolished, and independence, industry, thrift and self-respect be once more established amongst our people. The aim of the Church is to help the people help themselves. Work is to be re-enthroned as the ruling principle of the lives of our Church membership.[14]

Welfare Services, which now embraces the activities of personal and family preparedness, is most assuredly an application of the law of consecration as revealed to Joseph Smith. President Gordon B. Hinckley explained:

> The remarkable organization of the Church, which has received much attention, was framed by [Joseph Smith] as he was directed by revelation, and no modification or adaptation of that organization is ever considered without searching the revelations set forth by the Prophet.
> Even the welfare program, which some are prone to regard as of rather recent origin, is founded and operated strictly upon principles enunciated by Joseph Smith in the early years of the Church.[15]

This same plan, though admittedly not yet perfect in its application and administration, is still more perfectly administered and more extensive in its provident application than anything else done institutionally with the law of consecration in the history of the Church. Two members of the First Presidency, J. Reuben Clark, Jr., and Marion G. Romney, who over the years since 1935 gave careful watchcare to the welfare plan, characterized the welfare activities of the Church and its members as representing living the principles of the united order as taught by the Prophet Joseph Smith.[16]

President N. Eldon Tanner discussed how the "power of the priesthood" has miraculously been utilized with the welfare plan. President Harold B. Lee, he explained, was called in 1935 to organize the Church welfare program.

> He [President Lee] said that as he prayed fervently to the Lord for guidance as to the kind of organization that should be set up, he received the clear answer: "There is no new organization necessary to take care of the needs of this people. All that is necessary is to put the priesthood of God to work. There is nothing else you need as a substitute." This was done and the welfare program has gone forward and is a monument to the power of the priesthood and is a model for the world.[17]

Fast offerings have long constituted the means from which the needs of the poor in the Church have been provided. As President Spencer W. Kimball explained, "It has been, and now is, the desire and objective of the Church to obtain from fast offerings the necessary funds to meet the cash needs of the welfare program; and to obtain from welfare production projects the commodity needs."[18] Beginning with President Kimball's administration, Church members have been urged to contribute a generous fast offering. "Sometimes we have been a bit penurious . . . ," President Kimball chided. "I think that when we are affluent, as many of us are, that we ought to be very, very generous. . . . I think we should . . . give, instead of the amount we saved by our two meals of fasting, perhaps much, much more—ten times more where we are in a position to do it."[19]

President Kimball also discussed the overall value of Welfare Services:

> There are few activities in the Church that require more cooperation and concerted effort than Welfare Services. Whether it is rallying to find employment for a displaced quorum member, toiling on a production project, serving as a lead worker at a Deseret Industries, or accepting foster children in the home, it is cooperation and mutual concern that determines the overall success of the Storehouse Resource System.[20]

Living the Law of Consecration Today

How do we as Latter-day Saints further consecrate our time and talents to the building of the Kingdom of God and the establishment of Zion? The following counsel from the Doctrine and Covenants demonstrates attributes needed for living the law of consecration:

> Wherefore, be not weary in well-doing, for ye are laying the foundation of a great work. And out of small things proceedeth that which is great.
> Behold, the Lord requireth the heart and a willing mind; and the willing and obedient shall eat the good of the land of Zion in these last days. (D&C 64:33–34.)

> Wherefore, now let every man learn his duty, and to act in the office in which he is appointed, in all diligence.
> He that is slothful shall not be counted worthy to stand, and he that learns not his duty and shows himself not approved shall not be counted worthy to stand. (D&C 107:99–100.)

President Spencer W. Kimball enunciated the need to act with diligence according to the best spirit of the law of consecration in a sermon wherein he spoke of what the Saints must be doing to "bring again Zion":

> We must lay on the altar and sacrifice whatever is required by the Lord. We begin by offering a "broken heart and a contrite spirit." We follow this by giving our best effort in our assigned fields of labor and callings. We learn our duty and execute it fully. Finally we consecrate our time, talents, and means as called upon by our file leaders and as prompted by the whisperings of the Spirit. In the Church, as in the Welfare system also, we can give expression to every ability, every righteous desire, every thoughtful impulse. Whether a volunteer, father, home teacher, bishop, or neighbor, whether a visiting teacher, mother, homemaker, or friend—there is ample opportunity to give our all. And as we give, we find that sacrifice brings forth the blessings of heaven! And in the end, we learn it was no sacrifice at all.[21] (*Hymns*, no. 147.)

Let us not forget that we are under covenant to live the law of consecration. Elder Boyd K. Packer of the Council of the Twelve Apostles, frequently includes in his sermons emphasis on this idea: "We do it because we are under covenant to do it."[22] Elder Packer told this story to illustrate his point:

> Several years ago I installed a stake president in England. In another calling, he is here in the audience today. He had an unusual sense of direction. He was like a mariner with a sextant who took his bearings from the stars. I met with him each time he came to conference and was impressed that he kept himself and his stake on course.
>
> Fortunately for me, when it was time for his release, I was assigned to reorganize the stake. It was then that I discovered what that sextant was and how he adjusted it to check his position and get a bearing for himself and for his members.
>
> He accepted his release, and said: I was happy to accept the call to serve as stake president, and I am equally happy to accept my release. I did not serve just because I was under *call.* I served because I am under *covenant.* And I can keep my covenants quite as well as a home teacher as I can serving as stake president.[23]

President Ezra Taft Benson has counseled the Saints to diligently heed the "great commandment of life"—to love the Lord God with all our heart. "To love God with all your heart, soul, mind, and strength is all-consuming and all-encompassing. It is no lukewarm endeavor. It is total commitment of our very being—physically, mentally, emotionally, and spiritually—to a love of the Lord." He added that "the breadth, depth, and height of this love of God extend into every facet of one's life," whether spiritual or temporal.[24]

In March 1832, the Lord revealed to the Prophet Joseph Smith additional principles and clarification concerning the law of consecration. "For verily I say unto you," the revelation reads, "the time has come . . . that there be an organization of my people, in regulating and establishing the affairs of the storehouse for the poor of my people . . . to advance the cause, which ye have espoused, to the salvation of man, and to the glory of your Father who is in heaven." The revelation continues: "That you may be equal in the bonds of heavenly things, yea, and earthly things also, for the obtaining of heavenly things. For if ye are not equal in earthly things ye cannot be equal in obtaining heavenly things.'' The revelation also states that if these principles are not lived, we will have no ''place in the celestial world.'' (D&C 78:3–7.)

Reflecting upon these same verses, Elder Bruce R. McConkie left us with this thought: ''These are the principles underlying the establishment of Zion; these are the laws that must be lived in the New Jerusalem; these are the standards set by the Lord for the saints of latter days. Let every man judge for himself how nearly we approach them at this time.''[25]

Notes

1. *The Compact Edition of the Oxford English Dictionary* (Oxford: Oxford University Press, 1971), p. 848, s.v. ''consecrate.'' *Consecrate* in Noah Webster's 1828 *American Dictionary of the English Language* reflected essentially the same meaning: ''to appropriate to sacred uses; to set apart, dedicate, or devote, to the service and worship of God.'' This is undoubtedly the meaning that would have been understood by Joseph Smith and the Saints in the 1830s.

2. In Conference Report, Oct. 1977, p. 124.

3. Lyndon W. Cook, *Joseph Smith and the Law of Consecration* (Provo, Utah: Grandin Book Co., 1985), p. viii. My essay is in total harmony with Cook's thesis, and I am greatly indebted to him for his pathbreaking research.

4. John Whitmer, as the first official Church historian, kept a record called ''The Book of John Whitmer.'' The original is located in the RLDS Library-Archives in Independence, Mo. Discussion of ''the Family'' is found in the original ''The Book of John Whitmer,'' p. 11; in Cook, *Joseph Smith and the Law of Consecration*, pp. 6–7; and Milton V. Backman, Jr., *The Heavens Resound: A History of the Latter-day Saints in Ohio 1830–1838* (Salt Lake City: Deseret Book, Co., 1983), pp. 64–65.

5. *History of The Church of Jesus Christ of Latter-day Saints*, 7 vols., ed. B. H. Roberts (Salt Lake City: Deseret Book Co., 1957), 1:146–47.

6. Ibid., p. 148.

7. See Chapter 5, "The United Firm," in Cook, *Joseph Smith and the Law of Consecration,* pp. 57–70.

8. For a discussion of the economic problems besetting the Church and the "great apostasy" which followed, see chapter 17 "Conflict at Kirtland," in Backman, *The Heavens Resound,* pp. 310–41.

9. *History of the Church*, 3:87–89.

10. Ibid., 3:44.

11. Cook, *Joseph Smith and the Law of Consecration,* p. 77.

12. Joseph Smith to the Church in Caldwell County, 16 December 1838, as cited in Dean C. Jessee, ed., *The Personal Writings of Joseph Smith* (Salt Lake City: Deseret Book Co., 1984), p. 379.

13. For an extended discussion of applications of the law of consecration under Brigham Young and succeeding presidents, see Leonard J. Arrington, Feramorz Y. Fox, and Dean L. May, *Building the City of God* (Salt Lake City: Deseret Book Co., 1976).

14. In Conference Report, Oct. 1936, p. 3.

15. Gordon B. Hinckley, *Be Thou an Example* (Salt Lake City: Deseret Book Co., 1981), p. 118.

16. In Conference Report, Oct. 1942, pp. 55–59 (President Clark); and in Conference Report, Apr. 1966, pp. 95–101 (President Romney).

17. N. Eldon Tanner, "Six Questions About Priesthood," in *Priesthood* (Salt Lake City: Deseret Book Co., 1981), p. 15.

18. In Conference Report, Oct. 1977, p. 126.

19. Ibid., Apr. 1974, p. 184.

20. Ibid., Apr. 1978, p. 123.

21. Ibid., Apr. 1978, pp. 123–24.

22. Boyd K. Packer, *The Holy Temple* (Salt Lake City: Bookcraft, 1980), p. 170.

23. In Conference Report, Apr. 1987, p. 26; italics in original.

24. *Ensign*, May 1988, p. 4.

25. Bruce R. McConkie, *A New Witness for the Articles of Faith* (Salt Lake City: Deseret Book Co., 1985), p. 600.

6

The Second Coming of Jesus Christ

Larry E. Dahl

The Doctrine and Covenants is bulging with information about the second coming of the Savior and things pertaining thereto. At least forty of the 138 sections refer to it directly, and many other sections allude to it, speaking of events and conditions which will attend the Lord's coming—i.e., the world's ripening in iniquity, a day of judgment, millennial peace, and so on.

Although all the questions we may have about the Second Coming are not definitively answered in the Doctrine and Covenants, the revelations do provide much helpful information as we ponder a number of questions: When will he come? To whom will he appear? What are the signs that indicate his coming is near? What will happen to the living, the dead, Satan, world governments, and the earth when he comes? What are the Saints to do in preparation for his coming? Let us now consider each of these questions in turn.

Larry E. Dahl is Associate Professor of Church History and Doctrine and director of research in the Doctrine and Covenants for the Religious Studies Center at Brigham Young University.

When Will He Come?

Dozens of references in the Doctrine and Covenants note the nearness of the Second Coming. "It is the eleventh hour, and the last time that I shall call laborers into my vineyard" (33:3). "Therefore, the keys of this dispensation are committed into your hands; and by this ye may know that the great and dreadful day of the Lord is near, even at the doors" (110:16). Thirteen times the phrase "I come quickly" is used. "Nigh at hand" is repeated twelve times. And six times we are told the Lord's coming will be "soon."[1]

Even though we are reminded repeatedly of its nearness, we are told "the hour and the day no man knoweth, neither the angels in heaven, nor shall they know until he comes" (49:7; see also 39:21; 133:11). We are admonished to "gird up your loins and be watchful and be sober, looking forth for the coming of the Son of Man, for he cometh in an hour you think not" (61:38; see also 51:20; 124:10). "For the day of wrath shall come upon them [the unbelieving and rebellious] as a whirlwind" (63:6)—suddenly, powerfully, unexpectedly, destructively. The righteous will not be so surprised but will be anticipating his coming, looking forward to it, and praying for it (35:15; 45:39; 49:23; 61:38; 65:4–5).

Perhaps the most helpful verses in trying to narrow down the "when" of the Second Coming are D&C 77:6, 12, 13. Here we learn that the earth will have a temporal existence of seven thousand years, the last thousand of which will be the millennium.[2] We learn too that Christ will come "in the beginning of the seventh thousand years" (D&C 77:12). The term "in the beginning" has led some to believe that Christ will come immediately as the seventh seal is opened, or right at the close of the sixth period of time, which, if we can rely upon biblical chronology and our calendar system, is about A.D. 2000. Verse 13, however, makes plain that there is a period of time between the opening of the seventh seal and the Lord's coming. How long that will be is not specified, but it will be long enough for all the events spoken of in Revelation 9 to take place. Those are not happy events. They include wars and plagues and terrible wickedness —"murders," "sorceries," "fornication," and "thefts" (Revelation 9:21). "In those days shall men seek death, and shall not find it; and shall desire to die, and death shall flee from them" (Revelation 9:6). How long will such conditions prevail after the opening of the seventh seal and before the Savior comes—a few years, a generation, several generations? Any of these options would fit the "in the beginning of the seventh thousand years" designation, leaving room for uncertainty as to the precise time of the Lord's coming.

Not revealing the exact time of the Second Coming is purposeful (see Matthew 24:42–51). Not even the "angels in heaven" know (D&C 49:7). When the Prophet Joseph Smith prayed "very earnestly to know the time of the coming of the Son of Man" he was given a vague answer and told: "trouble me no more on this matter" (130:14–16). If the angels and the prophet of the Restoration cannot find out the time, it is unlikely that others know. Hence, a caution concerning those who claim to be privy to such things.

For those who truly love the Lord the "when" of the Second Coming really does not matter. They are not faithful simply because he may come in judgment any minute; they keep the commandments because they love the truth and want to do what is right. They do not fear his coming; they are "prepared" (38:30). They look forward to his coming, and pray for it, knowing that the Lord will bring a thousand years of peace and righteousness upon the earth when he does come.

To Whom Will He Appear?

In a sense, it is appropriate to speak of the second comings (plural) of the Lord. The Doctrine and Covenants specifies three groups to whom the Lord has appeared or will appear in the latter days—the Saints, the Jews, and the world.

To the Saints there have been and will yet be multiple appearances. He appeared to Joseph Smith in the First Vision (Joseph Smith—History 1:7–20). Joseph Smith and Sidney Rigdon saw and conversed with him in heavenly vision (D&C 76:14). He visited Joseph Smith and Oliver Cowdery, accepting the dedication of the Kirtland Temple and promising great blessings for the Saints (D&C 110:1–10). At some future time the Savior will attend a special meeting at Adam-ondi-Ahman where he will receive stewardship reports from those who have held priesthood keys upon the earth."[3] The Lord promised that he will come with the city of Enoch to the New Jerusalem and appear in the temple there (Moses 7:62–64; D&C 97:15–16). Undoubtedly there will be additional appearances to the faithful Saints.

The Savior will appear to the Jews on the Mount of Olives (D&C 45:48–53; see also Zechariah 14). "And then shall the Jews look upon me and say: What are these wounds in thine hands and in thy feet? Then shall they know that I am the Lord; for I will say unto them: These wounds are the wounds with which I was wounded in the house of my friends. I am he who was lifted up. I am Jesus that was crucified. I am the Son of God. And then shall they weep because of their iniquities; then shall they lament because they persecuted their king." (D&C 45:51–53.) What a marvelous reunion! A people who have been scattered, hated, persecuted, even slaughtered by the millions will finally find their true deliverer. The Jews' weeping will undoubtedly reflect a mixture of relief, sorrow, joy, and new hope. The Savior too may weep. Perhaps he will shed tears of joy because a special group of his covenant people will be "home" again—those who have now come unto him willingly safely gathered under his protective care, as chicks nestle securely under their mother's wings (see Matthew 23:37–39).

The Lord's appearance to the world, his appearance in glory, is the one that usually comes to mind when the Second Coming is mentioned. That appearance will be to all. "The curtain of heaven [shall] be unfolded, as a scroll is unfolded after it is rolled up, and the face of the Lord shall be unveiled" (D&C 88:95). "And all flesh shall see me together" (101:23). "And the Lord shall utter his voice, and all the ends of the earth shall hear it; and the nations of the earth shall mourn, and they that have laughed shall see their folly. And calamity shall cover the mocker, and the scorner shall be consumed; and they that have watched for iniquity shall be hewn down and cast into the fire." (D&C 45:49–50.) A world that is ripe in iniquity (see D&C 29:9;

86:7) will be harvested, burned "as stubble" (D&C 29:9; 64:24; 133:64). When the Lord comes at this harvest time he "shall be red in his apparel, and his garments like him that treadeth the wine vat (D&C 133:48). The "dyed garments" (D&C 133:46) are symbolic of the blood of the wicked, staining the garments of the Savior, as they are "trampled" like grapes in a wine vat (D&C 133:50–51). Not very comforting imagery! But God is a God of justice as well as a merciful God (see Alma 42:15). Joseph Smith taught:

> Our heavenly Father is more liberal in His views, and boundless in His mercies and blessings, than we are ready to believe or receive; and, at the same time, is more terrible to the workers of iniquity, more awful in the executions of His punishments, and more ready to detect every false way, than we are apt to suppose Him to be.[4]

From the beginning the Lord has revealed eternal truths in the form of commandments to mankind, specifying rewards for obedience and the consequences of disobedience. He has given agency, and provided as much help as individuals and groups were willing to receive. In the end there will be a time of accounting for all—the Saints, the Jews, and the world.

What Are the Signs of His Coming?

Doctrine and Covenants 29, 43, 45, 49, 87, 88, 101, 112, and 133 identify conditions and events that will signal the nearness of the Lord's second coming. Some of the signs appear in more than one of the sections, perhaps for emphasis. It is interesting and thought-provoking to carefully review the signs given by revelation to a prophet of God in this dispensation:

Social and Political Conflict

"Wars and rumors of wars" (D&C 45:26; see also 87:1–6); "the whole earth shall be in commotion" (D&C 45:26; 88:91); "and it shall come to pass among the wicked, that every man that will not take his sword against his neighbor must needs flee unto Zion for safety . . . and it shall be the only people that shall not be at war one with another" (D&C 45:68–69); "the wicked shall slay the wicked, and fear shall come upon every man" (D&C 63:33).

Fear and Despair

"There shall be weeping and wailing among the hosts of men" (D&C 29:15); "among the wicked, men shall lift up their voices and curse God and die" (D&C 45:32); "and surely, men's hearts shall fail them; for fear shall come upon all people" (D&C 88:91; 45:26).

Great Wickedness

"Darkness covereth the earth, and gross darkness the minds of the people, and all flesh has become corrupt before my face" (D&C 112:23); "the love of men shall wax cold, and iniquity shall abound" (D&C 45:27).

Famine, Pestilence, and Sickness

"And there shall be a great hailstorm sent forth to destroy the crops of the earth" (D&C 29:16); "and there shall be men standing in that generation, that shall not pass until they shall see an overflowing scourge; for a desolating sickness shall cover the land" (D&C 45:31); "flies . . . shall eat their flesh . . . maggots [shall] come in upon them . . . their flesh shall fall from off their bones, and their eyes from their sockets. . . . And it shall come to pass that the beasts of the forest and the fowls of the air shall devour them up" (D&C 29:18–20); "and there shall be . . . many desolations; yet men will harden their hearts against me" (D&C 45:33).

Extensive Natural Calamities

"For not many days hence and the earth shall tremble and reel to and fro as a drunken man. . . . For after your testimony cometh the testimony of earthquakes, that shall cause groanings in the midst of her, and men shall fall upon the ground and shall not be able to stand. And also cometh the testimony of the voice of thunderings, and the voice of lightnings, and the voice of tempests, and the voice of the waves of the sea heaving themselves beyond their bounds." (D&C 88:87–90; see also 43:25; 45:33; 87:6.)

Gospel Preached to Every Nation

"And this gospel shall be preached unto every nation, and kindred, and tongue, and people. And the servants of God shall go forth, saying with a loud voice: Fear God and give glory to him, for the hour of his judgment is come." (D&C 133:37–38.)

Gathering of Both the Righteous and the Wicked

"But my disciples shall stand in holy places, and shall not be moved" (D&C 45:32). Those holy places will be Zion and her stakes (D&C 101:16–23). "Zion shall flourish upon the hills and rejoice upon the mountains, and shall be assembled together unto the place which I have appointed" (D&C 49:25). There will also be a righteous remnant of believing Jews gathered at Jerusalem anticipating the coming of the Lord (D&C 45:43–44). In Zion there will be peace; in the rest of the world there will be conflict (see D&C 45:66–71). The Prophet Joseph Smith taught that "the time is soon coming, when no man will have any peace but in Zion and her stakes."[5]

The wicked will also be "gathered." They will be "bound in bundles" (D&C 86:7; 88:94; 101:66) of their own choosing, ripening in preparation for the final harvest. Neither the Spirit of God, nor the testimony of his servants, nor the terrible natural calamities, famines, plagues, or other events, will turn their hearts to God (D&C 43:23–25; 45:33). Some will "curse God and die" (D&C 45:32). Others will wish to curse God, but "their tongues shall be stayed that they shall not utter against me" (D&C 29:19). Generally, they will have turned their hearts from God "because of the precepts of men" (D&C 45:29), and experience the temporal and spiritual hopelessness of that decision.

"Jacob Shall Flourish in the Wilderness and the Lamanites Shall Blossom as the Rose" (D&C 49:24)

Perhaps "Jacob" in this instance means the Jews, and the "wilderness" refers to the land of Israel. The Jews have been restored to their homeland, and much is being done to make that land productive. It seems, however, that much of the motivation for what is happening in Israel is social and political—

rather than religious—at the present time. Is it possible that these descendants of Jacob must first flourish politically and temporally before they can turn their attention to spiritual matters?[6]

The Lamanites, the descendants of Lehi in Central and South America, are truly blossoming as the rose in accepting and living the gospel of Jesus Christ. Dozens of stakes exist with powerful local leadership, and they are increasingly providing missionaries to share the gospel with their countrymen.

Signs and Wonders in the Heavens and the Earth

"And it shall come to pass that he that feareth me shall be looking forth for the great day of the Lord to come, even for the signs of the coming of the Son of Man. And they shall see signs and wonders, for they shall be shown forth in the heavens above, and in the earth beneath. And they shall behold blood, and fire, and vapors of smoke. And before the day of the Lord shall come, the sun shall be darkened, and the moon be turned into blood, and the stars fall from heaven" (D&C 45:39–42; 29:14).

One of the signs to be given is "a great sign in heaven, and all people shall see it together" (D&C 88:93). In other scriptures this is referred to as the "sign of the Son of Man" (Matthew 24:30; Joseph Smith—Matthew 1:36). Concerning this sign, Joseph Smith said:

> Mr. Redding thinks that he has seen the sign of the Son of Man. But I shall use my right, and declare that, notwithstanding Mr. Redding may have seen a wonderful appearance in the clouds one morning about sunrise (which is nothing very uncommon in the winter season) he has not seen the sign of the Son of Man, as foretold by Jesus; neither has any man, nor will any man, until after the sun shall have been darkened and the moon bathed in blood; for the Lord hath not shown me any such sign; and as the prophet saith, so it must be—Surely the Lord God will do nothing, but He revealeth His secret unto His servants the prophets. (See Amos 3:7.) Therefore, hear this, O earth: The Lord will not come to reign over the righteous, in this world, in 1843, nor until everything for the Bridegroom is ready.[7]

On another occasion the Prophet observed:

> Judah must return, Jerusalem must be rebuilt, and the
> temple, and water come out from under the temple, and
> the waters of the Dead Sea be healed. It will take some
> time to rebuild the walls of the city and the temple, &c.;
> and all this must be done before the Son of Man will
> make His appearance. There will be wars and rumors of
> wars, signs in the heavens above and on the earth be-
> neath, the sun turned into darkness and the moon to
> blood, earthquakes in divers places, the seas heaving
> beyond their bounds; *then will appear one grand sign of
> the Son of Man in heaven. But what will the world do?
> They will say it is a planet, a comet, etc.* But the Son of
> Man will come as the sign of the coming of the Son of
> Man, which will be as the light of the morning cometh
> out of the east.[8]

One may argue that the world has always known wars and
rumors of wars, famines, earthquakes, and so on. How then are
such things signs of the Lord's second coming? In Doctrine and
Covenants 45 (verses 35 and 38) the Lord indicates that when
people see "all these things," not one or two or even several,
but "all" of them, "then shall they know that the hour is
nigh." The Lord further says that those that fear him will not
ignore the signs of the times, but "shall be looking forth for the
great day of the Lord to come, even for the signs of the coming
of the Son of Man" (D&C 45:39).

Perhaps a caution is in order for those who attempt to establish a clear and precise sequence of events among the signs of the
times. It appears that as with the "when" of the Second Coming, the exact sequence of events has been left deliberately ob-
scure.

> It is not possible for us, in our present relatively low
> state of spiritual understanding, to specify the exact
> chronology of all the events that shall attend the Second
> Coming. Nearly all of the prophetic word relative to our
> Lord's return links various events together without refer-
> ence to the order of their occurrence. Indeed, the same
> scriptural language is often used to describe similar events
> that will take place at different times.[9]

What Will Happen to the Living
When He Comes?

The Doctrine and Covenants describes what will happen to two groups living on the earth when the Savior comes—the "saints" and the "wicked." Nothing specifically is said of the "honorable men of the earth" (D&C 76:75) who have lived a terrestrial level of righteousness, but who have not as yet accepted the fullness of the gospel. Because the earth will be in a paradisiacal or terrestrial condition after the Savior comes, and because they have lived in harmony with terrestrial law, it is reasonable to believe that they will abide the day of his coming. Joseph Fielding Smith has written:

> When the reign of Jesus Christ comes during the millennium, *only those who have lived the telestial law will be removed*. The earth will be cleansed of all its corruption and wickedness. Those who have lived *virtuous lives*, who have been *honest* in their dealings with their fellow man and have *endeavored to do good* to the best of their understanding, shall remain. . . .
> The *honest* and *upright* of all nations, kindreds, and beliefs, who have kept the *terrestrial* or *celestial law,* will remain.[10]

Those who have lived the terrestrial or celestial law will be preserved from the forces that will destroy the wicked, or telestial people—"liars, and sorcerers, and adulterers, and whoremongers, and whosoever loves and makes a lie" (D&C 76:103). John adds "murderers" to the list (Revelation 22:15). Those guilty of such wickedness will die when Christ comes (D&C 29:9, 11; 63:34, 37, 54; 86:5–7; 88:94; 133:50–51). Their spirits will go into the spirit world where they suffer the consequences of their disobedience and prepare for the resurrection at the end of the millennium (see 76:84–85, 102–106). Sadly, their chosen path "shall leave them neither root nor branch" (D&C 133:64), meaning no eternal ties to either ancestry or posterity. (See D&C 131:1–4; 132:17.)

In contrast to the fate of the wicked, "the saints that are upon the earth, who are alive, shall be quickened and be caught up to meet him" (D&C 88:96). This "quickening" is not a change from mortality to immortality, but a transfiguration. These Saints will return to the earth as mortals, then "die at the age of man" (D&C 63:50), which Isaiah says is one hundred years (Isaiah 65:20). But when they die during the millennium "they shall not sleep in the dust, but they shall be changed in the twinkling of an eye" (D&C 63:51) from mortal beings to resurrected immortal beings.

To the righteous who are living on the earth the coming of the Lord will be a "great day" (D&C 45:39); to the wicked it will be "terrible" (45:74).

What Will Happen to the Dead When He Comes?

"For the day cometh that the Lord shall utter his voice out of heaven; the heavens shall shake and the earth shall tremble, and the trump of God shall sound both long and loud, and shall say to the sleeping nations: Ye saints arise and live; ye sinners stay and sleep until I shall call again" (D&C 43:18). Here again there is mention of only two groups, "saints" and "sinners." Sections 45 and 88, however, make clear that the dead who have earned either celestial or terrestrial rewards will be resurrected when Christ comes, with the celestial group coming forth first (D&C 45:54; 88:97–99). "The rest of the dead . . . live not again until the thousand years are ended" (D&C 88:101). That is, the "rest of the dead," those who have not qualified for celestial or terrestrial rewards, will not be resurrected until the thousand years are ended. They will live during the millennium, but in the spirit world. Their spirits will be called up at the beginning of the millennium, judged unworthy of resurrection at that time (D&C 88:100–101), then returned to the spirit world. "These are they who are thrust down to hell. These are they who shall not be redeemed from the devil until the last resurrection. . . . These are they who suffer the vengeance of eternal fire. These are they who are cast down to hell and suffer the wrath of Almighty God, until the fullness of times, when Christ shall have subdued all enemies under his feet, and shall have perfected his work" (D&C 76:84–85, 105–106). When the "fullness of times" has come, when the millennium is over, then those who have qualified for telestial rewards will be resurrected. Following them comes the resurrection of the sons of perdition who had received physical bodies on the earth (see D&C 88:101–102).

What Will Happen to Satan When the Lord Comes?

"And Satan shall be bound, that old serpent, who is called the devil, and shall not be loosed for the space of a thousand years" (D&C 88:110–111; see also 29:22; 43:31). Evidently he will be bound by a combination of two factors: he "shall not have power to tempt any man" (D&C 101:28), and he "shall have no place in the hearts of the children of men" (D&C 45:55)— i.e., "because of the righteousness of his [the Lord's] people, Satan has no power" (1 Nephi 22:26). Both the power of God and the righteousness of the people will bind Satan from having influence upon the earth.[11] But what about the spirit world? Will Satan have power there? If the telestial people who are in the spirit world during the millennium are not "redeemed from the devil until the last resurrection" (D&C 76:85), it may be that Satan's powers and buffetings will exist in that spirit realm.

Satan will be loosed and have influence upon the earth again "when the thousand years are ended, and men again begin to deny their God" (D&C 29:22; see also 43:31). This however, will be only "for a little season, that he may gather together his armies" in preparation for "the battle of the great God," the Battle of Gog and Magog, the final battle for the souls of men that began in the pre-earth life. Satan and his angels will lose that battle to Michael and the hosts of the righteous, and "shall be cast away into their own place, that they shall not have power over the saints any more at all" (D&C 88:111–14).[12]

What Will Happen to World Governments?

When the Lord comes again, he will "reign over all flesh" (D&C 133:25). In January 1831 he promised the Saints that they would have "no laws but my laws when I come" (D&C 38:22). A few months later he instructed them to "be subject to the powers that be, until he reigns whose right it is to reign, and subdues all enemies under his feet" (D&C 58:22). In the revelation and prophecy on war, the Lord declared that his coming would bring about "a full end of all nations" (D&C 87:6).

It seems clear that all who live upon the earth in the Millennium will be subject to a government directed by the Lord. Undoubtedly there will be organization and delegation, but the civil as well as ecclesiastical aspects of government will be in harmony with truth and righteousness. People will not have the right to ignore the Lord's authority, setting up independent nations and making unilateral decisions. Joseph Smith taught:

> While in conversation at Judge Adams' during the evening, I said, Christ and the resurrected Saints will reign over the earth during the thousand years. They will not probably dwell upon the earth, but will visit it when they please, or when it is necessary to govern it.[13]

Mortals, then, will be the administrators—under the direction of Christ and the resurrected Saints—of the millennial government. How they will receive their appointments is not mentioned. But we may be sure that the government will act with equity and justice for all who remain on the earth.

What Will Happen to the Earth?

The tenth Article of Faith indicates that when Christ returns to "reign personally upon the earth," the "earth will be renewed and receive its paradisiacal glory." As part of that renewal "the great deep . . . shall be driven back into the north countries, and the islands shall become one land; and the land of Jerusalem and the land of Zion shall be turned back into their own place, and the earth shall be like as it was in the days before it was divided" (D&C 133:23–24). In a revelation correcting some of the false notions of the Shakers about the second coming of the Lord, we are counseled to look for "the valleys to be exalted, and for the mountains to be made low, and for the rough places to become smooth" (D&C 49:23).

Another change in the earth itself is that "in the barren deserts there shall come forth pools of living water; and the parched ground shall no longer be a thirsty land" (D&C 133:29).

With all the geological changes it is likely that there will also be climatic adjustments. Elder Bruce R. McConkie has suggested that such will be the case. "Who knows but what the very axis of the earth will shift so that the seasons cease and the whole earth enjoys both seedtime and harvest at all times."[14]

What Are the Saints to Do in Preparation for His Coming?

Many times in the revelations, after information is given about the Second Coming, the word *wherefore* or *therefore* introduces what the Lord wants the Saints to do to prepare. (For examples of this see D&C 27:15; 33:17; 45:64; 63:36; and 87:8.) Three major themes that repeatedly surface are gathering, living righteously, and crying repentance to the inhabitants of the earth.

Gather to Zion and Her Stakes

Wherefore I, the Lord, have said, gather ye out from the eastern lands, assemble ye yourselves together ye elders of my church . . . gather up your riches . . . purchase an inheritance . . . And it shall be called the New Jerusalem, a land of peace, a city of refuge, a place of safety for the saints of the Most High God (D&C 45:64–66).

Wherefore, seeing that I, the Lord, have decreed all these things upon the face of the earth, I will that my saints should be assembled upon the land of Zion (D&C 63:36).

Zion shall not be moved out of her place, notwithstanding her children are scattered.

They that remain, and are pure in heart, shall return, . . . and then I have other places which I will appoint unto them, and they shall be called stakes, for the curtains or the strength of Zion. (D&C 101:17–18, 21.)

Behold, it is my will, that all they who call on my name, and worship me according to mine everlasting gospel, should gather together, and stand in holy places (D&C 101:22).

Gather ye together, O ye people of my church (D&C 133:4).

Be Steadfast in Righteousness

Take upon you my whole armor, . . . that ye may be able to stand (D&C 27:15).[15]

Be faithful, praying always, having your lamps trimmed and burning, and oil with you, that you may be ready at the coming of the Bridegroom (D&C 33:17).

I will that . . . every man should take righteousness in his hands and faithfulness upon his loins (D&C 63:36–37).

Stand ye in holy places, and be not moved, until the day of the Lord come (D&C 87:8).

Wherefore, prepare ye, prepare ye, O my people; sanctify yourselves . . . Go ye out from Babylon. Be ye clean that bear the vessels of the Lord . . . Go ye out . . . from the midst of wickedness, which is spiritual Babylon (D&C 133:4–5, 14).

Cry Repentance and Share the Gospel

Lift up your voice as with the sound of a trump, both long and loud, and cry repentance unto a crooked and perverse generation, preparing the way of the Lord for his second coming (D&C 34:6).

Wherefore, go forth, crying with a loud voice, saying: The kingdom of heaven is at hand; crying: Hosanna! blessed be the name of the Most High God.

Go forth baptizing with water, preparing the way before my face for the time of my coming. (D&C 39:19–20.)

Lift up your voices and spare not. Call upon the nations to repent, both old and young, both bond and free, saying: Prepare yourselves for the great day of the Lord (D&C 43:20).

Lift a warning voice unto the inhabitants of the earth; and declare both by word and by flight that desolation shall come upon the wicked (D&C 63:37).

Send forth the elders of my church unto the nations which are afar off; unto the islands of the sea; send forth unto foreign lands; call upon all nations, first upon the Gentiles, and then upon the Jews. . . . Yea, let the cry go forth among all people: Awake and arise and go forth to meet the Bridegroom. (D&C 133:8, 10.)

In addition to these three major themes, other things we are to do to prepare for the Lord's coming include "gird up your loins and be watchful and be sober" (D&C 61:38; see also 36:8; 50:46); "be patient in tribulation until I come" (D&C 54:10); "he that is tithed shall not be burned at his coming" (D&C 64:23); and "call upon the Lord" (D&C 65:5; see also 33:17, 88:126).

Though "the whole earth shall be in commotion, and men's hearts shall fail them" (D&C 45:26) as the time of the Second Coming draws near, the Saints of God have no need to fear or to be confused. It has been made abundantly clear what they are to do. And in the doing of it they will find purpose, peace, and happiness for themselves and for many other children of God whom they serve.

Conclusion

To have a proper view of the second coming of the Savior requires perspective and balance. Elder Neal A. Maxwell gave timely counsel at the April 1988 General Conference of the Church.

> Brothers and sisters, over the sweep of Christian history, some believers have, by focusing on a few prophecies while neglecting others, prematurely expected the Second Coming. Today, while we are obviously closer to that great moment, we are in the same danger.
>
> On the other hand, smugness is also a real danger. Of Jesus' first advent, the smug said, "It is not reasonable that such a being as a Christ shall come" (Helaman 16:18). Declared Jesus of His second coming, "Take heed . . . lest . . . that day come upon you unawares" (Luke 21:34–35; see also Matthew 24:37–38; Revelation 3:3; D&C 45:26).
>
> Peter wrote of the smug skeptics who would say, "Where is the promise of his coming," for do not "all things continue as they were from the beginning"? (2 Peter 3:4). . . .

Members of the Church need not and should not be alarmists. They need not be deflected from quietly and righteously pursuing their daily lives, "For God hath not given us the spirit of fear; but of power, and of love, and of a sound mind" (2 Timothy 1:7). . . .

Meanwhile, perhaps "summer is nigh" (Matthew 24:32; D&C 35:16; 45:37). We are here in mortality, and the only way to go is through; there isn't any around! Yet our Deliverer assures us, "Be of good cheer, for I will lead you along. The kingdom is yours and the blessings thereof are yours, and the riches of eternity are yours" (D&C 78:18).[16]

By carefully studying *all* the scriptural references as well as prophetic commentary pertaining to the second coming of the Lord, we can achieve a balanced, healthy perspective of the future and our present opportunities. The Doctrine and Covenants contributes a great deal to that quest.

Notes

1. See a concordance for references to the words *quickly*, *nigh*, and *soon*.

2. The "temporal existence" of the earth is usually interpreted to mean its existence from the fall of Adam to the end of the millennium, a period of seven thousand years. Doctrine and Covenants 77:6, 12, and 88:108–110 support such a view.

3. See Joseph Fielding Smith, *Doctrines of Salvation,* 3 vols., comp. Bruce R. McConkie (Salt Lake City: Bookcraft, 1955–56), 3:13–14; see also Doctrine and Covenants 116.

4. Joseph Smith, *Teachings of the Prophet Joseph Smith,* sel., Joseph Fielding Smith (Salt Lake City: Deseret Book Co., 1976), p. 257.

5. Ibid., p. 161.

6. See Bruce R. McConkie, *The Millennial Messiah* (Salt Lake City: Deseret Book Co., 1982), p. 229; see also *A New Witness for the Articles of Faith* (Salt Lake City: Deseret Book Co., 1985), pp. 511, 519–20, 564–65.

7. *Teachings of the Prophet Joseph Smith*, p. 280.

8. Ibid., pp. 286–87; emphasis added.

9. McConkie, *The Millennial Messiah,* p. 635.

10. Smith, *Doctrines of Salvation,* 3:62–63, emphasis in the original.

11. See George Q. Cannon, *Gospel Truths,* 2 vols. in one (Salt Lake City: Deseret Book Co., 1987), pp. 68–69; see also Joseph Fielding Smith, *Church History and Modern Revelation,* 2 vols. (Salt Lake City: Deseret Book Co. 1953), 1:192.

12. See *Teachings of the Prophet Joseph Smith,* p. 280.

13. Ibid., p. 268.

14. *A New Witness for the Articles of Faith* (Salt Lake City: Deseret Book Co., 1985), pp. 649–50.

15. It is interesting to contemplate the implications of the pieces of armor spoken of and the parts of the body they protect—helmet, breastplate, girdle about the loins, shoes, and to note that our "shield" against enemy blows is "faith," and the weapon we are to use to be successful in battle is "the sword of my Spirit."

16. *Ensign*, May 1988, pp. 7–9.

7

Priesthood, Keys, Councils, and Covenants

Monte S. Nyman

The keystone of our religion, the Book of Mormon, established that God does call men "to his holy work in this age and generation, as well as in generations of old" (D&C 20:11). The revelations of God that followed the publication of the Book of Mormon began to make known the nature of such matters as the directing power of the priesthood, the keys; the presiding councils of the priesthood; and the covenants that holders of the priesthood enter into. These revelations are now compiled in the Doctrine and Covenants for the membership of the Church to study and apply to their lives.

The Priesthood Keys Restored

President Joseph F. Smith defined the "Priesthood in general [as] the authority given to man to act for God" and the keys

---

Monte S. Nyman is Professor of Ancient Scripture and director of Book of Mormon research in the Religious Studies Center at Brigham Young University.

of that priesthood as "the power of directing these labors."[1] In
response to the desire of the Twelve for "a great revelation"
pertaining to their duties, the Lord revealed through Joseph
Smith the Prophet on 28 March 1835 that—

> There are, in the church, two priesthoods, namely, the
> Melchizedek and Aaronic, including the Levitical Priest-
> hood.
> Why the first is called the Melchizedek Priesthood is
> because Melchizedek was such a great high priest.
> Before his day it was called *the Holy Priesthood, after
> the Order of the Son of God.*
> But out of respect or reverence to the name of the Su-
> preme Being, to avoid the too frequent repetition of his
> name, they, the church, in ancient days, called that priest-
> hood after Melchizedek, or the Melchizedek Priesthood.
> All other authorities or offices in the church are ap-
> pendages to this priesthood.
> But there are two divisions or grand heads—one is the
> Melchizedek Priesthood, and the other is the Aaronic or
> Levitical Priesthood. (D&C 107:1–6.)

These two priesthoods had already been restored. On 15 May
1829, "an angel, who announced himself as John, the same that
is called John the Baptist in the New Testament," appeared to
Joseph Smith and Oliver Cowdery on the bank of the Susque-
hanna River, near Harmony, Pennsylvania, and conferred the
priesthood of Aaron upon them by the laying on of hands. He
explained that he operated "under the direction of Peter,
James, and John, the ancient apostles, who held the keys of the
higher priesthood, which was called the Priesthood of Melchizedek." He also promised them "that in due time the priesthood
of Melchizedek would be conferred upon them" (D&C 13, Preface). This promise was fulfilled in a few weeks, but unfortunately the exact date was not recorded in the annals of the
Church.[2]

The Aaronic Priesthood

John the Baptist informed Joseph and Oliver that the
Aaronic Priesthood held "the keys of the ministering of angels,

and of the gospel of repentance, and of baptism by immersion for the remission of sins" (D&C 13:1). The great revelation to the Twelve revealed that the priesthood of Aaron was conferred upon Aaron and his seed, throughout all their generations, and the literal descendants of Aaron had a legal right to it. Furthermore, the bishopric was "the same presidency of this priesthood, and holds the keys or authority of the same" (D&C 107:13).

Earlier the Lord had qualified that the "legal right to the bishopric" and "the presidency over this priesthood, and the keys or authority of the same 'belonged to' the firstborn among the sons of Aaron."[3] He must also be designated by the First Presidency and found worthy, and anointed and ordained under their hands. The Lord revealed that the legal heirs must "prove their lineage, or . . . ascertain it by revelation from the Lord under the hands of the above named Presidency (D&C 68:15–21).

This earlier revelation (November 1831) gives evidence that the lineage of the firstborn of Aaron was not known to the Church nor the world at that time nor has it been revealed publicly since that time. Therefore, the stipulation is still in force that "as a high priest of the Melchizedek Priesthood has authority to officiate in all the lesser offices, he may officiate in the office of bishop when no literal descendant of Aaron can be found, provided he is called and set apart and ordained unto this power by the hands of the Presidency of the Melchizedek Priesthood" (D&C 107:17; see also 107:68–71; 68:19).

In the great revelation to the Twelve, the Lord added some further descriptions of the keys of the Aaronic Priesthood to those given by John the Baptist. The Lord referred to administering the "outward ordinances, the letter of the gospel, the baptism of repentance for the remission of sins, agreeable to the covenants and commandments" (D&C 107:20; see also 84:26–27). He also stated that the office of bishop was to administer "all temporal things" (D&C 107:68).

Thus the keys of the Aaronic Priesthood, the lesser priesthood, the power to have angels minister, the power to preach the gospel of repentance, and to administer in all temporal things, has been restored in this dispensation. All of these powers, however, were in preparation for the greater priesthood that was to follow.

The Melchizedek Priesthood

As stated earlier, the exact date of the restoration of the keys of the Melchizedek Priesthood is not known. We do know from Doctrine and Covenants 18:9 that Oliver Cowdery and David Whitmer had received their apostolic calling by June 1829. As the revelation to the Twelve says, "the office of an elder comes under the priesthood of Melchizedek" (D&C 107:7).

Section 107 then gives four functions of that priesthood: (1) the right of presidency, (2) power and authority over all the offices in the Church in all ages of the world, (3) the right to administer in spiritual things, and (4) the right to officiate in all the offices in the Church (D&C 107:8−9). It then declares:

> The power and authority of the higher, or Melchizedek Priesthood, is to hold the keys of all the spiritual blessings of the church—
> To have the privilege of receiving the mysteries of the kingdom of heaven, to have the heavens opened unto them, to commune with the general assembly and church of the Firstborn, and to enjoy the communion and presence of God the Father, and Jesus the mediator of the new covenant (D&C 107:18−19).

Thus the Aaronic Priesthood administers the temporal matters of the Church and the Melchizedek Priesthood administers the spiritual. The Aaronic brings a person into the church of God upon the earth and the Melchizedek brings a person into the presence of God through the gospel and ordinances restored to the Church (D&C 84:19−22). Both priesthoods are functioning in the Church today.

The Patriarchal Order of Priesthood

Upon the completion of the Kirtland Temple, the Lord sent Elias and Elijah to restore the patriarchal authority and sealing power (D&C 110:13−15). Elias restored the keys or powers to organize eternal family units through the Abrahamic covenant, available through temples. Elijah then restored the keys or powers to seal this and all other ordinances, making them binding in the hereafter.

Elijah thus helped to provide "a welding link of some kind or other between the fathers and the children" (D&C 128:18). He brought the fulness of the priesthood, the power to make of men and women kings and priests, queens, and priestesses; the power to seal families up unto eternal life.[4] These keys, these sealing powers are functioning throughout the many temples that have been built and are being operated today by The Church of Jesus Christ of Latter-day Saints.

Other Keys

All priesthood is Melchizedek. "All other authorities or offices in the church are appendages to this priesthood" (D&C 107:5). Therefore all keys that have been restored are under the administration of this priesthood. In this dispensation of the fulness of times, Michael, or Adam; Gabriel, or Noah[5]; Moses the Lawgiver; Raphael; and "divers angels . . . down to the present time" appeared to Joseph Smith and declared "their dispensation, their rights, their keys, their honors, their majesty and glory, and the power of their priesthood" (D&C 128:21). The Doctrine and Covenants records many of these appearances but not all.

In the words of D&C 110:16, "Therefore, the keys of this dispensation are committed into your hands; and by this ye may know that the great and dreadful day of the Lord is near, even at the doors."

The President of the Office of the High Priesthood

The High Priesthood . . . is the greatest of all.

Wherefore, it must needs be that one be appointed of the High Priesthood to preside over the priesthood, and he shall be called President of the High Priesthood of the Church;

Or, in other words, the Presiding High Priest over the High Priesthood of the Church.

From the same comes the administering of ordinances and blessings upon the church, by the laying on of the hands. (D&C 107:64–67.)

The Lord revealed that the duty of the President of the high priesthood "is to preside over the whole church, and to be like unto Moses" (D&C 107:91). Moses was the Lord's spokesman, the man to whom he spoke "mouth to mouth, even apparently [directly], and not in dark speeches; and the similitude of the Lord [would Moses] behold" (Numbers 12:8). Such is the Lord's prophet today. He is to "be a seer, a revelator, a translator, and a prophet, having all the gifts of God which he bestows upon the head of the church" (D&C 107:92). He is the first elder and the presiding elder over all the church of Christ (D&C 20:2; 124:125). He is the only one who holds all the keys and powers of the high priesthood (D&C 124:123; 132:7).

The words that are spoken as the Prophet receives them from the Lord are to be received in patience and faith as if from the Lord's own mouth (D&C 21:4–5). "No one shall be appointed to receive commandments and revelations [for] this church except [the Prophet]" (D&C 28:2), and the Church is not to receive the teachings of any others who come before them as revelations or commandments for the entire church (D&C 43:3, 5).

The Prophet Joseph Smith held the keys of this dispensation and still presides over it (D&C 90:3; 112:15). His successors hold these keys while presiding upon the earth (D&C 28:7; 43:3; 90:4). We have a prophet, and therefore we need to take counsel from his hand.

The First Presidency

"Three Presiding High Priests, chosen by the body, appointed and ordained to that office, and upheld by the confidence, faith, and prayer of the church, form a quorum of the Presidency of the Church" (D&C 107:22). This quorum is designated as the First Presidency and is to "receive the oracles for the whole church" (D&C 124:126). "This is the highest council of the church of God, and a final decision upon controversies in spiritual matters" (D&C 107:80). These three men jointly hold the "keys of the kingdom, which belong always unto the Presidency of the High Priesthood" (D&C 81:2). Those who treat "the oracles" lightly are under condemnation and will fall if they do not repent (D&C 90:5). In the words of President Ezra Taft Benson: "The prophet and the presidency—the living prophet and the First Presidency—follow them and be blessed; reject them and suffer."[6] Peter, James, and John formed this quorum in the meridian of time (D&C 13, Preface), and they have passed their keys to this dispensation (D&C 27:12–13). They received these keys from Jesus himself (D&C 7:7). Today, three presiding high priests govern The Church of Jesus Christ of Latter-day Saints.

The Council of the Twelve

Oliver Cowdery and David Whitmer, when called as Apostles, were told that "there [were] others who [were] called to declare my gospel, both unto Gentile and unto Jew; yea, even twelve" (D&C 18:26–27). Cowdery and Whitmer were then, in June of 1829, called to search out the Twelve (v. 37). These Twelve were called and organized as a quorum on 14 February 1835 and then sought for a revelation pertaining to their duties. That revelation, already mentioned above, referred to "the twelve traveling counselors" being "called to be the Twelve Apostles, or special witnesses of the name of Christ in all the world—thus differing from other officers in the church in the duties of their calling" (D&C 107:23). President J. Reuben Clark has explained:

> . . . it should be in mind that some of the General Authorities have had assigned to them a special calling; they possess a special gift; they are sustained as prophets, seers, and revelators, which gives them a special spiritual endowment in connection with their teaching of the people. They have the right, the power, and authority to declare the mind and will of God to his people, subject to the over-all power and authority of the President of the Church. Others of the General Authorities are not given

this special spiritual endowment and authority covering their teaching; they have a resulting limitation, and the resulting limitation upon their power and authority in teaching applies to every other officer and member of the Church, for none of them is spiritually endowed as a prophet, seer and revelator. Furthermore, as just indicated, the President of the Church has a further and special spiritual endowment in this respect, for he is the Prophet, Seer, and Revelator for the whole Church.[7]

To qualify for this endowment, Cowdery and Whitmer were told the Twelve must desire to take upon them the name of Christ "with full purpose of heart" (D&C 18:27–28). The Lord then spoke to the yet-to-be-called Twelve (v. 31) and testified that:

> These words are not of men nor of man, but of me; wherefore, you shall testify they are of me and not of man;
> For it is my voice which speaketh them unto you; for they are given by my Spirit unto you, and by my power you can read them one to another; and save it were by my power you could not have them;
> Wherefore, you can testify that you have heard my voice, and know my words (D&C 18:34–36).

After choosing the Twelve, Oliver Cowdery instructed them that their ordination was not complete until the Lord himself had laid his hands upon their heads even as he had with his original Twelve.[8] Thus they were indeed chosen to qualify as special witnesses of the name of the Lord Jesus Christ.

As a council, these twelve men "form a quorum, equal in authority and power to the three presidents [First Presidency] previously mentioned" (D&C 107:24). As explained by the Prophet Joseph, this principle has reference to succession, and this council's authority is not fully exercised until the First Presidency is dissolved upon the death of the President.[9] The Twelve as a council then have authority to reorganize the First Presidency. This doctrine has been followed precisely since the death of Joseph Smith for every succeeding president of the Church.

An additional function of this council is "a Traveling Presiding High Council, to officiate in the name of the Lord, under the direction of the Presidency of the Church, agreeable to the institution of heaven; to build up the church, and regulate all the affairs of the same in all nations, first unto the Gentiles and secondly unto the Jews" (D&C 107:33). The institution of heaven is one of order carried out in solemnity before Christ, "according to truth and righteousness" (v. 84).

The building up and regulating the affairs of the Church was to be done "according to the power of the Holy Ghost . . . and according to the callings and gifts of God unto men" (D&C 18:32). The latter could imply that it is the calling of the Twelve to determine and ordain those who have been foreordained by the Lord to various callings. The Lord promised them sufficient grace (his blessings) to accomplish these duties if they walked uprightly before him and sinned not (D&C 18:31). Another major function of the Twelve is "in all large branches of the church, to ordain evangelical ministers [Patriarchs], as . . . designated unto them by revelation," an order "instituted in the days of Adam" and carried out in subsequent generations (D&C 107:39–57). All other officers of the Church were to be ordained and set in order by the Twelve "agreeable to the revelations" (D&C 107:58).[10]

The Twelve hold "the keys, to open the door by the proclamation of the gospel of Jesus Christ, . . . first unto the Gentiles and then unto the Jews" (D&C 107:35). The Lord revealed to Thomas B. Marsh that the keys for this work were held by the president of the Council of the Twelve, the position he held at the time. This responsibility was under the direction of the First Presidency who would counsel the president and the Twelve (D&C 112:16–20, 30). It is the duty of the president of the Twelve to delegate the authority to others of the Twelve to open the door of Christ's kingdom to the various nations of the world (D&C 112:21). Brigham Young was later called to be the president of the Council of the Twelve, and the Lord affirmed to him and the Twelve the responsibility of holding "the keys to open up the authority of my kingdom upon the four corners of the earth . . . to send [the Lord's] word to every creature" (D&C 124:28).

Oliver Cowdery and David Whitmer were told that the Twelve would have the desire to take upon them Christ's name "with full purpose of heart" and that they would know those that were to be chosen by "their desires and their works" (D&C 18:27–38). It is such men as this that have been chosen to be the special witnesses of the name of the Lord.

The Seventy

The third body of general Church administration is the Seventy. This quorum consists of seventy men who are to be presided over by seven presidents chosen from among the seventy, with one of the seven presidents presiding over the other six (D&C 107:93–94). This quorum is equal in authority to the quorum of the Twelve Apostles (D&C 107:25–26), meaning, of course, in the matter of succession. The members of this quorum "are to act in the name of the Lord, under the direction of the Twelve" and the Twelve are to call upon them when they need assistance in "building up the church and regulating all the affairs of the same" and in filling their "several calls for preaching and administering the gospel" (D&C 107:34, 38).

The members of the Seventy are "called to preach the gospel, and to be especial witnesses unto the Gentiles and in all the world—thus differing from other officers in the church in the duties of their calling" (D&C 107:25). President Gordon B. Hinckley thus spoke of the office of seventy as "an office that carries with it the responsibility of bearing apostolic witness of the name of Christ."[11] They "are to be traveling ministers, unto the Gentiles first and also unto the Jews" (v. 97; see also 124:139). As the kingdom grows and "the labor in the vineyard" requires more traveling ministers, the seven presidents are to call other seventy, even seven times seventy (D&C 107:95–96). The members of these quorums are called "to travel continually" rather than "to preside over the churches" at home (D&C 124:140).

The flexibility of this quorum, or eventually quorums, to meet the needs of a growing church has been demonstrated through the history of the Church and particularly in recent years. The First Quorum of the Seventy is gradually being filled, to the point that at the time of this writing it contains nearly its capacity of seventy members.

Other Quorums

The Lord left the door of Church organization open as he concluded the great revelation to the Twelve. He revealed that:

> Whereas other officers of the church, who belong not unto the Twelve, neither to the Seventy, are not under the responsibility to travel among all nations, but are to travel as their circumstances shall allow, notwithstanding they may hold as high and responsible offices in the church (D&C 107:98).

Such officers as Assistants to the Twelve, additional counselors to the First Presidency, or regional representatives of the Twelve would fall under this category.[12] The organization and functions of other quorums at stake and ward levels of both Aaronic and Melchizedek Priesthoods were also revealed in the revelations (D&C 107:85–90; 124:133–37), but they will not be treated here.

Quorum Decisions

The First Presidency, as stated earlier, is the final authority of the earthly kingdom. The Council of the Twelve and the First Quorum of the Seventy are said to be equal in authority in the matter of succession. All of their decisions "must be by the unanimous voice," or, "every member in each quorum must be agreed to its decisions, in order to make their decisions of the same power or validity one with the other" (D&C 107:27). "A majority may form a quorum when circumstances render it impossible to be otherwise" (D&C 107:28). Circumstances rendering it impossible to have the quorum at full capacity would be the death or unavailability of some of its members. The above statement also shows that a majority—more than one half—are required to make a decision.

> The decisions of these quorums [the Twelve and the Seventy] . . . are to be made in all righteousness, in holiness, and lowliness of heart, meekness and long suffering, and in faith, and virtue, and knowledge, temperance, patience, godliness, brotherly kindness and charity;

Because the promise is, if these things abound in them they shall not be unfruitful in the knowledge of the Lord.

And in case that any decision of these quorums is made in unrighteousness, it may be brought before a general assembly of the several quorums, which constitute the spiritual authorities of the church; otherwise there can be no appeal from their decision. (D&C 107:30–32.)

The Lord has revealed the organization of those who are to preside over his Church and has given the administrative policies and procedures that are to be followed by the officers and the members. Those who are slothful or do not learn their duties will not be approved of the Lord and not be counted worthy to stand (D&C 107:99–100).

The Oath and Covenant of the Priesthood

The Prophet Joseph designated section 84 of the Doctrine and Covenants as a "revelation on priesthood." In that revelation the Lord outlined several blessings "according to the oath and covenant which belongeth to the priesthood" (v. 39). On a later occasion, the Prophet referred to the Levitical Priesthood "made without an oath, but the Priesthood of Melchizedek is by an oath and covenant."[13]

A covenant involves two parties, and both must do something to make the covenant effective. In section 84 the Lord revealed his part, or agreements to those who were "faithful unto the obtaining these two priesthoods" (D&C 84:33)—the lesser being a preparatory, or schooling, order for the greater. He also stipulated that blessings were conditioned upon the recipient of the priesthood magnifying his calling; God later specified certain things required of him.

God's promises will be considered first. There are three blessings specified in section 84, but these are major ones, and others are also undoubtedly poured out upon the priesthood holder. The first blessing promised is that faithful priesthood holders are "sanctified by the Spirit unto the renewing of their bodies" (D&C 84:33). As revealed in the Book of Mormon, sanctification comes through the righteous exercise of the priesthood and the outpouring of the Holy Ghost (Alma 13:10–12). There are many examples of faithful priesthood holders on ward, stake, and General Authority levels of administration who have had their bodies renewed physically and been sanctified spiritually as they have accepted and labored in their callings.

The second blessing promised of the Lord is that the faithful priesthood bearers become "the seed of Abraham, and the Church and kingdom, and the elect of God" (D&C 84:34). To receive such a promise is a vital part of fulfilling the promise given to Abraham that his literal seed would bear the Lord's priesthood and ministry and thus bless all nations in the last days (see Abraham 2:9–11). Those addressed in this section are thus designated as inheritors of all of "the promises made to the fathers" (D&C 2:2). The "elect of God" here refers to those who live worthy of every trust; who live by every word of God; who hunger and thirst after righteousness; who make their callings and elections sure.[14]

The third blessing promised is that everything that the Father has will be given to the faithful priesthood holder. Through receiving the priesthood, a person is receiving Jesus Christ because the recipient is taking the name of Christ and acting with his authority. And those who receive Jesus are actually receiving the Father because all that Jesus does is by divine investiture of the Father. Those who receive the Father receive his kingdom; they receive the fulness of the glory of the Father. "Therefore all that [the] Father hath shall be given unto [them]" (D&C 84:34–38). In short, they shall receive eternal life. All that the Father has was given to Jesus, and he is willing to give the same to the faithful priesthood holder (John 15:16). As Isaiah foretold, "Therefore, will I [the Father] divide him a portion with the great, and he [Jesus Christ] shall divide the spoil with the strong" (Isaiah 53:12).

The great and eternal head has a nature of total righteousness (Helaman 13:38), therefore "all those who receive the priesthood, receive this oath and covenant of [the] Father, which he cannot break, neither can it be moved (D&C 84:40). God has given his oath, which he can guarantee because of his nature of righteousness. That is to say, to show the binding nature of his covenant to certify that God will keep his part of the covenant—the Lord swears with *an oath* (compare Psalm 110:4) that the righteous priesthood holder shall be an heir to all the Father has.[15]

The great blessings of the oath and covenant of the priesthood cannot be treated lightly. Those who make this covenant are sternly warned. "But whoso breaketh this covenant after he hath received it, and altogether turneth therefrom, shall not have forgiveness of sins in this world nor in the world to come" (D&C 84:41). This does not mean that man will become a son of perdition, but that he will not have the privilege of holding and exercising the priesthood in eternity.[16] To those who may be reluctant to enter such a serious covenant, the Lord also gives a warning: "And wo unto all those who come not unto this priesthood which ye have received, which I now confirm upon you who are present this day, by mine own voice out of the heavens; and even I have given the heavenly hosts and mine angels charge concerning you (D&C 84:42).

With these warnings as a background, the Lord outlined what is required of the priesthood holder to qualify for the eternal blessings that are promised. To magnify one's calling (v. 33) is to take the responsibility for the people with whom he labors or should labor upon his own head, teaching them and warning them so that their blood does not come upon his garments (Jacob 1:19; compare Ezekiel 33:1–9; 2 Nephi 9:44). It is to love his neighbor as himself as he administers the gospel and the ordinances to his fellowmen (D&C 84:19–22). The Lord followed his warnings with a commandment to the priesthood holder "to give diligent heed to the words of eternal life for you shall live by every word that proceedeth forth from the mouth of God" (D&C 84:43–44).

Conclusion

The priesthood has been restored in the last days. The Lord has given the keys to direct the use of the priesthood and established councils to govern the affairs of his Church. Those who receive the Aaronic priesthood are being trained to receive the Melchizedek. Those who enter into this higher priesthood do so by covenant, with the ultimate assurance that God's word is sure and his promises immutable. The Lord does indeed call men "to his holy work in this age and generation as well as in generations of old" (D&C 20:11).

Notes

1. Joseph F. Smith, *Gospel Doctrine* (Salt Lake City: Deseret Book Co., 1970), p. 136.

2. See Larry C. Porter, "The Priesthood Restored," in *Studies in Scripture, Vol. 2: The Pearl of Great Price,* eds. Robert L. Millet and Kent P. Jackson (Sandy, Utah: Randall Book Co., 1985), pp. 389–409.

3. This is a reference to the presiding bishop and has no reference to a local bishop today. See John Taylor, *Gospel Kingdom* (Salt Lake City: Bookcraft, 1964), pp. 195–96; Joseph Fielding Smith, *Doctrines of Salvation,* 3 vols., comp. Bruce R. McConkie (Salt Lake City: Bookcraft, 1954–56), 3:92; Bruce R. McConkie, *A New Witness for the Articles of Faith* (Salt Lake City: Deseret Book Co., 1985), p. 352.

4. See Joseph Smith, *Teachings of the Prophet Joseph Smith,* comp. Joseph Fielding Smith (Salt Lake City: Deseret Book Co., 1977), pp. 337–38.

5. *Teachings of the Prophet Joseph Smith,* p. 157.

6. From "Fourteen Fundamentals in Following the Prophet," in *1980 BYU Devotional Speeches of the Year* (Provo: Brigham Young University Press, 1980), p. 30.

7. David H. Yarn ed., *J. Reuben Clark: Selected Papers* (Provo, Utah: Brigham Young University Press, 1984), pp. 100–101.

8. *History of the Church,* 2:196.

9. Wilford Woodruff, in Conference Report, Apr. 1898, p. 89.

10. In recent years the right to recommend and (following the approval by the Council of the Twelve) ordain worthy men to serve as stake patriarchs has been delegated to stake presidents.

11. In Conference Report, Apr. 1984, p. 73; see also Smith, *Gospel Doctrine*, p. 183.

12. Harold B. Lee, *Stand Ye in Holy Places* (Salt Lake City: Deseret Book Co., 1974), p. 300.

13. *Teachings of the Prophet Joseph Smith,* p. 323.

14. See Marion G. Romney, in Conference Report, Apr. 1974, p. 116.

15. See Joseph Fielding Smith, in Conference Report, Apr. 1970, p. 59; Bruce R. McConkie, in Conference Report, Oct. 1977, p. 51.

16. Smith, *Doctrines of Salvation,* 3:141–42; Marion G. Romney, Conference Report, Apr. 1974, p. 116; Bruce R. McConkie, *A New Witness for the Articles of Faith,* p. 232.

8

A Quest for Zion

C. Max Caldwell

As part of an editorial in the *Times and Seasons,* 2 April 1842, the Prophet Joseph Smith wrote:

> The building up of Zion is a cause that has interested the people of God in every age; it is a theme upon which prophets, priests and kings have dwelt with peculiar delight; they have looked forward with joyful anticipation to the day in which we live; and fired with heavenly and joyful anticipations they have sung and written and prophesied of this our day; but they died without the sight; we are the favored people that God has made choice of to bring about the Latter-day glory.[1]

One of the most significant and frequently mentioned subjects in the Doctrine and Covenants is the establishment of Zion in the latter days. That this wonderful book of latter-day scrip-

---

C. Max Caldwell is Associate Professor of Church History and Doctrine at Brigham Young University.

ture is the major contributor to our understanding of Zion is apparent from the following:

The Book of Mormon contains forty-five references to Zion. All but nine of these, however, are either quotations from or commentary upon the writings of Isaiah. Only nine references in the book pertain to Zion or the establishment of Zion in the latter days. (See 1 Nephi 13:37; 2 Nephi 26:29–31; 28:21–24; 3 Nephi 21:1.)

The Pearl of Great Price contains sixteen references to Zion. However, all but two of these pertain to the ancient city of Zion and conditions pertaining to it as established under the inspired leadership of Enoch. Only two references in the book deal with the establishment of Zion in the last days (see Moses 7:62, 64).

The Doctrine and Covenants contains over two hundred references to Zion. One of these pertains to the City of Zion in Enoch's day (D&C 38:4). Four of them pertain to a prophetic injunction by the Lord through Isaiah pertaining to the latter days (D&C 113:7–9). These four and all of the others are divinely declared references to Zion in our day. Clearly, the Doctrine and Covenants is a "Zion handbook" for our day.

Without explanation of the term, the Savior spoke of Zion four times in the revelations given before the Church was organized in this dispensation. He directed a number of the brethren to "seek to bring forth and establish the cause of Zion" (D&C 6:6; 11:6; 12:6; 14:6). At that time, the intent and desires of the Lord for Zion were undefined. Then, on the day the Church was organized, the Lord said, speaking of the Prophet Joseph Smith, "Him have I inspired to move the cause of Zion in mighty power for good" (D&C 21:7). From the beginning, the Church and its leadership were intended to form an integral part of the establishing of a latter-day Zion.

Later, in September 1830, Joseph Smith recorded the first indication that the Lord intended to have a city built as part of this concept of Zion. A revelation containing such information came because Lucifer had deceived some of the brethren through false revelation into thinking they knew where such a city would be located. The Lord said that "no man knoweth where the city Zion shall be built, but it shall be given hereafter.

Behold, I say unto you that it shall be on the borders by the Lamanites" (D&C 28:9).

Approximately six months later instructions were given to the elders of the Church to go into the western lands, that they might purchase a land of inheritance which was to be appointed or identified by the Lord (see D&C 45:64–65). Then the Lord explained: "And it shall be called the New Jerusalem, a land of peace, a city of refuge, a place of safety for the saints of the Most High God; And the glory of the Lord shall be there, . . . and it shall be called Zion" (D&C 45:66–67).

The use of the name Zion to identify a latter-day city must have excited the early brethren, as they would have been reminded that this name was given to the city of Saints who attained great spiritual stature under the inspired leadership of the Prophet Enoch. This was the translated city about which the Savior said, "I am the same which have taken the Zion of Enoch into mine own bosom" (D&C 38:4). Enoch's Zion was unique, and so were the people who occupied it. They stand out in recorded history as a people who successfully lived the principles of celestial law that is required of a Zion people (see D&C 105:5). Enoch's city and the city of Zion of our day are widely separated in time, yet have many common characteristics, as described by Elder Orson Pratt:

> The Latter-day Zion will resemble, in most particulars, the Zion of Enoch; it will be established upon the same celestial laws—be built upon the same gospel, and be guided by continued revelation. Its inhabitants, like those of the antediluvian Zion, will be the righteous gathered out from all nations; the glory of God will be seen upon it; and His power will be manifested there, even as in the Zion of old. All the blessings and grand characteristics which were exhibited in ancient Zion will be shown forth in the Latter-day Zion.[2]

The purposes of the Lord were beginning to unfold. He planned to have a Zion city in this dispensation. Such grand plans could only find fulfillment by the developing of a people capable of living in such a glorious environment. He would develop them by revealing celestial laws and commanding the keeping of those laws. Then the faithful and obedient might become the inhabitants and custodians of the Lord's city of Zion.

The Place for Zion

A further step in the process came in June of 1831. The Prophet was instructed to take Sidney Rigdon and journey to Missouri as soon as possible. If they were faithful, the Lord would reveal to them the place for the city of the New Jerusalem, or Zion (see D&C 52:3–5).

In company with several others, Joseph Smith left Kirtland on 19 June, arrived safely in Missouri, and then asked the Lord the following question: "When will Zion be built up in her glory, and where will Thy temple stand, unto which all nations shall come in the last days?"[3] In response to his question, the Lord revealed the following to the Prophet Joseph in the land of Missouri:

> The land of Missouri . . . is the land which I have appointed and consecrated for the gathering of the saints. Wherefore, this is the land of promise, and the place for the city of Zion . . . the place which is now called Independence is the center place; and a spot for the temple is lying westward upon a lot which is not far from the courthouse. (D&C 57:1–3.)

A Temple

In pondering Joseph's question and the Lord's answer, one could hardly miss the significance of one matter. In the many revelations concerning Zion, there had been no previous mention of a temple in connection with the city of Zion. The first mention of a temple in our day was in a December 1830 revelation to Edward Partridge, in which the Lord stated he would come to his temple (D&C 36:8). A year later, he made a similar comment (42:36). Nothing had been said, however, that would link a temple with Zion. Yet Joseph included a reference to it in his inquiry. Why might he ask about a temple? Was he prompted to do so? Might he have learned of the need to have a temple in Zion from previously received, but perhaps, unpublished revelations? From his study of scriptural records describing previous societies of righteous people, had he recognized or visualized the need for a temple? One can only speculate. But one thing is certain: he knew a temple was to be a part of the establishment of a latter-day Zion. And, of course, the Lord's revealed answer confirmed the necessity of a temple whenever and wherever a Zion was built.

The Lord appointed Missouri as the land where the Saints were to be gathered. This was a new appointment, since previously, Kirtland, Ohio, had been designated as the gathering place for them (see D&C 37:3; 38:32). At least one major reason for the Lord's gathering his people together was identified by the Prophet Joseph when he said:

> What was the object of gathering the Jews, or the people of God in any age of the world? . . .
> The main object was to build unto the Lord a house whereby He could reveal unto His people the ordinances of His house and the glories of His kingdom, and teach the people the way of salvation; for there are certain ordinances and principles that, when they are taught and practiced, must be done in a place or house built for that purpose.[4]

Clearly the gathering Saints would need to build a temple in their quest for a latter-day Zion.

Within two years, however (by 1833), opposition to the Saints in Missouri became very visible. Mob action resulted in the destruction of the printing press, physical violence, and threats to exterminate the Mormons from Jackson County if they did not leave peaceably. The possibility of building a city of Zion seemed increasingly unlikely. But the Lord continued to provide direction, and in August of that same year directed that a temple should be built in Missouri for the salvation of Zion. He specifically indicated it should be built "speedily" (see D&C 97:10–12). It appears that any hope the Saints might have had to establish Zion was critically dependent upon their building a house unto the Lord. Such was the Lord's response to the threatenings of the enemies of the Church.

After explaining many of the valuable purposes to be served by their participation in temple ordinances, the Lord promised the Saints: "if Zion do these things she shall prosper, and spread herself and become very glorious, very great, and very terrible. And the nations of the earth shall honor her, and shall say: Surely Zion is the city of our God, and surely Zion cannot fall, neither be moved out of her place, for God is there, and the hand of the Lord is there." (D&C 97:18–19.)

Even though Satanic opposition was increasing, there still remained an opportunity for the building of a city of Zion. To do so would depend upon the development of a people whom the Lord described in the same revelation as "THE PURE IN HEART" (D&C 97:21). It was not enough to build a city of physical proportions. There must also be a people who were individually and collectively "pure in heart." They must be worthy of being called covenant people through their obedience to celestial principles and practices. In short, they must be desirous and capable of receiving and living by the instructions, standards, and covenants that are provided by the Lord in his holy house.

Whether one speaks of the mobs of Missouri in the early days of the Church, or of the enemies of righteousness in our own day, the benefits and purposes of the Lord's house are the same. It is within those sacred walls that Saints are instructed in the work of the ministry, regardless of their particular calling in the Church. It is in the temple that understanding is given concerning theory, principle, doctrine and all things that pertain to the Kingdom of God on the earth (see D&C 97:13–14). Without question, members of the Church receive great strength against worldly opposition, as well as spiritual power over the adversary through their participation in the ordinances and application of the principles presented in sacred temples.

Elder George Q. Cannon affirmed such a conclusion when he explained his feelings relative to the value of temples. Speaking of the uncompleted Salt Lake Temple, he said:

I fully believe that when that temple is once finished there will be a power and manifestations of the goodness of God unto this people such as they have never before experienced. Every work of this kind that we have accomplished has been attended with increased and wonderful results unto us as a people—an increase of power and of God's blessings upon us. It was so in Kirtland and at Nauvoo; at both places the Elders had an increase of power, and the Saints, since the completion of and the administration of ordinances in, those buildings have had a power they never possessed previously. . . .

. . . I fully believe also, as I have said, that when this and other temples are completed, there will be an increase of power bestowed upon the people of God, and that they will, thereby, be better fitted to go forth and cope with the powers of darkness and with the evils that exist in the world and to establish the Zion of God never more to be thrown down.[5]

We can never hope to establish a society of Zion without the benefits of temple experiences. Noting that it is as essential for the people of our day to enter into and keep the covenants of the temple as it was for the residents of Enoch's city of Zion, Brigham Young taught:

The Lord has declared it to be his will that his people enter into covenant, even as Enoch and his people did, which of necessity must be before we shall have the privilege of building the Centre Stake of Zion, for the power and glory of God will be there, and none but the pure in heart will be able to live and enjoy it. Go to now, with your might and with your means, and finish this [Salt Lake] Temple.[6]

Expulsion from Zion

Unfortunately, the early Saints who dwelt in Missouri were not adequately faithful to establish Zion. Perhaps they were unaware of the serious consequences of their disregard of the Lord's mandate to build a temple and do it speedily. The Lord certainly knew that any hope the Saints had of avoiding Satanic intervention in the aspirations for Zion depended upon their becoming involved in a temple-oriented style of life. Disobedience to this and other divine commandments preceded their expulsion from Jackson County in the fall of 1833. The Saints found themselves separated from the very land the Lord had appointed for the gathering place of his people and for the building of a city of Zion with an attendant temple of the Most High God.

On 16 December 1833, Joseph received a revelation concerning the Saints who were afflicted, persecuted, and cast out of the lands of their inheritance. The Lord explained that they were allowed to suffer "in consequence of their transgressions; . . . there were jarrings, and contentions, and envyings, and strifes, and lustful and covetous desires among them; therefore by these things they polluted their inheritances. They were slow to hearken unto the voice of the Lord their God; . . . In the day of their peace they esteemed lightly my counsel." (D&C 101:2, 6–8.)

They were not yet "pure in heart." Without such purity, they could not obtain heavenly powers sufficient to overcome the evil forces of opposition. Clearly, the people had brought upon themselves the tragic loss of opportunity to create a latter-day city of Zion. The time and place had been identified and provided. Instructions and commandments had been sufficient to accomplish divine purposes. But failure to follow divine directives had resulted in a separation of the people from the desired lands and a suspension of opportunity to establish Zion. In a pointed and powerful parable the Lord explained the cause of the Saints being driven out of the land of Zion (see D&C 101:43–62). To assist in understanding the meaning of the parable, the following comparison of the imagery may be helpful:

Nobleman	The Savior
Vineyard	Earth
Choice piece of land	Jackson County, Missouri
Servants	Church members
Olive trees	Settlements of the Saints
Watchmen	Officers of the Church
Watchman	The Prophet
Tower	Temple
Servant	Joseph Smith

Hyrum M. Smith and Janne Sjodahl have noted that "the Temple, the site of which was dedicated August 3, 1831, would have been the tower from which the movements of the enemy could have been observed by inspiration. But, as nothing more was done to complete that tower, the enemy came by night and broke down the hedge, and the servants of the nobleman fled, leaving the enemy in possession."[7]

From the parable we learn that the Saints took lightly the counsel given by the Lord concerning the need for a temple for the salvation of his people. They reasoned among themselves that there was no need for the temple. Twice in the parable the servants questioned the Lord's need for the tower. They seemingly did not consider that they, rather than the Lord, needed the tower. It is interesting that they consulted among themselves but did not bother to call upon the Lord. But the Lord of the vineyard called upon his servants, raised a crucial question, and provided his own answer:

> Why! what is the cause of this great evil?
> Ought ye not to have done even as I commanded you, and . . . built the tower also, and set a watchman upon the tower, and watched for my vineyard, and not have fallen asleep, lest the enemy should come upon you?
> And behold, the watchman upon the tower would have seen the enemy while he was yet afar off; and then ye could have made ready and kept the enemy from breaking down the hedge thereof, and saved my vineyard from the hands of the destroyer. (D&C 101:52–54.)

The Lord left no doubt that failure to build the temple was at the heart of the failure of the Saints to establish Zion. Any attempt on their part to establish a Zion society was fruitless without their also having the blessings of a holy temple. Speaking of the Lord's emphatic declaration to build a temple speedily in the face of Satan-inspired mob action that provided stiff opposition to the Lord's people and his work in Missouri, an interesting commentary has been given:

> God was, if we may say so reverently, anxious that His people should rear a Temple in which they could be endowed with power from on high before the conflict with the adversary. The history of Temples teaches us that the

people of God have been strong, or weak, in proportion to the faithfulness with which they have attended to their sanctuaries. . . . Speaking of the Temples in this dispensation, someone has declared that the completion of the Nauvoo Temple was the salvation of the Church from annihilation, although the Saints were forced to flee into the desert. Since the completion of the Salt Lake Temple, the adversary has had less power to injure the Church than he had before. If we remember that the Temples are the palaces of God, where His presence is manifested, we can understand why, when the adversary was marshalling his forces against the Church, [in Missouri] our Lord urged the Saints to build the Temple speedily. We can also understand why the evil one planned to have them scattered before they could rear that sacred edifice.[8]

Redemption of Zion Must Wait

Following the expulsion of the Saints from Jackson County, Lyman Wight and Parley P. Pratt journeyed to Kirtland, Ohio, to inquire of the Prophet what directions the Lord might have for the Saints in Missouri. They wondered about the possibility of being reinstated upon their lands and whether there was any possibility that Zion might be redeemed. In a revelation responding to their inquiry, the Lord assured them that Zion could still be redeemed, provided the Saints in Missouri and in Ohio would give strict and immediate obedience to his instructions:

> I have decreed a decree which my people shall realize, inasmuch as they hearken from this very hour unto the counsel which I, the Lord their God, shall give unto them.
>
> Behold, they shall, for I have decreed it, begin to prevail against mine enemies from this very hour. . . .
>
> . . . I have decreed that your brethren which have been scattered shall return to the lands of their inheritances, and shall build up the waste places of Zion. . . .
>
> Behold, this is the blessing which I have promised after your tribulations, and the tribulations of your brethren — your redemption, and the redemption of your brethren, even their restoration to the land of Zion, to be established, no more to be thrown down. (D&C 103:5–6, 11, 13.)

In this same revelation, the Lord instructed the Saints in Ohio to assist in the redemption of their brethren in Zion by sending a relief expedition. Ideally, this expedition was to consist of five hundred men with sufficient funds to purchase land as previously commanded by the Lord (see D&C 103:22–23, 30–34). This group, which finally numbered approximately two hundred men, was known as Zion's Camp. They were under-manned and underfunded to accomplish what the Lord had asked of them, yet they made the extremely difficult journey to Missouri under the leadership of Joseph Smith. The announced intention of the march was to seek restoration of the lands in Jackson County from which the members of the Church had been driven. Their desire and mandate was to reclaim the land of inheritance upon which they were to build a city of Zion.

Though the response to the Lord's call was inadequate to meet fully his expectations, many did go, at great effort and personal sacrifice. They arrived at Fishing River in Missouri on 22 June 1834, where the Lord gave a revelation to Joseph Smith declaring that Zion would not be redeemed at that time. To those who had faithfully responded to the Lord's requests, he promised "a blessing and an endowment" and indicated they had been participants in the cause of Zion "for a trial of their faith" (D&C 105:18–19). However, sufficient obedience had not been rendered by the majority of the Saints, in Ohio, in branches of the Church in the East, or in Missouri. The Lord rebuked the disobedient, postponing the establishment of Zion to some future time. He said:

> Were it not for the transgressions of my people, speaking concerning the church and not individuals, they might have been redeemed even now.
> But behold, they have not learned to be obedient to the things which I required at their hands, but are full of all manner of evil, and do not impart of their substance, as becometh saints, to the poor and afflicted among them;
> And are not united according to the union required by the law of the celestial kingdom;
> And Zion cannot be built up unless it is by the principles of the law of the celestial kingdom; otherwise I cannot receive her unto myself. And my people must needs

be chastened until they learn obedience, if it must needs be, by the things which they suffer. . . .

Therefore, in consequence of the transgressions of my people, it is expedient in me that mine elders should wait for a little season for the redemption of Zion. (D&C 105:2–6, 9.)

The Saints failed in their efforts to establish Zion. An opportunity was lost. One of the great events of the world's history had to be deferred to a future time. Though the revelations of the Savior had authorized the time, the place, and the people, led by one of the greatest prophets of all time, the Saints did not have sufficient faith to render obedience and follow their living prophet. The members of the Church had not proven worthy of their celestial trust. As a group, they were not prepared to develop a Zion society nor build the city in which such a society might be established by a "pure in heart" people. At least temporarily the Church lost its opportunity to create a city of Zion like the Zion of Enoch's day.

After Much Tribulation and Preparation

In suspending this project "for a little season" several conditions were described as being prerequisite to the redemption of Zion. The Lord said the people need to:

1. Learn obedience
2. Be united
3. Be prepared
4. Be taught
5. Have experience
6. Know their duty
7. Be endowed with power
8. Become very great
9. Be sanctified
10. Purchase lands
    (D&C 105:3–4, 10–11, 28, 31)

The Lord certainly knew the fledgling Church would not reach such lofty goals. Why then were the Saints requested to seek for such seemingly unattainable objectives at that time?

The Lord has revealed at least part of the answer to our question.

First of all, we should acknowledge Zion could have been established by those early Saints. Repeatedly such was declared to be a real possibility, provided that the Saints rendered strict obedience to the celestial laws governing such a society. The opportunity was provided. Unfortunately Church members closed the door on their own privileges.

Second, an interesting statement is contained in a revelation received by Joseph Smith when he first journeyed to Missouri to learn of the location of the latter-day city of Zion. To those early Saints, eager with anticipation, the Lord said:

> Ye cannot behold with your natural eyes, for the present time, the design of your God concerning those things which shall come hereafter, and the glory which shall follow after much tribulation. . . .
> The hour is not yet, but is nigh at hand. . . .
> For this cause I have sent you—that you might be obedient, and that your hearts might be prepared to bear testimony of the things which are to come;
> And also that you might be honored in laying the foundation. (D&C 58:3–4, 6–7.)

Armed with historical perspective, one can safely conclude that the establishment of settlements in Missouri served many purposes that were essential to the development of the Lord's people and the ultimate redemption of Zion. But it is also apparent that those people were not then, collectively, intended to do more than that which is described in the above revelation, namely, lay the foundation. Elder B. H. Roberts has observed that the Lord did not expect to establish a Zion city at that time:

> The immediate and triumphant establishment of Zion, though expected by many of the Saints, was nowhere contemplated in the revelations of God to the Church. That hope of immediate establishment and glorification of Zion was the result of faulty deductions from the revelations of God; but the Lord was not blind respecting the events about to take place on the land of Zion, nor did He hold out any false hope to His people had they but read His revelations aright. . . . the Lord said to them through His Prophet: [quotes D&C 58:1–7, 13, 44–45]

These statements, when rightly considered, dispel all notion of the immediate establishment of Zion. The Lord distinctly warns His servants against any such supposition. He predicts "tribulation" before the glory shall come. It is only after "much tribulation" that the blessings are promised.[9]

Why, then, were the Saints sent to Missouri at that time? They were to learn obedience, bear testimony of things to come, and establish a foundation upon which the Lord could then build his church and the membership thereof. To build a temple or a Zion city, one must begin with a sure foundation. That spiritual foundation consists of unconditional, unsolicited, self-imposed obedience to the spiritual laws that structure celestial societies. The Saints were to learn obedience in the midst of tribulation. The Apostle Paul said the Savior learned obedience "by the things which he suffered" (Hebrews 5:8). The Saints have to do the same. Unless we face and overcome opposition by the full and free use of our agency, we don't really learn obedience.

With unerring foresight, the Lord anticipated the failure to establish Zion but assured the struggling Saints of the honor of "laying the foundation." They were given the opportunity of initiating this great work and played a significant, God-ordained role in so doing.

Conclusion

As Church history unfolded, the Saints were ultimately driven out of the state of Missouri. They settled temporarily in Illinois and then were again driven from their homes to settle in the western territories of the country. Many of the members who had been a part of the effort to establish Zion in Jackson County, Missouri, were also in companies of pioneers trekking west. Every step westward was one step further away from the originally designated place for the Lord's city and temple. It must have come as a great comfort and assurance that their efforts had not been in vain and that the future would yet include the building of the New Jerusalem, when a revelation was received by their prophet-leader, Brigham Young, stating: "Go thy way and do as I have told you, and fear not thine enemies;

for they shall not have power to stop my work. Zion shall be redeemed in mine own due time." (D&C 136:17–18.)

The present is a time for striving to become "pure in heart." We recognize the vital role of the temple in providing us the same protection from spiritual enemies of our own day that the Lord offered the struggling Saints in Missouri when they were faced with evil-inspired mobs. It is imperative that we associate ourselves with temple ordinances and experiences, that we prepare for and participate in those spiritually strengthening ways the Lord has ordained. If we are to build homes and stakes of Zion quality now, we must follow the same course the Lord revealed in an earlier day. At the dedication of the Logan Temple, President John Taylor offered the following inspired prayer:

> We have now completed this, another house, which we this day dedicate and consecrate unto Thee, that we may be further prepared to carry out Thy will, to administer in Thine ordinances, to purify and instruct Thy Church, and to build up and establish Thy Zion on the earth, which Thou hast decreed should be accomplished in the dispensation of the fullness of times.[10]

We also note that the future still holds in store the building of the New Jerusalem in Jackson County. Elder Joseph Young, brother of President Brigham Young and one of the first members of the First Quorum of the Seventy, said:

> The saints are looking for a modern Zion which shall be after the identical order of the ancient one; and for a time when the Apostles with their President at their head, will rise up and thunder so loud, that if they do not shake the mountains from their foundations, they will have the effect of shaking pride and covetousness out of the hearts of the Saints, who will be filled with righteousness—their only motive, the building up of Zion; making their faith and their works, their means and their substance to bow to that end, and that only, and so continuing their labors in this good work, answering to the Zion within them, and erecting and adorning temples and mansions; building cities, and spreading abroad, until they shall become a model of Zion of old, built by Enoch.[11]

Though the forces of opposition are rampant about us and present challenging barriers to the establishment of the level of righteousness required for a city of Zion, President Marion G. Romney has provided the following encouragement:

> Remember that Enoch's Zion was built in a day when wickedness was as rampant as it is among us today. Among those who rejected the word of God in that day "there were wars and bloodshed;" they were ripening in that iniquity which brought the flood. "But the Lord came and dwelt with his people, and they dwelt in righteousness . . . [And the Lord called his people Zion,] because they were of one heart and one mind." (Moses 7:16.)[12]

We can be certain that the Lord will accomplish his proclaimed purposes and objectives of this dispensation. He stated, "I will raise up unto myself a pure people, that will serve me in righteousness" (D&C 100:16). The quest for Zion continues.

Notes

1. *History of The Church of Jesus Christ of Latter-day Saints*, 7 vols., ed. B. H. Roberts (Salt Lake City: Deseret Book Co., 1957), 4:609.

2. *The Seer*, vol. 2, (May 1854), p. 265.

3. *History of the Church,* 1:189.

4. Ibid., 5:423.

5. In *Journal of Discourses*, 14:125–26.

6. In *Journal of Discourses,* 18:263.

7. Hyrum M. Smith and Janne M. Sjodahl, *Doctrine and Covenants Commentary* (Salt Lake City: Deseret Book Co., 1951), p. 647.

8. Smith and Sjodahl, *Doctrine and Covenants Commentary,* p. 612.

9. *History of the Church*, 3:xxxv–xxxvi.

10. *Millennial Star*, 46:388.

11. History of the Organization of the Seventies, p. 11.

12. In Conference Report, Apr. 1976, p. 169.

Trials and Tribulations: The Refiner's Fire

Keith W. Perkins

O ne of the age-old questions in the world has been, "Why do the wicked seem to prosper and the righteous suffer?" The book of Job is one of the great literary masterpieces that deals with the question of why the righteous suffer. The Lord himself clarified this issue in his great Sermon on the Mount: "That ye may be the children of your Father which is in heaven: for he maketh his sun to rise on the evil and on the good, and sendeth rain on the just and on the unjust" (Matthew 5:45). In addition to Job, many individuals who have lived on earth have demonstrated by their personal lives why the righteous suffer and have trials and tribulations. In fact, the greatest being who ever lived on this earth, the Lord Jesus Christ, suffered more than any other. In this dispensation a prime example of a righteous man facing great trials and tribulations is the Prophet Joseph Smith. In our own day we have seen a similar example in

---

Keith W. Perkins is Professor and Chairman of the Department of Church History and Doctrine at Brigham Young University.

the life of President Spencer W. Kimball. Perhaps no better answer can be found to this age-old question than can be found in the Doctrine and Covenants.

The following are some brief excerpts from the Doctrine and Covenants that give the Lord's teachings about trials and tribulations:

> Be patient in afflictions, revile not against those that revile. Govern your house in meekness, and be steadfast. (D&C 31:9.)
>
> And again, be patient in tribulation until I come; and, behold, I come quickly, and my reward is with me, and they who have sought me early shall find rest to their souls. Even so. Amen. (D&C 54:10.)
>
> For verily I say unto you, blessed is he that keepeth my commandments, whether in life or in death; and he that is faithful in tribulation, the reward of the same is greater in the kingdom of heaven.
>
> Ye cannot behold with your natural eyes, for the present time, the design of your God concerning those things which shall come hereafter, and the glory which shall follow after much tribulation.
>
> For after much tribulation come the blessings. Wherefore the day cometh that ye shall be crowned with much glory; the hour is not yet, but is nigh at hand. (D&C 58:2–4.)
>
> [The righteous dead in the spirit world were they] who had offered sacrifice in the similitude of the great sacrifice of the Son of God, and had suffered tribulation in their Redeemer's name (D&C 138:13).

Sometimes, however, sufferings, trials, and afflictions come upon us because of our own sins and transgressions. Such was the case with the early Saints who were driven out of Jackson County, Missouri, in 1833. Even though they had been driven out, the Lord still held out the promise of eternal life if they repented.

> Verily I say unto you, concerning your brethren who have been afflicted, and persecuted, and cast out from the land of their inheritance—
>
> I, the Lord, have suffered the affliction to come upon them, wherewith they have been afflicted, in consequence of their transgressions;

Yet I will own them, and they shall be mine in that day when I shall come to make up my jewels (D&C 101: 1–3).

People generally react in one of two ways to trials and tribulations: either they become more kind, gentle, and loving or else they become bitter. Christ cried out in the Garden of Gethsemane: "O my Father, if it be possible, let this cup pass from me: nevertheless not as I will, but as thou wilt" (Matthew 26:39). And on the cross he further pleaded, "Eli, Eli, lama sabachthani? that is to say, My God, my God, why hast thou forsaken me?" (Matthew 27:46.) Even though his suffering was beyond our comprehension, he accepted the will of the Father and suffered for our sins, pains, temptations, sicknesses, and afflictions. By this suffering his love and capacity to succor were increased (Alma 7:11). His love is so great that when the prophets speak of the ultimate love, they call it the "pure love of Christ" (Moroni 7:47).

In this dispensation the best contrasting example of what trials and tribulations do to two men is Joseph Smith and Sidney Rigdon. In the dark days of betrayal and apostasy these two men, along with others, were illegally thrown into the foul jails of Richmond and Liberty, Missouri. They spent almost four months in Liberty Jail—an ironic name for a jail. In prison they suffered all kinds of abuse. They were poisoned three or four times and fed human flesh.[1] After a few months Sidney Rigdon was released from jail, but before leaving he declared "that the sufferings of Jesus Christ were a fool to his."[2] This seemed to be the turning point in Sidney's life. After this experience he was no longer the great leader of the Church that he had been. Joseph Smith no longer wanted him as a counselor because of his unfaithfulness; the Prophet later remarked that if Sidney Rigdon led the Church he "would lead the Church to destruction in less than five years."[3] Finally, after the death of the Prophet Joseph Smith, Sidney returned to Nauvoo, after going to Pittsburgh contrary to the Lord's counsel (D&C 124:108), and claimed he should be the "guardian" for the Church. When he secretly began plotting against the Twelve after originally agreeing to support them, he was excommunicated. Thus Sidney's reactions to the trials and tribulations he faced made him a bitter man, one who finally lost his testimony and faith.

Contrast this with the Prophet Joseph Smith who went through the same experiences as Sidney, and even more, and yet he became more kind and gentle. Besides the other terrible conditions that the rest of the prisoners suffered, he also was very sick at times with a toothache and a terrible pain in his face in consequences of a severe cold.[4] It is from the Prophet's letter in Liberty Jail that we can learn the most about his response to trials and tribulations.

The Letter from Liberty Jail

The letter from Liberty Jail came about in a very interesting way. The brethren had been in prison for four long months. They had been sentenced to be shot, only to have a brave man, General Alexander Doniphan, refuse to carry out that order. They had listened to the foul oaths and boastings of the terrible deeds of murder, rape, abuse, and foul language of their guards. "We are compelled to hear nothing but blasphemous oaths, and witness a scene of blasphemy, and drunkenness and hypocrisy, and debaucheries of every description," wrote the Prophet Joseph Smith.[5] In addition, they had heard, through the personal visits of their family and friends to their lonesome prison, of other atrocities. The immediate prompter was, however, a heart-rending letter from the Prophet's wife, Emma. She told of not only her personal suffering, but of the suffering of all the Saints: "The daily sufferings of our brethren in travelling and camping out nights, and those on the other side of the river would beggar the most lively description."[6] She also informed Joseph of the growth and progress of his family, especially their baby son, who was growing and learning to walk without his father there to enjoy those precious moments. "We are all well at present, except Frederick, who is quite sick. Little Alexander who is now in my arms is one of the finest little fellows, you ever saw in your life, he is so strong that with the assistance of a chair he will run all round the room."[7] This must have torn at the heartstrings of this tender, loving man, a person made more tender and loving because of his experience within his lonesome prison.

His return letter to his beloved Emma tells why he wrote another letter he enclosed, which he had written to the Church: "I have sent an Epistle to the church directed to you because I wanted you to have the first reading of it and then I want Father and Mother to have a copy of it keep the original yourself as I dictated the matter myself and shall send another as soon as possible."[8] This letter to the Church has become a classic in Mormon literature. Portions were selected by Elder Orson Pratt in 1877 when he was assigned to prepare a new edition of the scriptures, and have become sections 121, 122, and 123 of the Doctrine and Covenants. These are some of the finest words of counsel extant on the purpose and benefits of trials and tribulation. They help answer the questions of the ages and give us answers to these perplexing queries that no other generation has had. Truly the Lord fulfilled his promise that he would reveal those things "that [had] not been revealed since the world was until now; which our forefathers have awaited with anxious expectation. . . . A time to come in the which nothing shall be withheld." (D&C 121:26–28; see also Matthew 13:11; D&C 28:7; 42:61; 90:14; 101:32–33.) Certainly one of the "mysteries" to be revealed was an answer to this age-old question of why the righteous suffer and the wicked seem to prosper.

Not only is the timeless question answered in those parts of the letter from Liberty that were excerpted by Orson Pratt and have become scripture, but also some of the best answers to this question were not mined out by Elder Pratt and are left there like gold nuggets—left for us to mine out for ourselves. In the material I have quoted, those portions which are found in both the Doctrine and Covenants and *History of the Church* appear in brackets ([]). I have included with these the scriptural reference from the Doctrine and Covenants. Now let us look at the Lord's answer to this timeless question of why the righteous suffer.

In the letter Joseph Smith first reminded the Saints of what characteristics they must have if they were going to be able to accept and come away stronger from the trials and tribulations they were going through. "May faith and virtue, and knowledge and temperance and patience and godliness, and brotherly kindness and charity be in you and abound, that you may not be barren in anything, nor unfruitful."⁹

Then he shared with them some of his most intimate and heartrending prayers that he had uttered while in prison:

> O God, where art thou? And where is the pavilion that covereth thy hiding place?
>
> How long shall thy hand be stayed, and thine eye, yea thy pure eye, behold from the eternal heavens the wrongs of thy people and of thy servants, and thine ear be penetrated with their cries?
>
> Yea, O Lord, how long shall they suffer these wrongs and unlawful oppressions, before thine heart shall be softened toward them, and thy bowels be moved with compassion toward them?
>
> O Lord God Almighty, maker of heaven, earth, and seas, and of all things that in them are, and who controllest and subjectest the devil, and the dark and benighted dominion of Sheol—stretch forth thy hand; let thine eye pierce; let thy pavilion be taken up; let thy hiding place no longer be covered; let thine ear be inclined; let thine heart be softened, and thy bowels moved with compassion toward us.
>
> Let thine anger be kindled against our enemies; and, in the fury of thine heart, with thy sword avenge us of our wrongs.
>
> Remember thy suffering saints, O our God; and thy servants will rejoice in thy name forever. (D&C 121:1–6.)

How long Joseph Smith must have prayed—how many hours, weeks, months—we do not know. But finally the loving answer from his Heavenly Father came. To appreciate why the answer must have taken so long and to understand the spiritual environment in which the revelation came, I will include his preliminary remarks before the answer comes from the Lord:

> And we need not say to you that the floodgates of our hearts were lifted and our eyes were a fountain of tears, but those who have not been enclosed in the walls of prison without cause or provocation, can have but little idea how sweet the voice of a friend is; one token of friendship from any source whatever awakens and calls into action

every sympathetic feeling; it brings up in an instant everything that is passed; it seizes the present with the avidity
of lightning; it grasps after the future with the fierceness
of a tiger; it moves the mind backward and forward, from
one thing to another, until finally all enmity, malice and
hatred, and past differences, misunderstandings and mis-
managements are slain victorious at the feet of hope; and
when the heart is sufficiently contrite, then the voice of
inspiration steals along and whispers, [My son, peace be
unto thy soul; thine adversity and thine afflictions shall be
but a small moment; and then if thou endure it well, God
shall exalt thee on high; thou shalt triumph over all thy
foes; thy friends do stand by thee, and they shall hail thee
again, with warm hearts and friendly hands; thou art not
yet as Job; thy friends do not contend against thee, neither charge thee with transgression, as they did Job; and
they who do charge thee with transgression, their hope
shall be blasted and their prospects shall melt away as the
hoar frost melteth before the burning rays of the rising
sun.] (D&C 121:7–11.)[10]

Note that the answer to even the Prophet's prayer does not
come until "all enmity, malice and hatred . . . are slain victorious at the feet of hope." Then, and only then, does the answer
come, and so it is with all of us. The other great message in this
portion of the letter is that our life on this earth is very short; the
Lord calls it "a small moment." Elder Neal A. Maxwell has
given us some excellent insights into this portion of the Lord's
revelation to Joseph Smith:

In the Apocryphon of James, Jesus reportedly told an afflicted Peter and James, "If you consider how long the
world existed before you, and how long it will exist after
you, you will find that your life is one single day and your
sufferings one single hour." ("The Apocryphon of
James," in *The Nag Hammadi Library in English,* ed.
James M. Robinson, San Francisco: Harper and Row,
1978, p. 31.)
How like what the Lord told suffering Joseph in jail:
"My son, . . . thine adversity and thine afflictions shall be
but a small moment" (D&C 121:7).
One's life, therefore, is brevity compared to eternity—
like being dropped off by a parent for a day at school.
But what a day![11]

In his letter from Liberty Jail, Joseph Smith continued his counsel to the Saints, informing them that the suffering in Missouri was only the crucible of the Lord to refine them into pure gold.

> And now, beloved brethren, we say unto you, that inasmuch as God hath said that He would have a tried people, that He would purge them as gold, now we think that this time He has chosen His own crucible, wherein we have been tried; and we think if we get through with any degree of safety, and shall have kept the faith, that it will be a sign to this generation, altogether sufficient to leave them without excuse; and we think also, it will be a trial of our faith equal to that of Abraham, and that the ancients will not have whereof to boast over us in the day of judgment, as being called to pass through heavier afflictions; that we may hold an even weight in the balance with them; but now, after having suffered so great sacrifice and having passed through so great a season of sorrow, we trust that a ram may be caught in the thicket speedily, to relieve the sons and daughters of Abraham from their great anxiety.[12]

It may sound strange to us for the Prophet Joseph Smith to state that this trial of their faith would be equal to Abraham's (compare D&C 132:49–50), but we must remember that in the case of Abraham, the ultimate sacrifice was not required, only asked, while many of the Saints had sacrificed their very lives and the lives of their loved ones. The Prophet also spoke to this issue:

> Behold this is like Abraham. A striking evidence of their acceptance before the Lord in this thing, but this is not all, they are called to contend with the beast of the wilderness for a long time whose jaws are open to devour them. Thus did Abraham and also Paul at Ephesus. Behold thou art like them. And again the affliction of my Brethren reminds me of Abraham offering up Isaac his only son but my Brethren have been called to give up even more than this, their wives and their children, yea and their own life also. O Lord what more dost thou require at their hands before thou wilt come and save them. May I not say . . . Lord thou wilt save them out of the hands of their enemies. Thou hast tried them in the furnace of affliction a furnace of thine own choosing and couldst thou have tried

them more then thou hast. O Lord then let this suffice and from henceforth let this be recorded in heaven for thine angels to look upon and for a testimony against all those ungodly men who have committed those ungodly deeds [forever and] ever.[13]

The purpose of our trials and tribulations and what they do for us begins to be revealed like a hidden pearl. The first thing we learn from the Lord is that suffering helps make us more refined. Just as when gold is refined it glistens and glows, so we become more loving, kind, and considerate. Second, by suffering we are able to "hold an even weight in the balance with them" (the ancient Saints); i.e., we are worthy of the same reward because we paid as heavy a price as they did.

Third, the Prophet tells us that after our tribulations and after we—

exercise fervent prayer and faith in the sight of God always, [He shall give unto you knowledge by His Holy Spirit, yea by the unspeakable gift of the Holy Ghost, that has not been revealed since the world was until now; which our forefathers have awaited with anxious expectation to be revealed in the last times, which their minds were pointed to by the angels, as held in reserve for the fullness of their glory; a time to come in the which nothing shall be withheld] (D&C 121:26–28).[14]

Thus one of the greatest gifts that God can give us, precious knowledge from the Holy Ghost, comes as a direct result of our trials and tribulations.

The ultimate purpose for trials and tribulations the voice of the Lord described to the Prophet Joseph Smith in minute detail.

If thou art called to pass through tribulation; if thou art in perils among false brethren; if thou art in perils among robbers; if thou art in perils by land or by sea;

If thou art accused with all manner of false accusations; if thine enemies fall upon thee; if they tear thee from the society of thy father and mother and brethren and sisters; and if with a drawn sword thine enemies tear thee from the bosom of thy wife, and of thine offspring, and thine elder son, although but six years of age, shall cling to thy garments, and shall say, My father, my

father, why can't you stay with us? O, my father what are
the men going to do with you? and if then he shall be thrust
from thee by the sword, and thou be dragged to
prison, and thine enemies prowl around thee like wolves
for the blood of the lamb;

And if thou shouldst be cast into the pit, or into the
hands of murderers, and the sentence of death passed
upon thee; if thou be cast into the deep; if the billowing
surge conspire against thee; if fierce winds become thine
enemy; if the heavens gather blackness, and all the ele-
ments combine to hedge up the way; and above all, if the
very jaws of hell shall gape open the mouth wide after
thee, know thou, my son, that all these things shall give
thee experience, and shall be for thy good.

The Son of Man hath descended below them all. Art
thou greater than he?

Therefore, hold on thy way, and the priesthood shall
remain with thee; for their bounds are set, they cannot
pass. Thy days are known, and thy years shall not be
numbered less; therefore, fear not what man can do, for
God shall be with you forever and ever. (D&C 122:5–9.)

For the most part this is not a prediction to the Prophet of
what could or would happen, but it is a rehearsal by the Lord of
his history. We have the remembrance of that six-year-old son,
Joseph Smith, III, of what this experience was like.

I remember vividly the morning my father came to
visit his family after the arrest that took place in the fall
of 1838. When he was brought to the house by an armed
guard I ran out of the gate to greet him, but was roughly
pushed away from his side by a sword in the hand of the
guard and not allowed to go near him. My mother also
was not permitted to approach him and had to receive his
farewell by word of lip only. The guard did not permit
him to pass into the house nor her to pass out, either because he feared an attempt would be made to rescue his
prisoner or because of some brutal instinct in his own
breast. Who shall say?[15]

Thus the Lord gives us the ultimate reasons for trials and
tribulations. "All these things shall give thee experience, and
shall be for thy good." What experience! But when we know
that our suffering will give us the experience that is necessary for
us to have in order to be exalted, and will ultimately be for our

good—when such perspective comes, then such experiences become easier to bear. And, once again no matter how bad our trials and tribulations have been, we still know there is one who has suffered far more than we, and therefore he can bear our infirmaties, our pain, and our sorrow because he knows what we are going through; indeed, the Son of Man hath descended below them all.

President Marion G. Romney helps us appreciate the tremendous growth that came to Joseph Smith during this "brief moment" of suffering in Liberty Jail and gives us an increased appreciation for his greatness as a result of this experience.

> Speaking for himself and his fellow prisoners, he said: ". . . in His Almighty name we are determined to endure tribulation as good soldiers unto the end." (*DHC*, vol. 3, p. 297.) And counseling the Saints to do likewise, he said: ". . . let thy bowels . . . be full of charity towards all men. . . ." (*DHC*, vol. 3, p. 300.)
>
> This admonition, considered in light of the circumstances under which it was given, seems to me to almost equal the Master's statement from the cross: "Father, forgive them; for they know not what they do" (Luke 23:34). . . .
>
> No wonder the Lord could say to him, as he did, ". . . I seal upon you your exaltation, and prepare a throne for you in the kingdom of my Father, with Abraham your father.
>
> "Behold, I have seen your sacrifices, and will forgive all your sins; I have seen your sacrifices in obedience to that which I have told you. . . ." (D&C 132:49–50.)[16]

No wonder Joseph Smith understood so much about suffering. Very early the Lord had told him: "Be patient in afflictions, for thou shalt have many; but endure them, for, lo, I am with thee, even unto the end of thy days" (D&C 24:8). Near the end of his life he could, like Paul (see 2 Timothy 4:7), report how he had finished the course which the Lord had laid out for him:

> And as for the perils which I am called to pass through, they seem but a small thing to me, as the envy and wrath of man have been my common lot all the days of my life; and for what cause it seems mysterious, unless

I was ordained from before the foundation of the world for some good end, or bad, as you may choose to call it. Judge ye for yourselves. God knoweth all these things, whether it be good or bad. But nevertheless, deep water is what I am wont to swim in. It all has become a second nature to me; and I feel, like Paul, to glory in tribulation; for to this day has the God of my fathers delivered me out of them all, and will deliver me from henceforth; for behold, and lo, I shall triumph over all my enemies, for the Lord God hath spoken it. (D&C 127:2.)

It is no wonder Orson F. Whitney could say of Joseph Smith:

It remained for the Prophet Joseph Smith to . . . set forth the why and wherefore of human suffering; and in revealing it he gave us a strength and power to endure that we did not before possess. For *when men know why they suffer,* and realize that it is for a good and wise purpose, they can bear it much better than they can in ignorance. . . .

It is for our development, our purification, our growth, our education and advancement, that we buffet the fierce waves of sorrow and misfortune; and we shall be all the stronger and better when we have swam the flood and stand upon the farther shore. . . .

When we want counsel and comfort, we do not go to children, nor to those who know nothing but pleasure and self-gratification. We go to men and women of thought and sympathy, men and women who have suffered themselves and can give us the comfort that we need. Is not this God's purpose in causing [allowing] his children to suffer? He wants them to become more like himself. God has suffered far more than man ever did or ever will, and is therefore the great source of sympathy and consolation. "Who are these arrayed in white, nearest to the throne of God?" asked John the Apostle, wrapt in his mighty vision. The answer was: "These are they who have come up through great tribulation, and washed their robes and made them white in the blood of the Lamb." [Revelation 7:14.]

There is always a blessing in sorrow and humiliation. They who escape these things are not the fortunate ones. "Whom God loveth he chasteneth." When he desires to make a great man he takes a little street waif, or a boy in the back-woods, such as Lincoln or Joseph Smith, and brings him up through hardship and privation to be the grand and successful leader of a people. Flowers shed most of their perfume when they are crushed. Men and women have to suffer just so much in order to bring out the best that is in them.[17]

It has been the author's privilege to know a number of people who have faced terrible trials and tribulations and have learned from these experiences, and it truly has been for their good. When my wife and I were newly married, we were asked by a sweet sister if we would like to live in their home rent free by taking care of it. Her husband was dying and they were living in a cooler climate for the summer. This was too much for a newly married couple to resist. Periodically this dear sister would drop in for a visit. One night we asked her to stay for dinner. She rehearsed some of her life. She had lost two grandchildren in a very tragic fire while she and the parents stood outside of the burning home, unable to reach the two little girls. Not only was her husband now dying, but her son was also. As we visited that night, we expressed our sympathy for all that she was experiencing. I was shocked when she said, "But I am the most blessed of all people." I asked her how she could say this with all the tragedy she had gone through and was even now experiencing in her life. She then related the many blessings that she experienced in her life. I looked at this saintly woman sitting before me; she was one of the most kind and loving persons I had ever met. She truly had been sanctified by her suffering in a way that I would never reach.

A number of years later I had a similar experience with my own brother. When he and his wife had their first baby we were all thrilled. After a short period of time, however, we noticed that something was different about their son. His head seemed to be abnormally large. Our worse fears were confirmed by the doctor who said he was a hydrocephalic (he had water on the brain). Before he was two years old he had undergone over fifteen operations on the brain. Many times he went into the operating room and the family was told that he would never survive the operation. They braced for his death, only to have him come out of the surgery stronger than he had gone into it. When things were looking the worst for their son we decided to have a family prayer with my parents, my brothers and sister, and all the grandchildren. My father asked each of the priesthood holders to pray in turn according to age, beginning with him. My eldest brother prayed next, followed by myself, then my brother-in-law, until it finally came to my brother, whose boy we were praying for. Each of us in turn had pleaded with the Lord for little David, but when it came time for my youngest brother to pray, instead of praying for his son he prayed for several minutes for all those others who were suffering, without mentioning his son at all. Only at the end did he pray for his son. He and his wife had developed a love and concern for others that none of the rest of us had. Surely their sensitivity had come because of all the suffering they had gone through. I am certain that they have a love and gentleness that the rest of us will never have who have not gone through the trials and tribulations they have experienced.

Probably no prophet in recent times had suffered the trials and tribulations that President Spencer W. Kimball experienced. I think it is therefore significant that one of the finest addresses given on the subject was delivered by him at Brigham Young University when he was a member of the Quorum of the Twelve. He entitled this great address, "Tragedy or Destiny?" A few brief excerpts from this masterful address also help us to answer the question of the ages concerning suffering:

> Is there not wisdom in his giving us trials that we might rise above them, responsibilities that we might achieve, work to harden our muscles, sorrows to try our souls? Are we not exposed to temptations to test our strength, sickness that we might learn patience, death that we might be immortalized and glorified? . . .

I like also the words of these verses, the author of which I do not know:

> Pain stayed so long I said to him today,
> "I will not have you with me any more,"
> I stamped my foot and said, "Be on your way,"
> And paused there, startled at the look he wore.
> "I, who have been your friend," he said to me,

"I, who have been your teacher—all you know
Of understanding love, of sympathy,
And patience, I have taught you. Shall I go?"
He spoke the truth, this strange unwelcome guest;
I watched him leave, and knew that he was wise.
He left a heart grown tender in my breast,
He left a far, clear vision in my eyes.
I dried my tears, and lifted up a song—
Even for one who'd tortured me so long.[18]

President Kimball gave us a fourth reason why people suffer: accidents. After relating a number of tragic accidents, he asked the following questions:

Could the Lord have prevented these tragedies? The answer is, Yes. The Lord is omnipotent, with all power to control our lives, save us pain, prevent all accidents, drive all planes and cars, feed us, protect us, save us from labor, effort, sickness, even from death. . . .

We should be able to understand this, because we can realize how unwise it would be for us to shield our children from all effort, from disappointments, temptations, sorrows, suffering.

The basic gospel law is free agency and eternal development. To force us to be careful or righteous would be to nullify that fundamental law and make growth impossible. . . .

Is there not wisdom in his giving us trials that we might rise above them, responsibilities that we might achieve, work to harden our muscles, sorrows to try our souls? Are we not exposed to temptations to test our strength, sickness that we might learn patience, death that we might be immortalized and glorified? . . .

I spoke at the funeral service of a young Brigham Young University student who died during the World War II. There had been hundreds of thousands of young men rushed prematurely into eternity through the ravages of that war.[19]

We have reviewed the four major reasons for suffering: (1) experience; (2) for our good; (3) our own transgression; and (4) accidents. Regardless of how our trials, tribulations, and sufferings come upon us, it is our attitude towards them that will determine whether they become stumbling blocks or stepping-stones. We need to remind ourselves of the promises the Lord made to the Prophet Joseph Smith as he neared the end of his months of ordeal in the jails in Missouri:

> And although their influence shall cast thee into trouble, and into bars and walls, thou shalt be had in honor; and but for a small moment and thy voice shall be more terrible in the midst of thine enemies than the fierce lion, because of thy righteousness; and thy God shall stand by thee forever and ever. . . .
>
> Therefore, hold on thy way, and the priesthood shall remain with thee; for their bounds are set, they cannot pass. Thy days are known, and thy years shall not be numbered less; therefore, fear not what man can do, for God shall be with you forever and ever. (D&C 122:4, 9.)

When we handle the trials, tribulations, and suffering as did most of those we mentioned in this article, especially the Prophet Joseph Smith, then we will be able to claim the blessings the Lord has in store for us:

> Ye cannot behold with your natural eyes, for the present time, the design of your God concerning those things which shall come hereafter, and the glory which shall follow after much tribulation.
>
> For after much tribulation come the blessings. Wherefore the day cometh that ye shall be crowned with much glory; the hour is not yet, but is nigh at hand. (D&C 58:3–4.)

Notes

1. See *History of The Church of Jesus Christ of Latter-day Saints*, 7 vols., ed. B. H. Roberts (Salt Lake City: Deseret Book Co., 1957), 3:420.

2. *History of the Church*, 3:264; see also *Times and Seasons*, 6 vols. (Nauvoo: The Church of Jesus Christ of Latter-day Saints, 1830–46), 5:666.

3. *History of the Church*, 6:592–93.

4. Ibid., 3:418.

5. Ibid., 3:290.

6. In Dean C. Jessee, ed., *The Personal Writings of the Prophet Joseph Smith* (Salt Lake City: Deseret Book Co., 1971), p. 389.

7. Ibid., p. 388.

8. Ibid., p. 408, spelling has been modernized, original punctuation retained.

9. *History of the Church,* 3:290.

10. Ibid., 3:293.

11. Neal A. Maxwell, in Conference Report, Oct. 1985, pp. 20–21.

12. *History of the Church*, 3:294.

13. Jessee, *Personal Writings,* p. 284; punctuation has been added and spelling modernized.

14. *History of the Church,* 3:296.

15. *The Saints' Herald,* 6 Nov. 1934, p. 1414.

16. Marion G. Romney, in Conference Report, Oct. 1969, pp. 58–59.

17. Orson F. Whitney, *Improvement Era*, Nov. 1918, pp. 5–7.

18. Spencer W. Kimball, *Faith Precedes the Miracle*, (Salt Lake City: Deseret Book Co., 1973), pp. 97, 101.

19. Kimball, *Faith Precedes the Miracle,* pp. 96–97, 101.

10

A New and Everlasting Covenant of Marriage

Robert L. Millet

T he whole subject of the marriage relation," President
Brigham Young stated, "is not in my reach, nor in any
other man's reach on this earth.

> It is without beginning days or end of years; it is a hard
> matter to reach. We can tell some things with regard to it;
> it lays the foundation for worlds, for angels, and for the
> Gods; for intelligent beings to be crowned with glory, im-
> mortality, and eternal lives. In fact, it is the thread which
> runs from the beginning to the end of the holy Gospel of
> salvation—of the Gospel of the Son of God; it is from
> eternity to eternity.[1]

The profound truths contained in section 132 of the Doctrine
and Covenants (when read in conjunction with other revelations, particularly section 131) constitute the scriptural
authority for the unique and exalted concept of marriage and

Robert L. Millet is Associate Professor and Chairman of the Department of Ancient Scripture at Brigham Young University.

family among the Latter-day Saints. In a day when iniquity abounds and love of many has begun to wax cold (see D&C 45:27), the revelations of God through his prophets provide an anchor to the troubled soul. Doctrine and Covenants 132 is a message which is both peaceful and penetrating, a revelation which can bring order and organization to things on earth, as well as point man toward his infinite possibilities among the Gods.

The eternal marriage covenant is a critical part of the "new and everlasting covenant" which is the fulness of the gospel. In a revelation given in October, 1830, Joseph Smith was told: "Verily I say unto you, blessed are you for receiving mine everlasting covenant, even the fulness of my gospel, sent forth unto the children of men, that they might have life and be made partakers of the glories which are to be revealed in the last days, as it was written by the prophets and apostles in days of old" (D&C 66:2; compare 39:11; 45:9; 133:57). Elder Bruce R. McConkie has written:

> The gospel is the *everlasting* covenant because it is ordained by Him who is Everlasting and also because it is everlastingly the same. In all past ages salvation was gained by adherence to its terms and conditions, and that same compliance will bring the same reward in all future ages. Each time this everlasting covenant is revealed it is *new* to those of that dispensation. Hence the gospel is the *new and everlasting covenant.*[2]

Some four to five hundred years before the coming of Christ, the Lord Jehovah spoke through Malachi: "Behold, I will send my messenger, and he shall prepare the way before me: and the Lord, whom ye seek, shall suddenly come to his temple, even the messenger of the covenant, whom ye delight in: behold, he shall come, saith the Lord of hosts" (Malachi 3:1). This prophecy was surely fulfilled in the meridian of time in the coming of John the Baptist as an Elias and forerunner before his Master, Jesus Christ. Its ultimate fulfillment, however, would await the final dispensation, a time wherein God would gather together in one all things in Christ (Ephesians 1:10). In our day the Lord made known through his modern seer, Joseph

Smith, that the restored gospel was itself a "messenger" sent to prepare the people of the earth for his second coming. "I came unto mine own," the Savior said, "and mine own received me not; but unto as many as received me gave I power to do many miracles, and to become the sons of God; and even unto them that believed on my name gave I power to obtain eternal life. And even so *I have sent mine everlasting covenant into the world to be a light to the world, and to be a standard for my people, and for the Gentiles to seek to it, and to be a messenger before my face to prepare the way before me.*" (D&C 45:8–9; italics added.)

Backgrounds to the Revelation on Marriage

Eternal marriage, the ordinance by which couples enter into the patriarchal order, is called in Doctrine and Covenants 131:2 a "new and everlasting covenant." It is *a* new and everlasting covenant within *the* new and everlasting covenant or fulness of the gospel. In our day it is a crucial element in the restitution of all things (D&C 132:40, 45). Eternal marriage is the ordinance and covenant which leads to the consummate blessings of the gospel of Jesus Christ; it is that order of the priesthood which, when put into effect, will bind ancestry to posterity and thus prevent the earth from being utterly wasted at the time of the Savior's second coming (D&C 2).

It would appear that Joseph Smith the Prophet learned of the doctrine of eternal marriage—as he did in so many other matters—in a gradual, line-upon-line fashion. Joseph Noble, a close associate of the Prophet, observed that the revelation on eternal marriage was given to Joseph "while he was engaged in the work of translation of the Scriptures."[3] More specifically, the first inklings of understanding concerning *plural* marriage would have come as early as 1831, while the Prophet was engaged in a careful study of Genesis.[4] The opening verse of section 132 suggests that Joseph had inquired concerning Old Testament personalities and their participation in plural marriage. Elder B. H. Roberts has given the following extended explanation:

There is indisputable evidence that the revelation making known this marriage law was given to the Prophet as early as 1831. In that year, and thence intermittently up to 1833, the Prophet was engaged in a revision of the English Bible text under the inspiration of God, Sidney Rigdon in the main acting as his scribe. As he began his revision with the Old Testament, he would be dealing with the age of the Patriarchs in 1831. He was doubtless struck with the favor in which the Lord held the several Bible Patriarchs of that period, notwithstanding they had a plurality of wives. What more natural than that he should inquire of the Lord at that time, when his mind must have been impressed with the fact—Why, O Lord, didst Thou justify Thy servants, Abraham, Isaac, and Jacob; as also Moses, David, and Solomon, in the matter of their having many wives and concubines (see opening paragraph of the Revelation)? In answer to that inquiry came the revelation, though not then committed to writing.[5]

It is difficult to know at what point in the history of the Church Joseph Smith began to understand and teach the principles associated with *eternal* marriage. By 1839, however, he was teaching the doctrine to others. Parley P. Pratt has left us the following account of an experience with Joseph the Seer in Philadelphia in 1839. "In Philadelphia," he writes, "I had the happiness of once more meeting with President Smith, and of spending several days with him and others, and with the Saints in that city and vicinity.

> During these interviews he taught me many great and glorious principles concerning God and the heavenly order of eternity. It was at this time [we note again that it was in 1839] that I received from him the first idea of eternal family organization, and the eternal union of the sexes in those inexpressibly endearing relationships which none but the highly intellectual, the refined and pure in heart, know how to prize, and which are at the very foundation of everything worthy to be called happiness.
> Till then I had learned to esteem kindred affections and sympathies as appertaining solely to this transitory state, as something from which the heart must be entirely weaned, in order to be fitted for its heavenly state.
> It was Joseph Smith who taught me how to prize the endearing relationship of father and mother, husband and wife; of brother and sister, son and daughter.

It was from him that I learned that the wife of my bosom might be secured to me for time and all eternity; and that the refined sympathies and affections which endeared us to each other emanated from the fountain of divine eternal love. It was from him that I learned that we might cultivate these affections, and grow and increase in the same to all eternity; while the result of our endless union would be an offspring as numerous as the stars of heaven, or the sands of the sea shore.

It was from him that I learned the true dignity and destiny of a son of God, clothed with eternal priesthood, as the patriarch and sovereign of his countless offspring. It was from him that I learned that the highest dignity of womanhood was, to stand as a queen and priestess to her husband, and to reign for ever and ever as the queen mother of her numerous and still increasing offspring.

I had loved before, but I knew not why. But now I loved — with a pureness — an intensity of elevated, exalted feeling, which would lift my soul from the transitory things of this grovelling sphere and expand it as the ocean. I felt that God was my heavenly Father indeed; that Jesus was my brother, and that the wife of my bosom was an immortal, eternal companion; a kind of ministering angel, given to me as a comforter, and a crown of glory for ever and ever. In short, I could now love with the spirit and with the understanding also.[6]

The Prophet Joseph Smith shared many of the details of the revelation concerning plural marriage, with intimate associates, particularly when he felt one could be trusted to value and preserve a sacred matter. Between 1831 and 1843 a number of the leaders of the Church were instructed concerning the plurality of wives and were told that eventually many of the faithful would be called upon to comply with the will of the Lord. In speaking to a gathering of the Reorganized Church of Jesus Christ of Latter Day Saints in Plano, Illinois, in 1878, Orson Pratt

explained the circumstances connected with the coming forth of the revelation on plural marriage. Refuted the statement and belief of those present that Brigham Young was the author of the revelation; showed that Joseph Smith the Prophet had not only commenced the practice of that principle himself, and taught it to others, before President Young and the Twelve had returned from their mission in Europe, in 1841, but that Joseph actually received revelations upon that principle as early as 1831.[7]

As one might expect, the doctrine of plural marriage was not easily received, even by those who were otherwise counted as faithful. Elder John Taylor, known to be one of the purest men who ever lived, explained that "when this system [plural marriage] was first introduced among this people, it was one of the greatest crosses that ever was taken up by any set of men since the world stood."[8] Helen Mar Whitney, one of Joseph Smith's plural wives, recalled that Joseph "said that the practice of this principle would be the hardest trial the Saints would ever have to test their faith."[9] One of those for whom the principle was particularly difficult was Emma Smith, wife of the Prophet. It appears, therefore, that one of the major reasons for the formal recording of the revelation in 1843 was to assist Emma to recognize the divine source of this doctrine. William Clayton, private secretary to Joseph Smith, recorded the following:

> On the morning of the 12th of July, 1843, Joseph and Hyrum Smith came into the office of the upper story of the "Brick-store," on the bank of the Mississippi River. They were talking of the subject of plural marriage, [and] Hyrum said to Joseph, "If you will write the revelation on celestial marriage, I will take and read it to Emma, and I believe I can convince her of its truth, and you will hereafter have peace." Joseph smiled and remarked, "You do not know Emma as well as I do." Hyrum repeated his opinion, and further remarked, "The doctrine is so plain, I can convince any reasonable man or woman of its truth, purity, and heavenly origin," or words to that effect. . . . Joseph and Hyrum then sat down, and Joseph commenced to dictate the Revelation on Celestial Marriage, and I wrote it, sentence by sentence, as he dictated. After the whole was written, Joseph asked me to read it through slowly and carefully, which I did, and he pronounced it correct.[10]

The following entry from William Clayton's diary for 12 July 1843 is interesting: "This A.M. I wrote a Revelation consisting of 10 pages on the order of the priesthood, showing the designs in Moses, Abraham, David and Solomon having many wives and concubines &c. After it was wrote Prests. Joseph & Hyrum presented it and read it to E[mma] who said she did not believe a word of it and appeared very rebellious.''[11]

The Lord's Justification

Doctrine and Covenants 132 is a revelation dealing with celestial marriage. It also contains information and explanations concerning the practice of plural marriage. One latter-day historian, Danel Bachman, has suggested that section 132 consists largely of the Lord's answers to three critical questions posed by the Prophet Joseph Smith.[12]

The first question asked by the Prophet Joseph was simply why the polygamous actions of notable Old Testament prophet-leaders had received divine approval. Why was it, the Prophet wanted to know, that prophets, patriarchs, and kings could have many wives and concubines?[13] In the Lord's response, Joseph was told to prepare his heart for the instructions about to be given (D&C 132:3) in this instance the explanation for the ancient phenomenon was to be accompanied by a commandment to institute the practice in modern times. Seeking further light and knowledge had led the Prophet to further and greater obligations; much was about to be given, and much would soon be required (compare D&C 82:3). Salvation in the highest heaven was at stake. Those who received this command to take additional wives and were obedient qualified themselves — through the eternal principle of obedience (compare D&C 130:20–21) — for the fulness of the glory of the Father, "which glory shall be a fulness and a continuation of the seeds forever and ever" (D&C 132:19). These are they who shall be enlarged, that is, have an increase—spirit children—into the eternities. They enjoy eternal lives (D&C 131:1–4; 132:17, 24). Joseph had taught these principles only two months earlier on 16 May 1843: "Except a man and his wife enter into an everlasting covenant and be married for eternity, while in this probation, by the power and authority of the Holy Priesthood, they will cease to increase when they die; that is, they will not have any children after the resurrection. But those who are married by the power and authority of the priesthood in this life, and continue without committing the sin against the Holy Ghost, will continue to increase and have children in the celestial glory."[14]

Salvation consists in the blessing of eternal lives, the continuation of the family unit in eternity. Damnation is the result of rejecting this new and everlasting covenant and is due largely to pursuing the broad and wide ways of the world; the punishment is "the deaths," the dissolution of the family unit beyond the grave (D&C 132:17, 24–25).

Marriage in the Lord: Sealed by the Holy Spirit of Promise

The second question posed by the Prophet Joseph Smith seems to be associated with the cryptic statement by Jesus in response to a Sadducean trap: "Ye do err, not knowing the scriptures, nor the power of God. For in the resurrection they neither marry, nor are given in marriage, but are as the angels of God in heaven" (Matthew 22:29–30; compare Luke 20:34–36). This expression, little understood in the days of the Prophet, is repeatedly given today as scriptural evidence against the Latter-day Saint doctrine of eternal marriage. Joseph Smith's question concerning its meaning led to a modern revealed commentary upon the passage and pointed us to the reality that Jesus Christ had taught the doctrine of eternal marriage during his mortal ministry.[15]

From section 132 we learn that they who neither marry nor are given in marriage in eternity are they who choose not to enter in by the strait gate and partake of the new and everlasting covenant of marriage. Even persons who qualify in every other way for the glories of the celestial kingdom, but who reject opportunities for celestial marriage, cannot attain unto the highest degree of the celestial glory (compare D&C 131:1–4). Such persons are "appointed angels in heaven, which angels are ministering servants, to minister for those who are worthy of a far more, and an exceeding, and an eternal weight of glory." The Lord continued: because they did not abide by his law, "they cannot be enlarged, but remain separately and singly, without exaltation, in their saved condition, to all eternity; and from henceforth are not gods, but are angels of God forever and ever." (D&C 132:16–17.) In commenting upon the status of angels, Joseph Smith said: "Gods have an ascendancy over the angels, who are ministering servants. In the resurrection, some are raised to be angels, others are raised to become Gods."[16]

The Holy Spirit of Promise is the Holy Ghost, the Holy Spirit promised to the faithful. The Holy Ghost is a member of the Godhead with vital and important roles in the salvation of the people of the earth. He is a revelator and a testator, the means by which a witness of the truth is obtained. He is a sanctifier, the means by which filth and dross are burned out of the human soul as though by fire. One of the highest functions the Holy Ghost serves is to be a sealer, as the Holy Spirit of Promise. In this capacity he searches the heart, certifies a person is just, and thereafter seals an exaltation upon that person. In commenting on verse 7 in section 132 (regarding all covenants, contracts, bonds, and so on having the seal of the Holy Spirit of Promise), Elder Bruce R. McConkie has written:

> By way of illustration, this means that baptism, partaking of the sacrament, administering to the sick, marriage, and every covenant that man ever makes with the Lord . . . must be performed in righteousness by and for people who are worthy to receive whatever blessing is involved, otherwise whatever is done has no binding and sealing effect in eternity.
>
> Since "the Comforter knoweth all things" (D&C 42:17), it follows that it is not possible "to lie to the Holy Ghost" and thereby gain unearned or undeserved blessings, as Ananias and Sapphira found out to their sorrow (Acts 5:1–11). And so this provision that all things must be sealed by the Holy Spirit of Promise, if they are to have "efficacy, virtue, or force in and after the resurrection of the dead" (D&C 132:7), is the Lord's system for dealing with absolute impartiality with all men, and for giving all men exactly what they merit, neither adding nor diminishing from.
>
> When the Holy Spirit of Promise places his ratifying seal upon a baptism, or a marriage, or any covenant, ex-

cept that of having one's calling and election made sure, the seal is a conditional approval or ratification; it is binding in eternity only in the event of subsequent obedience to the terms and conditions of whatever covenant is involved.

But when the ratifying seal of approval is placed upon someone whose calling and election is thereby made sure —because there are no more conditions to be met by the obedient person—this act of being sealed up unto eternal life is of such transcendent import that of itself it is called being sealed by the Holy Spirit of Promise, which means that in this crowning sense, being so sealed is the same as having one's calling and election made sure.[17]

Sin, Repentance, and the Holy Spirit of Promise

Without question, one of the most misunderstood (and misquoted) verses of scripture is Doctrine and Covenants 132:26. Some members of the Church have wrested the scriptures to the point where they have concluded that a temple marriage alone (which they equate with being sealed by the Holy Spirit of Promise) will assure them of an exaltation, in spite of "any sin or transgression of the new and everlasting covenant whatever, and all manner of blasphemies." When it is fully understood, however, that the marriage ceremony performed in the House of the Lord—though performed by worthy priesthood bearers granted sacred sealing powers—is a conditional ordinance, a rite whose eventual blessings are contingent upon the faithfulness of the participants in years to come, then verse 26 is recognized as being consistent with other related principles—obedience, endurance to the end, and appropriate reward. Verse 26 has reference to those who have received the new and everlasting covenant of marriage, have complied with all its conditions, and have passed the tests of mortality. These are they who, paraphrasing Joseph Smith, have lived by every word of God, and are willing to serve the Lord at all hazards. They have made their callings and elections sure to eternal life.[18] Persons who attain this level of righteousness "are sealed up against all manner of sin and blasphemy except the blasphemy against the Holy Ghost and the shedding of innocent blood."[19]

The Prophet Joseph Smith extended the challenging invitation to the Saints: "I would exhort you to go on and continue to call upon God until you make your calling and election sure for yourselves, by obtaining this more sure word of prophecy, and wait patiently for the promise until you obtain it."[20] Latter-day Saints who are married in the temple must press forward in the work of the Lord and with quiet dignity and patient maturity seek to be worthy of the certain assurance of eternal life before the end of their mortal lives. But should one not formally receive the more sure word of prophecy in this life, he has the scriptural promise that faithfully enduring to the end — keeping the covenants and commandments from baptism to the end of his life (Mosiah 18:8–9) — results in the promise of eternal life, whether that promise be received here or hereafter (D&C 14:7; compare 2 Nephi 31:20; Mosiah 5:15).

All men are subject to temptation and mortal weaknesses and therefore commit some sin, even those whose callings and elections have been made sure (see D&C 20:32–34; 124:124). Though the disposition to commit grievous sin would certainly be less among such individuals, the principles of repentance and forgiveness are as highly treasured by these as by any of our Father's children. At the same time, where much is given, much is expected and required. Joseph Smith taught: "If men sin wilfully after they have received the knowledge of the truth, there remaineth no more sacrifice for sin."[21] In the words of a modern Apostle: "Suppose such persons become disaffected and the spirit of repentance leaves them — which is a seldom and almost unheard of eventuality — still, what then? The answer is — and the revelations and teachings of the Prophet Joseph Smith so recite! — they must then pay the penalty of their own sins, for the blood of Christ will not cleanse them."[22]

One who is guilty of serious transgression and loses the right to the Spirit and the protective blessings of the priesthood is essentially "delivered unto the buffetings of Satan" (D&C

132:26), such that "Lucifer is free to torment, persecute, and afflict such a person without let or hindrance. When the bars are down, the cuffs and curses of Satan, both in this world and in the world to come, bring indescribable anguish typified by burning fire and brimstone"[23] (compare D&C 78:12; 82:20–21; 104:9–10; 1 Corinthians 5:1–5).

Once one has been sealed by the Holy Spirit of Promise, he is in a position to either rise to exaltation or (through rebellion and apostasy) fall to perdition. Doctrine and Covenants 132:27 has specific reference to those who have received the new and everlasting covenant of marriage and proven faithful enough to have the final stamp of approval from the Holy Ghost. One who has been sealed up unto eternal life and thereafter proves to be a total enemy to the cause of righteousness is guilty of "shedding innocent blood," the innocent blood of Christ, and assenting unto his death.[24] Such a vicious disposition would lead the transgressor to reject and crucify the Son of God afresh (compare Hebrews 6:4–6).

The revelation on marriage teaches that those who are sealed by the Holy Spirit of Promise—who have proven worthy of the consummate blessings associated with the eternal marriage covenant—and who then "commit any sin or transgression of the new and everlasting covenant whatever, and all manner of blasphemies" and yet "commit no murder wherein they shed innocent blood" shall come forth in the first resurrection and enter into exaltation. Of such persons; however, the revelation states: "But they shall be destroyed in the flesh, and shall be delivered unto the buffetings of Satan unto the day of redemption, saith the Lord God" (D&C 132:26). "To be destroyed in the flesh," explained Joseph Fielding Smith, "means exactly that. We cannot destroy men in the flesh, because we do not control the lives of men and do not have power to pass sentences upon them which involve capital punishment. In the days when there was theocracy on the earth, then this decree was enforced. What the Lord will do in lieu of this, because we cannot destroy in the flesh, I am unable to say, but it will have to be made up in some other way."[25]

Among the most beautiful and touching verses in section 132 are verses 49–50, wherein the Lord seals an exaltation upon the head of Joseph the Seer. What a comfort to a troubled and weary mind to hear such words as these: "Verily I seal upon you your exaltation, and prepare a throne for you in the kingdom of my Father, with Abraham your father." The reader of this revelation is also given a meaningful insight into how to qualify for such a transcendent promise: "Behold, I have seen your sacrifices, and will forgive all your sins; I have seen your sacrifices in obedience to that which I have told you. Go, therefore, and I make a way for your escape, as I accepted the offering of Abraham of his son Isaac." The key element in obtaining the promise of exaltation is sacrifice. It was to the School of the Prophets in the winter of 1834–35 that Joseph had given profound counsel: only through the sacrifice of all things could one come to the point of faith or confidence wherein he could have an actual knowledge that the course in life he was pursuing was according to the divine will. "Those, then, who make the sacrifice," the Prophet had taught, "will have the testimony that their course is pleasing in the sight of God; and those who have this testimony will have faith to lay hold on eternal life."[26] That principle of truth was now realized and confirmed directly upon the head of the one who had declared it less than ten years earlier; no matter what the eventuality, nothing could separate the man of God from the love of his God.

Marriage Among the Ancients

As a type of follow-up on his first question, Joseph Smith was given additional insights into requirements made of individuals in ancient times. The Patriarch Abraham was instructed to take Hagar, the servant of Sarah, as a second wife, as a part of fulfilling the promises made earlier to the Father of the Faithful that his posterity would be as numerous as the stars in the heavens or the sands upon the seashore (Genesis 22:17; Abraham 3:14). This modern revelation helps to clarify the Old Testament story considerably (see Genesis 16), and shows that the decision to take an additional wife was a God-inspired directive, and not simply a desperate move by Sarah to ensure mortal posterity for her grieving husband. Joseph Smith was told that because of Abraham's perfect obedience he was granted the privilege of eternal increase. The Lord then said to Joseph: "This promise is yours also, because ye are of Abraham, and the promise was made unto Abraham" (D&C 132:31). Then came the command to Joseph Smith, who had in 1836 received the keys necessary to become a modern father of the faithful (D&C 110:12): "Go ye, therefore, and do the works of Abraham; enter ye into my law and ye shall be saved" (D&C 32:32; compare 124:58).

The Lord further explained that Abraham, Isaac, and Jacob had attained godhood because of their implicit obedience. More specifically, because they only took additional wives as those wives were given by God, they have entered into their exaltation. David and Solomon were also given directions (through the legal administrators of their day) to take additional wives and enjoyed the approbation of the heavens as they stayed within the bounds the Lord had set. When they moved outside the divinely given channel, however, and began to acquire wives and concubines for selfish or lustful reasons (e.g., David in the case of Bathsheba, 2 Samuel 11; Solomon in the case of taking "strange women" as wives, women who "turned away his heart" from the things of righteousness, 1 Kings 11), they offended God and forfeited the eternal rewards that might have been theirs. Jacob in the Book of Mormon, speaking in behalf of the Lord, warned his people: "Behold, David and Solomon truly had many wives and concubines, which thing was abominable before me, saith the Lord" (Jacob 2:24). When both scriptural passages (Jacob 2 and D&C 132) are read together, it becomes clear that the Lord was condemning—in no uncertain terms—unauthorized plural marriages, and not the principle of plurality of wives per se. Later in that same chapter of Jacob the word of the Lord came: "For if I will, saith the Lord of Hosts, raise up seed unto me [through plural marriage] I will command my people; otherwise they shall hearken unto these things"

(Jacob 2:30). Note the words of Joseph Smith as late as October of 1843: "[I] gave instructions to try those persons who were preaching, teaching, or practicing the doctrine of plurality of wives; for, according to the law, I hold the keys of this power in the last days; for there is never but one on earth at a time on whom the power and its keys are conferred; and I have constantly said no man shall have but one wife at a time, unless the Lord directs otherwise."[27] The instruction of the Lord to the Saints of our own day is also to "go and do the works of Abraham," not through the practice of plural marriage—such has been discontinued by divine command—but by entering into holy temples and participating in the new and everlasting covenant of marriage.

Concerning Adultery

Verse 41 of section 132 suggests the third question that Joseph Smith must have asked of the Lord. In essence, the question of the Prophet was: "Why were not such polygamous relationships violations of the law of chastity? Why was this not considered adultery?" The Lord's answer was simple and forthright, although considerable space was devoted to the issue in the revelation: any action inspired, authorized, or commanded of God is moral and good. More specifically, marriages approved of the Almighty are recognized and acknowledged as sacred institutions, despite the values or opinions of earth or hell. Joseph wrote in 1839: "How much more dignified and noble are the thoughts of God, than the vain imaginations of the human heart!"[28] Verse 36 of this section sheds light on this principle, the idea that whatever God requires is right: "Abraham was commanded to offer his son Isaac; nevertheless, it was written: Thou shalt not kill. Abraham, however, did not refuse, and it was accounted unto him for righteousness." In a letter written to Nancy Rigdon in 1842, Joseph sought to explain (albeit in veiled language) the appropriateness of plural marriage when divinely sanctioned:

Happiness is the object and design of our existence, and will be the end thereof if we pursue the path that leads to it; and this path is virtue, uprightness, faithfulness, holiness, and keeping all the commandments of God. But we cannot keep all the commandments without first knowing them, and we cannot expect to know all, or more than we now know, unless we comply with or keep those we have already received. That which is wrong under one circumstance, may be and often is, right under another. God said thou shalt not kill, — at another time he said thou shalt utterly destroy. This is the principle on which the government of heaven is conducted — by revelation adapted to the circumstances in which the children of the kingdom are placed. Whatever God requires is right, no matter what it is, although we may not see the reason thereof till long after the events transpire. If we seek first the kingdom of God, all good things will be added. So with Solomon — first he asked wisdom, and God gave it him, and with it every desire of his heart, even things which may be considered abominable to all who do not understand the order of heaven only in part, but which, in reality, were right, because God gave and sanctioned by special revelation. . . . Every thing that God gives us is lawful and right, and 'tis proper that we should enjoy his gifts and blessings whenever and wherever he is disposed to bestow; but if we should seize upon these same blessings and enjoyments without law, without revelation, without commandment, those blessings and enjoyments would prove cursings and vexations in the end, and we should have to go down in sorrow and wailings of everlasting regret. . . . Blessings offered, but rejected are no longer blessings, but become like the talent hid in the earth by the wicked and slothful servant — the proffered good returns of the giver, the blessing is bestowed on those who will receive.[29]

In section 132 Emma Smith was encouraged to submit to the will of the Lord pertaining to her husband — to yield her heart to the mind of God with regard to the matter of plural marriages. Obedience would lead to glorious blessings; disobedience would lead to damnation, for the covenant people are to abide by this ''law of the priesthood'' whenever it is specifically given to them by new revelation through the living prophet.

Summary

We may rest assured that whatever God reveals is given for the benefit and fulfillment of his children—for their happiness. Celestial, or eternal, marriage has been given to man, according to the word of the Master, in order that man might "multiply and replenish the earth, according to my commandment, and . . . fulfill the promise which was given by my Father before the foundation of the world, and for their exaltation in the eternal worlds, that they may bear the souls of men; for herein is the work of my Father continued, that he may be glorified" (D&C 132:63; compare v. 31). One of the most popular and important scriptural passages in the church is found in the Pearl of Great Price. The Lord explained to Moses the purpose of creation and existence: "For behold, this is my work and my glory—to bring to pass the immortality and eternal life of man" (Moses 1:39). That the Prophet understood early in his ministry that God's progression and development was accomplished through the exaltation of his children is evident from an early recording of Moses 1:39. Note a variant rendering of this statement in the Prophet's first draft of the Bible translation: "Behold, this is my work To my glory, to the immortality and eternal life of man."[30] In short, God's work—creating worlds without number, peopling them with his spirit sons and daughters, and providing the truths of the gospel for their edification and salvation (Moses 1:27–38)—not only benefits his children, but further glorifies himself. In speaking by the inspiration of the Lord, Joseph the Prophet explained the following in the famous King Follett Sermon of 7 April 1844:

> What did Jesus do? Why, I do the things I saw my Father do when worlds came rolling into existence. My Father worked out His kingdom with fear and trembling, and I must do the same; and when I get my kingdom, I shall present it to my Father, so that He may obtain kingdom upon kingdom, and it will exalt him in glory. He will then take a higher exaltation, and I will take His place, and thereby become exalted myself. So that Jesus treads in the tracks of his Father, and inherits what God did before;

and God is thus glorified and exalted in the salvation and exaltation of all His children.[31]

Notes

1. In *Journal of Discourses*, 26 vols. (Liverpool: F.D. Richards, 1855–86), 2:90.

2. Bruce R. McConkie, *Mormon Doctrine,* 2d ed. (Salt Lake City: Bookcraft, 1966), pp. 529–30.

3. See minutes of the Davis Stake conference, published under "Plural Marriage," in *Millennial Star* 16:454; cited by Danel Bachman in "New light on an Old Hypothesis: The Ohio Origins of the Revelation on Eternal Marriage," *Journal of Mormon History* 5 (1978): 22.

4. See Robert J. Matthews, *"A Plainer Translation" Joseph Smith's Translation of the Bible, A History and Commentary* (Provo: Brigham Young University Press, 1975), pp. 96, 257.

5. *History of The Church of Jesus Christ of Latter-day Saints*, 7 vols., ed. B. H. Roberts (Salt Lake City: Deseret Book Co., 1957), 5:xxix–xxx.

6. *Autobiography of Parley P. Pratt* (Salt Lake City: Deseret Book Co., 1976), pp. 297–98.

7. *Millennial Star*, 9 Dec. 1878, p. 788; see also Matthews, "A Plainer Translation," p. 258.

8. In *Journal of Discourses*, 11:221.

9. "Scenes and Incidents in Nauvoo," *Women's Exponent* 10 (1 Nov. 1881): 83.

10. *The Historical Record,* pp. 225–26 as cited in Hyrum M. Smith and Janne M. Sjodahl, *Doctrine and Covenants Commentary* revised ed. (Salt Lake City: Deseret Book Co., 1951), pp. 820–21.

11. Cited in Lyndon W. Cook, *The Revelations of the Prophet Joseph Smith* (Salt Lake City: Deseret Book Co., 1985), p. 294.

12. See "New Light on an Old Hypothesis," pp. 19–32.

13. A concubine was a wife who came from a position of lower social standing, and who thus did not enjoy the same status as one of

higher birth. Under ancient practice, where caste systems were much more common than at present, a man could take a slave or non-citizen as a legal wife, but it was understood that she was of a lower status. This was the case with Sarah (the first wife) and Hagar (the servant who became a concubine).

14. Joseph Smith, *Teachings of the Prophet Joseph Smith,* comp. Joseph Fielding Smith (Salt Lake City: Deseret Book Co., 1976), pp. 300–301.

15. See Bruce R. McConkie, *Doctrinal New Testament Commentary,* 3 vols. (Salt Lake City: Bookcraft, 1966–73), 1:604–6; *The Mortal Messiah,* 4 books (Salt Lake City: Deseret Book Co., 1979–81), 3:374–81.

16. *Teachings of the Prophet Joseph Smith,* p. 312.

17. McConkie, *Doctrinal New Testament Commentary,* 3:335–36.

18. *Teachings of the Prophet Joseph Smith,* pp. 150–51.

19. McConkie, *Mormon Doctrine,* p. 110.

20. *Teachings of the Prophet Joseph Smith,* p. 299.

21. Ibid., p. 128.

22. McConkie, *Doctrinal New Testament Commentary,* 3:343.

23. McConkie, *Mormon Doctrine,* p. 108.

24. McConkie, *Doctrinal New Testament Commentary,* 3:161, 345; *The Mortal Messiah,* 2:216.

25. Joseph Fielding Smith, *Doctrines of Salvation,* 3 vols., comp. Bruce R. McConkie (Salt Lake City: Bookcraft, 1954–56), 2:96– 97. The concept of being "destroyed in the flesh" has given rise to a host of spurious ideas, not the least of which is the mistaken notion that a person guilty of a capital crime may, through assuring that his execution involves the shedding of his own blood, in some way mitigate or atone for his heinous actions. In a letter written by Elder Bruce R. McConkie regarding the Church's position in regard to "blood atonement," we read the following: "There simply is no such thing among us as a doctrine of blood atonement that grants a remission of sins or confers any other benefit upon a person because his own blood is shed for sins. Let me say categorically and unequivocally that this doctrine can only operate in a day when there is no separation of Church and State and when the power to take life is vested in the ruling theocracy as was the case in the day of Moses.

From the day of Joseph Smith to the present there has been no single instance of so-called blood atonement of Christ . . . , and except for the use of the term 'blood atonement' as a synonym—nothing more—of 'capital punishment' where 'enlightened' members of the Church are concerned, there is no such thing as blood atonement . . . since there is no such thing as blood atonement, except as indicated above, the *mode* of execution could have *no* bearing on the matter of atoning for one's sins.'' (Bruce R. McConkie to Thomas B. McAffee, 18 Oct. 1978, pp. 2, 3, 4, copy in writer's possession.)

26. *Lectures on Faith,* N.B. Lundwall, comp. (Salt Lake City: Bookcraft, n.d.), 6:10.

27. *Teachings of the Prophet Joseph Smith,* p. 324.

28. Ibid., p. 137.

29. From *The Personal Writings of Joseph Smith,* ed. Dean C. Jessee (Salt Lake City: Deseret Book Co., 1984), pp. 507–9; see also *History of the Church,* 5:134–36; Smith, *Teachings,* pp. 255–57.

30. In Matthews, *A Plainer Translation,* p. 222, emphasis in Matthews.

31. *History of the Church,* p. 306.

11

Church and State

Donald Q. Cannon

In the meridian of time Jesus said, "Render therefore unto Caesar the things which are Caesar's; and unto God the things that are God's" (Matthew 22:21). In this oft-quoted passage of scripture the Savior told us what to do in matters of church and state. The New Testament tells us what to do but not how to do it. Modern revelation to the Prophet Joseph Smith provides information on how to behave in relation to civil government and on how government should be conducted. In the course of this essay some important political principles contained in the Doctrine and Covenants will be identified and discussed.

The principles found in revelation may be conveniently divided into two categories: Responsibilities of governments, and responsibilities of citizens.

Donald Q. Cannon is Associate Dean of Religious Education and Professor of Church History and Doctrine at Brigham Young University.

Responsibilities of Government

The principles related to the responsibilities of government set limits on governmental power and identify spheres of legitimate activity for governments. Seven such principles are discussed below.

1. *Governments Are Accountable to God*

This principle is found in section 134 of the Doctrine and Covenants, a statement of belief about governments.

This statement of belief was accepted by the vote of a general assembly of the Church held at Kirtland, Ohio, on 17 August 1835. Prior to this meeting the Saints had been subjected to mobbings, plunderings, and murders in the state of Missouri. In the midst of this commotion and turmoil the Saints were falsely accused of being opposed to law and order. Thus, section 134 served as a rebuttal to the enemies of the Church as well as a guideline for political behavior for Church members.

Authorship of section 134 has generally been attributed to Oliver Cowdery. The statement on government was first published in the *Messenger and Advocate* in August 1835 and included as section 102 in the 1835 edition of the Doctrine and Covenants.

If governments are accountable to God, they must also find their origin in God. Doctrine and Covenants 134 affirms that governments are instituted by God and that men are answerable to God for their actions in relation to them. Joseph Smith taught that "God puts up one, and sets down another" government at his will and pleasure and that such governments are subject to the will of God.[1]

2. *Governments Were Instituted "for the Benefit of Man"*

This principle is also found in section 134 of the Doctrine and Covenants. It served as a reminder of the ultimate goodness of government for the Saints who had suffered at the hands of mobs in Missouri.

Historically, governments have not seemed to exist for the benefit of mankind. More often than not governments have taken advantage of their subjects. Certainly Church members who had experienced mob violence in Ohio and Missouri were unsure about the beneficial nature of government. In contrast to their experience, Church leaders declared that governments had an obligation and duty to provide for the benefit of their subjects. Governments did not exist for the aggrandizement of rulers but for the well-being of their people.

This inspired declaration on government supported the notion that the existence of government was far superior to the absence of government. Even a bad government was better than no government at all. Apostle Erastus Snow taught this concept in an address he gave over a century ago. Although his examples are necessarily dated, the fundamental ideas are correct.

> Anarchy—shall I say, is the worst of all governments? No: Anarchy is the absence of all government; it is the antipodes [at opposite points] of order; it is the acme of confusion; it is the result of unbridled license, the antipodes of true liberty. The Apostle Paul says truly: "For there is no power but of God: the powers that be are ordained of God." At first this is a startling statement. Even the monopoly of the one-man-power as in Russia [the Czar], or the monopoly of the aristocracy as in other parts of Europe, or the imbecility and sometimes stupidity of a republic like our own, is far better than no government at all. And for this reason, says the Apostle Paul, "The powers are ordained of God," not that they are always the best forms of government for the people, or that they afford liberty and freedom to mankind, but that any and all forms of government are better than none at all, having a tendency as they do to restrain the passions of human nature and to curb them, and to establish and maintain order to a greater or less degree. One monopoly is better than many; and the oppression of a king is tolerable, but the oppression of a mob, where every man is a law to himself and his own right arm, is his power to enforce his own will, is the worst form of government.[2]

3. *The United States Constitution Was Inspired by God*

Closely related to the principles of governments being accountable to God and existing for the benefit of mankind is the belief that the Constitution was inspired by and instituted by God.

This idea is found in section 101, which was received on 16 December 1833 in Kirtland, Ohio. It came soon after a whole series of mob actions had occurred against the Saints in Missouri. Church members had been expelled from Jackson County and had taken refuge in Clay County. This revelation explained why the Saints had been persecuted and then held out the promise of the redemption of Zion. It also stressed the Lord's role in the establishment of the Constitution and government of the United States. This information concerning the Constitution was designed to encourage the Saints.

When the Lord proclaims that he established the Constitution of this land (101:77), it implies several things. The Lord's involvement shows that it is an inspired document. He accomplished his work through "wise men" (98:10) he raised up or prepared for that purpose. It also means that governments have a responsibility to God, as brought out in the very first principle discussed in this essay.

The idea that God inspired the Constitution has caught the attention of all of the presidents of the Church in this dispensation. All of the presidents from Joseph Smith to Ezra Taft Benson have commented on this subject, particularly John Taylor and Ezra Taft Benson. Each of these two presidents commented at least eight different times on this concept.

Known for his love of America, President Benson has provided stirring commentary on the Constitution both as an Apostle and as President. In a general conference of the Church he said:

> I am grateful that the God of heaven saw fit to put his stamp of approval upon the Constitution and to indicate that it had come into being through wise men whom he raised up unto this very purpose. He asked the Saints, even in the dark days of their persecution and hardship to continue to seek for redress from their enemies "According," he said, "to the laws and constitution . . . which I have suffered to be established and should be maintained for the rights and protection of all flesh" (D&C 101:77). And then he made this most impressive declaration:

"And for this purpose have I established the Constitution of this land, by the hands of wise men whom I raised up unto this very purpose, and redeemed the land by the shedding of blood." (*Ibid.*, 101:80.)[3]

4. *Governments Must Protect the Agency of Man*

This principle is found in section 134, which we have already discussed. The basic issue here is the matter of freedom of conscience. People should be allowed to worship according to the dictates of their conscience, not in some government-prescribed manner. Church leaders throughout this dispensation have emphasized the importance of free agency. They have said, in essence: take away this right and man is a slave. With this principle in place man is free to make the best of his situation.

In a keynote address delivered at a Book of Mormon symposium, sponsored by the Religious Studies Center at Brigham Young Univesity, Elder Dallin H. Oaks addressed the issue of free agency. In defining free agency, Elder Oaks said: "When I say free agency, I refer to what scripture calls agency, which means an exercise of the will, the power to choose." In its purest sense, Elder Oaks said, free agency cannot be taken away. However, our freedom, "the power to act upon our choices" can be taken away. We may lose our freedom in three ways: "(1) by physical laws, (2) by our own action, and (3) by the actions of others, including governments."[4]

Governments can—and some do—restrict freedom. This article on government, in section 134, enjoins governments to protect the agency of man.

5. *Governments Have an Obligation to Guarantee Freedom of Religion*

Closely related to the principle of guaranteeing man's agency is the principle of freedom of religion. This principle is also found in section 134.

Religious freedom is one of the most fundamental and important rights civil government should guarantee. Freedom of religion differs from the protection of agency because it deals with the general institution, i.e. the Church organization, rather than the individual. Religious institutions must be free to teach and promote their beliefs and principles without interference by government. Indeed, the restoration of the gospel and the reestablishment of the Church of Jesus Christ in our time was made possible largely because freedom of religion existed in the United States of America. It was at least easier for the Lord to restore his church and kingdom in America than it might have been elsewhere.

Several Church leaders have commented on this subject. George Albert Smith, who served as President of the Church immediately after World War II, spoke frequently about the fact that America provided a haven for the Restoration. He said, for example:

> During the great struggle for independence in the country under the leadership of George Washington, our Heavenly Father was preparing the way for the restoration of the gospel of Jesus Christ in its purity.
> He gave to certain individuals the inspiration to frame the Constitution of the United States that has been referred to in this conference, the greatest palladium of human rights that we know anything about. Under such a Constitution the gospel of Jesus Christ was restored to the earth one hundred nineteen years ago.[5]

6. *Separation of Church and State Is Essential*

This important principle is also found in section 134. When the new government was created following the American Revolution, great pains were taken to avoid the threat of a state church. Consequently, the Constitution provided for a strict separation of church and state. Neither the state nor any religion should have undue influence or control of the other entity. This provision of separation protects both government and religion.

In 1907 the First Presidency (Joseph F. Smith, John R. Winder, and Anthon H. Lund) made the following official statement on the principle of separation of church and state.

> The Church of Jesus Christ of Latter-day Satins holds to the doctrine of the separation of church and state; the non-interference of church authority in political matters;

and the absolute freedom and independence of the individual in the performance of his political duties. . . .
    We declare that from principle and policy, we favor:
    The absolute separation of church and state;
    No domination of the state by the church;
    No church interference with the functions of the state;
    No state interference with the functions of the church,
or with the free exercise of religion;
    The absolute freedom of the individual from the dom-
ination of ecclesiastical authority in political affairs;
    The equality of all churches before the law.[6]

7. *"When the Wicked Rule the People Mourn"*

This principle is found in section 98 of the Doctrine and
Covenants, a revelation received 6 August 1833 at Kirtland,
Ohio. It came just seventeen days after the first mobbings in
Missouri. Knowing the Saints' pain and frustration, the Lord
counseled them on the laws of war, retaliation, and forgiveness.
Within that broader context he also advised them that wicked
rulers bring misery.

The concept that wicked rulers cause the people to mourn is
certainly consistent with world history. Even the slightest
knowledge of historical events furnishes evidence of this pattern. It would seem that no civilization has escaped this plague.
Certainly the Mormons in nineteenth-century Missouri had
ample cause to mourn. Concerning this matter, Elder Brigham
Young, Jr., said in 1900:

> I tell you one thing that I will do: I will support good
> men in every position. I care not what proposition may be
> submitted to me, I will sustain good men. For it is writ-
> ten, "When the wicked rule, the people mourn." When
> the righteous rule, the people rejoice. . . .
> . . . What do I care about party feeling! A lot of men
> meet together and get up names, among them some
> shyster that has foisted himself into notice through some
> means or other of his own making, and they rush that
> upon me, and because I would not vote for such men two
> or three years ago, they said, "You are a mugwump."
> Well, I would rather be a know-nothing than to subscribe
> to conditions which will make me responsible for the ac-
> tions of the wicked. I will not do it, I do not care who it

cuts, nor what the consequences may be. I say it to the nation, I say it to the world: As God lives, I will never support a man that I know is a wicked man, for any office. The word of the Prophet of God has been given to me, as it has to you, and we have got to take cognizance of these things.[7]

Responsibilities of Citizens

In addition to outlining correct principles for governments to follow, the revelation in the Doctrine and Covenants provide a correct course of action for citizens to follow. They set limits on the rights and powers of citizens and outline steps which citizens should take to ensure that they will have good government. I have identified seven principles which properly fit into the category of citizens' responsibilities.

1. *Citizens Should Obey the Laws of the Land*

This principle forms a foundation upon which all the other political responsibilities of citizens rests. It is found in section 58 of the Doctrine and Covenants.

The revelation contained in section 58 was received 20 July 1831 and was one of the first revelations in this dispensation received in Jackson County, Missouri. The occasion was Joseph Smith's first visit to Missouri. As he discovered Missouri for himself, Joseph Smith reported that he was favorably impressed with the land but had reservations about the people. For him, they seemed too far removed from the ways of God. Perhaps his assessment of the people of Missouri was a harbinger of troubles the Church later experienced in Missouri.

When the Lord explained, "Let no man break the laws of the land, for he that keepeth the laws of God hath no need to break the laws of the land" (D&C 58:21), he may have been preparing the Saints for a time when they might be tempted to break the laws of the land. This principle extends beyond the time when they were in Missouri. It applies to all Church members everywhere. In a word, the Lord is telling his people to obey the law. The Prophet Joseph Smith reiterated this principle in the Articles of Faith, and he also frequently included it in his speeches. In January of 1843, for example, he said, "We will keep the laws of the land."[8]

2. *Citizens Should Uphold the Constitutional Laws of the Land*

This principle of political behavior is obviously a companion principle and refinement of the first principle on obeying the law. While the Saints had an obligation to obey all laws, they had a special obligation to honor the Constitution. This principle was presented to the people in section 98.

All but one of the Church presidents has commented on upholding the constitutional law of the land. John Taylor, the most prolific writer on this subject, touched on it at least thirty-eight times. Studying his comments on this subject, one readily concludes that he believed it was the sacred duty of every Latter-day Saint in the United States to vigorously support the tenets of the U.S. Constitution. Two brief examples from his writings and speeches will enable us to capture the essence of his thinking on this subject.

> We are citizens of the United States, and profess to support the Constitution of the United States; and wherein that binds us, we are bound.[9]
> The Constitution of the United States has ever been respected and honored by us. We consider it one of the best national instruments ever formed. Nay, further, Joseph Smith in his day said it was given by inspiration of God. We have ever stood by it, and we expect when the fanaticism of false, blatant friends shall have torn it shred from shred, to stand by the shattered ruins and uphold the broken, desecrated remnants of our country's institutions in all their primitive purity and pristine glory.[10]

During the struggle with the United States government over statehood and polygamy, the Church made every effort to establish the constitutionality of the laws of the land. One of the most celebrated cases to come before the Supreme Court was the Reynolds case, involving George Reynolds, a secretary to the First Presidency.[11] In this case the Supreme Court ruled that the Morrill Anti-Polygamy Act was constitutional. As other laws, such as the Edmunds-Tucker Act, were declared constitu-

tional, the Church faced a serious dilemma: the law ran counter
to earlier revelations of God. President Wilford Woodruff
pleaded with the Lord to know what to do. He was inspired to
stop the practice of plural marriage, thus honoring the constitutional law of the land.[12]

3. *Citizens Should Be Actively Involved in Government*

The principles related to sustaining the law and the Constitution are closely related to the principle of being actively involved
in government. This important principle was made known in
section 134.

Latter-day Saints have been counseled to be actively involved in the political process in order to ensure that laws and
governmental actions are both constitutional and acceptable to
God and man. If we are involved, we have an opportunity to
shape our government rather than simply react to its edicts.

Joseph Smith set the example for political involvement by
running for President of the United States. He became a third
party candidate in the 1844 presidential election. Since his time
many Latter-day Saints have run for office. Today, all of the
United States Senators and congressmen from Utah are members of the Church.

Political involvement includes more than running for office.
The Church encourages grass roots participation, such as at-
tending local party caucuses and mass meetings. It likewise encourages us to be involved in public hearings on issues which
concern our communities. In recent years, the Church has encouraged its members to be involved in supporting moral issues.
Thus, many Mormons have been active in anti-pornography efforts in locations around the world. Most of the leaders of the
Church in this dispensation have urged members to be actively
involved in political affairs. Joseph Smith taught:

> It is our duty to concentrate all our influence to make
> popular that which is sound and good, and unpopular
> that which is unsound. 'Tis right, politically, for a man
> who has influence to use it, as well as for a man who has
> no influence to use his. From henceforth I will maintain
> all the influence I can get.[13]

4. *We Should Seek Honest, Wise Men*

An important part of being actively involved in politics is choosing good men and women for political office. The counsel that "honest men and wise men should be sought for diligently" was given in the revelation found in section 98, verse 10.

A belief in the possibility of electing honest, wise men and women to political office is an affirmation of faith in the democratic process. Latter-day Saints believe in the fundamental goodness of a democratic republic and of the attendant practice of voting for elected officials. During almost every election Church leaders encourage members to vote—to participate in the privilege of the franchise. Generally, this counsel to vote is coupled with the instructions to vote one's own conscience; there is no attempt to dictate in matters of parties, or candidates. Elder Hartman Rector, Jr., wrote, for example:

> The Lord has made plain that we have a solemn obligation to choose good and honest men to represent us in secular governmental service. It is obvious that a man's spiritual and moral qualifications should be considered before his academic record or his oratorical ability. It is a sobering thought that whatever laws the elected enact, we are obligated then to obey.[14]

5. *Citizens Should Renounce War and Proclaim Peace*

This principle for governing the behavior of Church members and other citizens sets a high standard of conduct. The principle concerning war and peace was given in the revelation now known as section 98. As indicated earlier, this revelation was received 6 August 1833 at Kirtland, Ohio, and came just a few days after the first mob attacks against the Mormons took place in Missouri. The desire for retaliation was intense. Here, the Lord told the Saints to follow the higher road and avoid the desire for revenge. This principle follows the New Testament model of turning the other cheek and returning good for evil. In this, as in all matters, the Saints are instructed to follow the example of Jesus Christ.

Elder Hugh B. Brown appealed for peace on the eve of World War II.

The Lord has revealed again in these latter days the charge to His followers to—"Renounce war, and proclaim peace." To endeavor in every proper way, through example and influence, to promote peace everywhere, that the way may be prepared so that "nations shall not lift up the sword against nations" but be prepared for the coming of the reign of the Lord, that peace and good will toward men shall prevail everywhere. This, we are confident, will eventually occur.[15]

6. Church Members Are Justified in Defending Themselves

This principle is a refinement of the principle of renouncing war and proclaiming peace, giving guidelines for how members are to defend themselves. These guidelines on defense are found in the Doctrine and Covenants, sections 98 and 134.

In the instructions given in section 134, we learn that there are certain things which are worth defending. Specifically, it is correct to defend ourselves, our friends, property, and government. These instructions would include, of course, one's family and beliefs, as well. Concerning this principle President David O. McKay said,

> There are, however, two conditions which may justify a truly Christian man to enter—mind you, I say *enter, not begin*—a war: (1) An attempt to dominate and to deprive another of his free agency, and, (2) Loyalty to his country. Possibly there is a third, viz., Defense of a weak nation that is being unjustly crushed by a strong, ruthless one. . . .
>
> Paramount among these reasons, of course, is the defense of man's freedom. An attempt to rob man of his free agency caused dissension even in heaven.[16]

7. Sedition and Rebellion Are Unbecoming

This political principle, found in Doctrine and Covenants 134, is especially appropriate for members of a worldwide Church. In many areas of the world political oppression exists, and there is very little freedom. In such circumstances rebellion may seem warranted and even desirable. However, Church leaders have consistently taught that such behavior is inappropriate. Further, they have urged members to help maintain peace and stability, even in the face of oppressive government. In many area conferences, held in various places around the world, Church leaders have taught that members should recognize the established authority in the countries where they reside. In this regard, President Joseph Fielding Smith taught that "no member of the Church can be accepted as in good standing whose way of life is one of rebellion against the established order of decency and obedience to law. We cannot be in rebellion against the law and be in harmony with the Lord."[17]

Conclusion

In this essay we have identified fourteen principles from the Doctrine and Covenants concerning political conduct. Seven of these principles apply to the behavior of governments, and seven apply to the conduct of citizens. An analysis of these fourteen principles shows clearly that God is interested in civil government and the relationship between church and state. Governments are a necessary fact of life, necessary to preserve order and stability in society. Citizens have a responsibility to obey the law and to be actively involved in political affairs. According to modern revelation, both governments and individual citizens have a responsibility to God in political matters.

Notes

1. *Teachings of the Prophet Joseph Smith,* comp. Joseph Fielding Smith (Salt Lake City: Deseret Book Co., 1976), p. 251.

2. *Journal of Discourses,* 26 vols. (Liverpool: F.D. Richards and Sons, 1855–86), 22:151.

3. In Conference Report, Oct. 1954, p. 120.

4. "Free Agency and Freedom," talk delivered by Elder Dallin H. Oaks, BYU Religious Studies Center Symposium on the Book of Mormon, 11 October 1987.

5. In Conference Report, Apr. 1949, pp. 167–68.

6. Appendix to Conference Report, Apr. 1907, p. 14.

7. In Conference Report, Oct. 1900, p. 44.

8. *The Words of Joseph Smith*, eds. Andrew F. Ehat and Lyndon W. Cook (Provo, UT: Religious Studies Center, Brigham Young University, 1980), p. 156.

9. *Journal of Discourses,* 5:154.

10. John Taylor Papers, volume one (10 July 1861).

11. See Edward Leo Lyman, *Political Deliverance: The Mormon Quest for Mormon Statehood* (Chicago: University of Illinois Press, 1986), pp. 20–21.

12. Ibid., pp. 42–44, 135–40.

13. *History of The Church of Jesus Christ of Latter-Day Saints,* 7 vols., ed. B. H. Roberts (Salt Lake City: Deseret Book Co., 1957), 5:286.

14. *Ensign*, Nov. 1975, p. 11.

15. In Conference Report, Apr. 1940, p. 27.

16. In Conference Report, Apr. 1942, pp. 72–73.

17. *Ensign*, June 1971, p. 50.

Latter-day Insights into the Life Beyond

Robert L. Millet

Certainly no subject has captivated the interest and attention of men and women like that of the life beyond. The high and the low of all classes of mankind have sought, with Job, to know, "If a man die, shall he live again?" (Job 14:14).

The spring of 1820 heralded the dawning of a brighter day, as celestial light pierced the blackness of the long night of heaven's silence. In the midst of that light stood two eternal beings whose very presence attested to the reality of the life beyond, as would the subsequent appearances of various messengers who would be sent to bestow the knowledge, keys, and powers pertaining to the eternal worlds. Through the Restoration, the mysteries of God have begun to be unfolded, and the Saints of the Most High are made partakers of that knowledge which few eyes have seen, few ears heard—knowledge which soothes and sanctifies the soul.

Robert L. Millet is Associate Professor and Chairman of the Department of Ancient Scripture at Brigham Young University.

The Vision: Many Mansions of the Father

Less than two years passed from the time of the formal organization of the restored Church until the God of Glory chose to open the heavens and expand the spiritual horizons of the Saints in a transcendent manner. It was the winter of 1832. Joseph Smith had been engaged in his work of inspired translation of the Bible since June of 1830, and since April of 1831 he had concentrated on the New Testament. Joseph and Emma were living in the home of John Johnson in Hiram, Ohio. On 16 February in the year 1832 Joseph the prophet and Sidney Rigdon his scribe prayerfully pondered the fifth chapter of John's gospel, particularly verse 29. By the power of the Spirit, the translators felt impressed to alter the King James verse so as to refer to the "resurrection of the just" and the "resurrection of the unjust," instead of the resurrections "of life" and "of damnation." The implications of this change "caused us to marvel," the Prophet said, "for it was given unto us of the Spirit. And while we meditated upon these things, the Lord touched the eyes of our understandings and they were opened, and the glory of the Lord shone round about." (D&C 76:18–19.)

That which burst upon the minds and hearts of Joseph Smith and Sidney Rigdon also burst the shackles of ignorance and fear and provided specific doctrinal instruction concerning the Great Plan of the Eternal God. The Vision of the Glories consists of a series of manifestations: (1) a glorious vision of the throne of God, Christ at his right hand, and holy angels praising and worshiping their God; (2) a dramatically contrasting scene —the fall of Lucifer and the sons of perdition, those who chose to deny and defy the Lord and his plan, and who with malevolent mentality seek to crucify the Christ anew; (3) then, as the glory of the day follows the darkness of night, a vision of the celestial world, as well as an understanding of those who qualify for such wonders and blessings; (4) a vision of the terrestrial world with its honorable hosts; (5) a vision of the telestial world and its inhabitants, those who lived in dishonor and were untouched by spiritual truths; and (6) an understanding of hell— its composition and duration. The vision takes us from premortality to residence in the eternal worlds and thus provides through its breadth and depth the answers to a multitude of questions. "Nothing could be more pleasing to the Saints upon the order of the kingdom of the Lord," Joseph Smith exulted, "than the light which burst upon the world through the foregoing vision."

> Every law, every commandment, every promise, every truth, and every point touching the destiny of man, from Genesis to Revelation, where the purity of the scriptures remains unsullied by the folly of men, go to show the perfection of the theory [of different degrees of glory in the future life] and witnesses the fact that that document is a transcript from the records of the eternal world. The sublimity of the ideas; the purity of the language; the scope for action; the continued duration for completion, in order that the heirs of salvation may confess the Lord and bow the knee; the rewards for faithfulness, and the punishments for sins, are so much beyond the narrow-mindedness of men, that every honest man is constrained to exclaim: *"It came from God."*[1]

Subsequent revelations to Joseph Smith made known the fact that "he who is not able to abide the law of a celestial kingdom cannot abide a celestial glory" (D&C 88:22), and that the type and quality of body with which one is resurrected determines the kingdom to which he will be assigned in the eternal worlds (see D&C 88:21–32). Further, it was in Nauvoo that Joseph the Prophet made known that "in the celestial glory there are three heavens or degrees; and in order to obtain the highest, a man must enter into this order of the priesthood [meaning the new and everlasting covenant of marriage]; and if he does not, he cannot obtain it. He may enter into the other, but that is the end of his kingdom; he cannot have an increase." (D&C 131:1–4.)

Vision of the Celestial Kingdom

The headquarters of the Saints had moved from New York and Pennsylvania to Ohio. By 1831 two Church centers were organized, one in Kirtland and the other in Missouri (Zion). Joseph Smith and his people received a commandment as early as 1833 to build a temple in Kirtland and were given profound promises. The Lord instructed that they "should build a house, in the which house I design to endow those whom I have chosen with power from on high" (D&C 95:8). Truly the sacrifices of the Saints brought forth the blessings of heaven as God rewarded the works of his chosen people with a marvelous outpouring of light and truth.

Joseph and the early leaders of the Church had begun to meet in the temple before its completion, and had participated in washings, anointings, and blessings, all in preparation for what came to be known as the Kirtland Endowment. On Thursday evening, 21 January 1836, the Prophet and a number of Church leaders from Kirtland and Missouri had gathered in the third, or attic, floor of the Kirtland Temple (in the translating, or "President's Room"). After anointings and after all the presidency had laid their hands upon the Prophet's head and pronounced many glorious blessings and prophecies, a mighty vision burst upon the assembled leadership.[2]

> The heavens were opened upon us, and I beheld the celestial kingdom of God, and the glory thereof, whether in the body or out I cannot tell.
> I saw the transcendent beauty of the gate through which the heirs of that kingdom will enter, which was like unto circling flames of fire;
> Also the blazing throne of God, whereon was seated the Father and the Son.
> I saw the beautiful streets of that kingdom, which had the appearance of being paved with gold. (D&C 137:1–4.)

Joseph had learned by vision in February of 1832 the nature of those who would inherit the highest heaven, the celestial. These persons are they who "overcome by faith, and are sealed by the Holy Spirit of promise . . . they into whose hands the Father has given all things" (D&C 76:53, 55). The Prophet's vision of the Celestial Kingdom was not unlike John the Revelator's vision of the holy city, the earth in its sanctified and celestial state. "The foundations of the wall of the city," writes John, "were garnished with all manner of precious stones." Further, "the street of the city was pure gold, as it were transparent glass." (Revelation 21:19, 21.)

Joseph's account of the vision continues: "I saw Father Adam and Abraham; and my father and my mother; my brother Alvin, that has long since slept; And marveled how it was that he had obtained an inheritance in that kingdom, seeing that he had departed this life before the Lord had set his hand to gather Israel the second time, and had not been baptized for the remission of sins" (D&C 137:5–6). Joseph Smith's brief view of the celestial kingdom permitted him to witness specific persons who had proven true and faithful in all things, and thus had qualified for exaltation. Adam, the first man and father of the race, had sought the Lord and found him. "Abraham received all things," a revelation stated, "whatsoever he received, by revelation and commandment, . . . and hath entered into this exaltation and sitteth upon his throne" (D&C 132:29). That Joseph's vision was a glimpse into the future celestial realm is evident from the fact that he saw his parents—Joseph, Sr., and Lucy Mack—in the kingdom of the just, when in fact both were still living in 1836. Father Smith was, interestingly, in the same room with his son at the time the vision was received.

Alvin Smith was born on 11 February 1798 in Tunbridge, Vermont, the firstborn of Joseph, Sr., and Lucy Mack Smith. His was a pleasant and loving disposition, and he always sought out opportunities to aid the family in their continual financial struggles. Joseph, Jr., later described his oldest brother as one in whom there was no guile.[3] "He was a very handsome man, surpassed by none but Adam and Seth."[4] Lucy Mack Smith writes that on the morning of 15 November 1823, "Alvin was taken very sick with the bilious colic." One physician hurried to the Smith home and administered calomel to Alvin. The dose of calomel "lodged in his stomach," and on the third day of sickness, Alvin became aware of the fact that death was near. He asked that each of the Smith children come to his bedside for his parting counsel and final expression of love. As his mother later recalled, "When he came to Joseph, he said, 'I am now going to die, the distress which I suffer, and the feelings that I have, tell me my time is very short. I want you to be a good boy, and do everything that lies in your power to obtain the Record. [Joseph had been visited by Moroni less than three months before this time.] Be faithful in receiving instruction, and in keeping every commandment that is given you.' "[5] Alvin died on 19 November. His mother wrote of the pall of grief surrounding his passing: "Alvin was a youth of singular goodness of disposition —kind and amiable, so that lamentation and mourning filled the whole neighborhood in which he resided."[6] Joseph wrote painfully of Alvin's passing many years later: "I remember well the pangs of sorrow that swelled my youthful bosom and almost burst my tender heart when he died. He was the oldest and noblest of my father's family. . . . He lived without spot from the time he was a child. . . . He was one of the soberest of men, and when he died the angel of the Lord visited him in his last moments."[7]

Inasmuch as Alvin had died some seven years before the formal organization of the Church (and thus had not been baptized by proper authority), Joseph wondered how it was possible for Alvin to have attained the highest heaven. Alvin's family had been shocked and saddened at his funeral when they heard the Presbyterian minister announce that Alvin would be consigned to hell, having never officially been baptized or involved in the church. William Smith, Alvin's younger brother, recalls: "Hyrum, Samuel, Katherine, and mother were members of the Presbyterian Church. My father would not join. He did not like it because of Rev. Stockton had preached my brother's funeral sermon and intimated very strongly that he had gone to hell, for Alvin was not a church member, but he was a good boy and my father did not like it."[8] What joy and excitement must have filled the souls of both Joseph, Jr., and Joseph, Sr., as they learned a comforting truth from an omniscient and omni-loving God: "Thus came the voice of the Lord unto me, saying: All who have died without a knowledge of this gospel, who would have received it if they had been permitted to tarry, shall be heirs of the celestial kingdom of God; Also all that shall die henceforth without a knowledge of it, who would have received it with all their hearts, shall be heirs of that kingdom; for I, the Lord, will judge all men according to their works, according to the desire of their hearts." (D&C 137:7–9.)

God does not and will not hold anyone accountable for a gospel law of which he was ignorant. Every person will have opportunity—here or hereafter—to accept and apply the principles of the gospel of Jesus Christ. Only the Lord, the Holy One of Israel, is capable of "keeping the gate" and thus discerning completely the hearts and minds of mortal men; he alone knows when a person has received sufficient knowledge or impressions to constitute a valid opportunity to receive the gospel message. Joseph had reaffirmed that the Lord will judge men not only by their actions, but also by their attitudes—the desires of their hearts (compare Alma 41:3) and their opportunities.

One of the most profoundly beautiful of doctrines is that enunciated in the Vision of the Celestial Kingdom regarding the status of children who die before the time of accountability: "And I also beheld that all children who die before they arrive at the years of accountability are saved in the celestial kingdom of heaven" (D&C 137:10). King Benjamin had learned from an angel that "the infant perisheth not that dieth in his infancy" (Mosiah 3:18). A revelation given to Joseph Smith in September of 1830 specified that "little children are redeemed from the foundation of the world through mine Only Begotten" (D&C 29:46; compare JST, Matthew 19:13–15). Joseph Smith taught in 1842 that "the Lord takes many away even in infancy, that they may escape the envy of man, and the sorrows and evils of this present world; they were too pure, too lovely, to live on earth; therefore, if rightly considered, instead of mourning we have reason to rejoice as they are delivered from evil, and we shall soon have them again."[9] By virtue of his infinite understanding of the human family, "we may assume that the Lord knows and arranges beforehand who shall be taken in infancy and who shall remain on earth to undergo whatever tests are needed in their cases."[10] These children will come forth from the grave as they lie down—as children—[11]and will grow to maturity in the Millennium. They will not be expected to face tests or temptations in their resurrected state, but will go on to enjoy the highest and grandest blessings of exaltation associated with the everlasting continuation of the family unit.[12]

The Vision of the Celestial Kingdom opened the door to the glorious reality that men and women who may have died without the privileges of gospel blessings here will not be eternally

disadvantaged hereafter. Four and one-half years after Joseph
Smith's Vision of the Celestial Kingdom the Prophet delivered
his first public discourse on the subject of baptism for the dead
at the funeral of Seymour Brunson, a member of the Nauvoo
High Council. One man who was in attendance at the funeral
has left us the following account:

> I was present at the discourse that the Prophet Joseph
> delivered on baptism for the dead 15 August 1840. He
> read the greater part of the 15th chapter of Corinthians
> and remarked that the Gospel of Jesus Christ brought
> glad tidings of great joy. . . . He also said the apostle
> [Paul] was talking to a people who understood baptism
> for the dead, for it was practiced among them. He went
> on to say that people could now act for their friends who
> had departed this life, and that the plan of salvation was
> calculated to save all who were willing to obey the require-
> ments of the law of God. He went on and made a very
> beautiful discourse.[13]

One month later, on 14 September 1840, Joseph Smith, Sr.,
passed away. Just before his death, Father Smith requested that
someone be baptized for and in behalf of his oldest son, Alvin.
Hyrum Smith complied with his father's last wishes and was
baptized by proxy for Alvin in 1840 and again in 1841.[14] Alvin
received the endowment by proxy on 11 April 1877, and was
sealed to his parents on 25 August 1897.[15]

Vision of the Redemption of the Dead

The knowledge of salvation for the living and the dead revealed initially through the Prophet Joseph Smith continued to
be expanded and elaborated as the ongoing Restoration made
further truths available "line upon line." It is to the Prophet's
nephew—Joseph F. Smith—that we now turn for precious insights into the manner in which the gospel is preached in the
world of spirits.

During the last six months of his life, President Joseph F.
Smith suffered from the effects of advancing years (he was in
his eightieth year) and spent much of his time in his personal
study in the Beehive House. President Smith did manage to gar-

ner enough strength to attend the eighty-ninth semi-annual conference of the Church (October 1918). At the opening session of the conference (Friday, 4 October) he arose to welcome and address the Saints, and with a voice filled with emotion, spoke the following:

> As most of you, I suppose, are aware, I have been undergoing a siege of very serious illness for the last five months. It would be impossible for me, on this occasion, to occupy sufficient time to express the desires of my heart and my feelings, as I would desire to express them to you. . . .
> I will not, I dare not, attempt to enter upon many things that are resting upon my mind this morning, and I shall postpone until some future time, the Lord being willing, my attempt to tell you some of the things that are in my mind, and that dwell in my heart. I have not lived alone these [last] five months. I have dwelt in the spirit of prayer, of supplication, of faith and of determination; and I have had my communication with the Spirit of the Lord continuously.[16]

According to his son, Joseph Fielding Smith, the prophet was here expressing (albeit in broadest terms) the fact that during the past half-hear he had been the recipient of numerous manifestations, some of which he had shared with his son, both before and following the conference. One of these manifestations, the Vision of the Redemption of the Dead, had been received just the day before, on 3 October, and was recorded immediately following the close of the conference.[17]

The aged prophet's attention was perhaps drawn to the world beyond mortality by his frequent confrontation with death. His parents, Hyrum and Mary Fielding Smith, both died while he was a young man. Among the great trials of his life none was more devastating than the passing of many of his children into death. President Smith was possessed of an almost infinite capacity to love, and thus the sudden departure of dear ones brought extreme anguish and sorrow. Joseph Fielding Smith later wrote: "When death invaded his home, as frequently it did, and his little ones were taken from him, he grieved with a broken heart and mourned, not as those who mourn who live without hope, but for the loss of his 'precious jewels' dearer to him than life itself.''[18]

On 20 January 1918 Hyrum Mack Smith, oldest son of Joseph F. and then a member of the Council of the Twelve Apostles, was taken to the hospital for a serious illness. The physicians diagnosed a ruptured appendix. Despite constant medical attention and repeated prayers, Hyrum M.—then only 45 years of age—died on the night of 23 January. This was a particularly traumatic affliction for the President. Hyrum had been called as an Apostle at the same conference when his father had been sustained as the Church's sixth president (October 1901). Hyrum Mack was a man of depth and wisdom beyond his years, and his powerful sermons evidenced his unusual insight into gospel principles. ''His mind was quick and bright and correct,'' remarked President Smith. ''His judgment was not excelled, and he saw and comprehended things in their true light and meaning. When he spoke, men listened and felt the weight of his thoughts and words.'' Finally, the prophet observed: ''He has thrilled my soul with his power of speech, as no other man ever did. Perhaps this was because he was my son, and he was filled with the fire of the Holy Ghost.''[19] The prophet was already in a weakened physical condition due to age, and his sudden sense of loss caused him ''one of the most severe blows that he was ever called upon to endure.''[20]

President Smith indicated in October of 1918 that the preceding six months had been a season of special enrichment; in fact it may be shown that the last thirty months of his life (specifically, from April 1916 to October 1918) represent an era of unusual spiritual enlightenment in which he delivered to the Church some of the most important and inspiring insights of this dispensation.

At the April 1916 general conference President Joseph F. Smith delivered a remarkable address, the thrust of which established a theme for the next thirty months of his life; it laid the foundation for his final doctrinal contribution—the Vision of the Redemption of the Dead. In his opening sermon entitled ''In the Presence of the Divine,'' President Smith spoke of the nearness of the world of spirits and of the interest and concern for us and our labors exercised by those who have passed beyond the veil. He stressed that those who labored so diligently in their mortal estate to establish the cause of Zion would not be denied the privilege of "looking down upon the results of their own labors" from their post-mortal estate. In fact, the President insisted, "they are as deeply interested in our welfare today, if not with greater capacity, with far more interest behind the veil, than they were in the flesh." Perhaps the keynote statement of the prophet in this sermon was the following: "Sometimes the Lord expands our vision from this point of view and this side of the veil, that we feel and seem to realize that we can look beyond the thin veil which separates us from that other sphere."[21]

Another significant dimension of the life beyond was stressed in a talk delivered by President Joseph F. Smith in February of 1918 at a temple fast meeting, entitled "The Status of Children in the Resurrection." In this address we are allowed a brief glimpse into the heart of a noble father who—having lost little ones to death and having mourned their absence—rejoices in the sure knowledge that: (1) mortal children are immortal beings, spirits who continue to live and progress beyond the veil; and (2) as the Prophet Joseph Smith taught, children will come forth from the grave as they lie down—as children—and such persons will thereafter be nurtured and reared to physical maturity by worthy parents. "O how I have been blessed with these children," exulted President Smith, "and how happy I shall be to meet them on the other side!"[22]

Further evidence that the veil had become thin for Joseph F. Smith is to be found in his recording (on 7 April 1918) of a dream vision he had received many years earlier, while on his first mission to Hawaii. The dream had served initially to strengthen the faith and build the confidence of a lonely and weary fifteen-year-old on the slopes of Haleakala on the island of Maui; it had, through the years that followed, served to chart a course for Joseph F. and give to him the assurance that his labors were acceptable to the Lord, and that he also had the approbation of his predecessors in the presidency of the restored Church. In the dream young Joseph F. encountered his uncle, the Prophet Joseph, and was fortified in his desire to remain free from the taints of the world. In addition, he learned at an early age that the separation between mortality and immortality is subtle, and that the Lord frequently permits an intermingling of the inhabitants of the two spheres.[23]

As finite man stands in the twilight of life, he is occasionally able to view existence with divine perspective and is thus capable of opening himself to the things of infinity. "If we live our holy religion," President Brigham Young taught in 1862, "and let the Spirit reign," the mind of man "will not become dull and stupid, but as the body approaches dissolution the spirit takes a firmer hold on the enduring substance behind the veil, drawing from the depths of that eternal Fountain of Light sparkling gems of intelligence which surround the frail and sinking tabernacle with a halo of immortal wisdom."[24] This poignant principle was demonstrated beautifully in the life of President Joseph F. Smith. Here was a man who met death and sorrow and persecution with a quiet dignity, and, like his Master, grew toward perfection through the things which he suffered. On Thursday, 3 October 1918, President Smith, largely confined to his room because of illness, sat meditating over matters of substance. On this day the prophet specifically began to read and ponder upon the universal nature of the Atonement, and the Apostle Peter's allusions to Christ's postmortal ministry. The stage was set: preparation of a lifetime and preparation of the moment were recompensed with a heavenly endowment— the Vision of the Redemption of the Dead. In the words of the President: "As I pondered over these things which are written, the eyes of my understanding were opened, and the Spirit of the Lord rested upon me, and I saw the hosts of the dead, both small and great" (D&C 138:11).

Joseph F. Smith saw in vision "an innumerable company of the spirits of the just," the righteous dead from the days of Adam to the meridian of time. These all were anxiously awaiting the advent of the Christ into their dimension of life, and were exuberant in their anticipation of an imminent resurrection (D&C 138:12–17). Having consummated the atoning sacrifice on Golgotha, the Lord of the living and the dead passed into the world of the departed. The dead, having "looked upon the long absence of their spirits from their bodies as a bondage" (D&C 138:50; compare 45:17), were, in a sense, in prison. Yes, even the righteous sought "deliverance" (D&C 138:15, 18); the Master came to declare "liberty to the captives who had been faithful" (D&C 138:18). As Peter had said, Christ went beyond the veil to preach "unto the spirits in prison" (1 Peter 3:19). Joseph Smith had taught: "Hades, Sheol, paradise, spirits in prison, are all one: it is a world of spirits."[25] And as Elder Bruce R. McConkie has explained, in this vision "it is clearly set forth that the whole spirit world, and not only that portion designated as hell, is considered to be a spirit prison."[26]

To the congregation of the righteous the Lord appeared, and "their countenances shone, and the radiance from the presence of the Lord rested upon them." President Smith observed as the Lord taught "the everlasting gospel, the doctrine of the resurrection and the redemption of mankind from the fall, and from individual sins on conditions of repentance." In addition, Christ extended to the righteous spirits "power to come forth, after his resurrection from the dead, to enter into his Father's kingdom, there to be crowned with immortality and eternal life." (D&C 138:24, 19, 51.)

It was while pondering the question of how the Savior could have taught the gospel to so many in the spirit world in so short a time (the time intervening between his death on Friday and his rising from the tomb on Sunday morning) that President Smith received a most significant doctrinal insight. The President came to understand "that the Lord went not in person among the wicked and the disobedient"—those in hell or outer darkness (see Alma 40:13)—but rather "organized his forces and appointed messengers, clothed with power and authority," that such representatives might carry the message of the gospel "unto whom he [the Lord] could not go personally, because of their rebellion and transgression." The chosen messengers "declare the acceptable day of the Lord." They carried the gospel message to those who had no opportunity to accept or reject the truth and also to those who rejected the message on earth. These who were visited by messengers were taught the principles and ordinances of the gospel (including the vicarious nature of the ordinances), in order that the inhabitants of the world of spirits might be judged and rewarded by the same divine standards as those who inhabit the world of mortals (D&C 138:29, 30–31, 37). The insight that Christ did not personally visit the disobedient is a doctrinal matter introduced to the Church for the first time in October of 1918 and does much to broaden our understanding and answer questions with regard to the work within that sphere.

By the power of the Holy Ghost President Smith perceived the identity of many of the noble and great from the beginning of time, including Adam, Seth, Noah, Abraham, Isaiah, the Nephite prophets before Christ, and many more. In addition, the President recognized Mother Eve and many of her faithful daughters. President Smith had taught a number of years earlier that women minister to women in the spirit world, even as they do in holy places on earth.[27]

It is at this point in the vision that President Smith stated: "The Prophet Joseph Smith, and my father, Hyrum Smith, Brigham Young, John Taylor, Wilford Woodruff, and other choice spirits who were reserved to come forth in the fulness of times . . . were also in the spirit world. I observed that they were also among the noble and great ones who were chosen in the beginning to be rulers in the Church of God. Even before they were born, they, with many others, received their first lessons in the world of spirits and were prepared to come forth in the due time of the Lord." (D&C 138:53–56.) In the absence of available prophetic commentary upon this passage, it is difficult to know exactly what President Smith saw and what he meant. At least two possibilities suggest themselves. First, it could be that Joseph F. Smith observed that the leaders of the final dispensation (then living and preparing in their premortal state) were allowed to witness and be a part of the glorious scenes in the premortal world of spirits in A.D. 34. This occasion would thus represent a mingling of the unembodied and the disembodied. A second possibility is simply that President Smith's vision of the postmortal spirit world shifted in time—from a first century A.D. gathering to a scene of workers in the spirit world during the final gospel dispensation. In short, President Smith became an eyewitness of that realm where he would soon — within six weeks — be at work.

President Joseph F. Smith's vision confirms another doctrine that had been taught by Joseph Smith: the faithful in this life continue to teach and labor in the world of spirits in behalf of those who know not God (D&C 138:57). As recorded in George Laub's journal under date of 12 May 1844, the Prophet Joseph declared: "Now all those who die in the faith go to the prison of Spirits to preach to the dead in body, but they are alive in the spirit, and those spirits preach to the spirits that they may live according to God in the spirit and men do minister for them in the flesh."[28] President Smith had taught this doctrine on a number of occasions;[29] here he became an eyewitness of the same.

Having laid before us his remarkable vision — "a complete and comprehensive confirmation of the established doctrine of the Church where salvation for the dead is concerned"[30] — President Smith climaxed his doctrinal contribution with testimony: "Thus was the vision of the redemption of the dead revealed to me, and I bear record, and I know that this record is true, through the blessing of our Lord and Savior, Jesus Christ, even so. Amen." (D&C 138:60.)

The Vision of the Redemption of the Dead was dictated by President Smith to his son — Joseph Fielding Smith — after the close of the October 1918 conference. The vision was presented to the First Presidency, Twelve, and Patriarch in a council meeting on Thursday, 31 October 1918. Because of his weakened condition, the President was not able to be in attendance but asked Joseph Fielding to read the revelation to the gathered General Authorities. Note the following from the journal of Anthon H. Lund, first counselor to President Smith: "In our Council Joseph F. Smith, Jr. read a revelation which his father had had in which he saw the spirits in Paradise preach to the spirits in prison, but did not go himself. It was an interesting document and the apostles accepted it as true and from God."[31] Elder James E. Talmage of the Council of the Twelve Apostles recorded the following in his personal journal:

Attended meeting of the First Presidency and the Twelve. Today President Smith who is still confined to his home by illness, sent to the Brethren the account of a vision through which, as he states, were revealed to him important facts relating to the work of the disembodied Savior in the realm of departed spirits, and of the missionary work in progress on the other side of the veil. By united action the Council of the Twelve, with Counselors in the First Presidency, and the Presiding Patriarch accepted and endorsed the revelation as the word of the Lord. President Smith's signed statement will be published in the next issue (December) of the Improvement Era, which is the organ of the Priesthood quorums of the church.[32]

The text of the vision first appeared in the 30 November edition of the *Deseret News*. It was printed in the December *Improvement Era*, and in the January 1919 editions of the *Relief Society Magazine,* the *Utah Genealogical and Historical Magazine,* the *Young Women's Journal*, and the *Millennial Star.*

President Smith's physical condition worsened during the first weeks of November 1918. On Sunday, 17 November he was taken with an attack of pleurisy, which finally developed into pleuro-pneumonia. Tuesday morning, 19 November 1918 his work in mortality was completed. It was fitting that at the next general conference Elder James E. Talmage should deliver the following touching and appropriate tribute to the President. Elder Talmage asked: "Well, where is he now?" The Apostle answered: "He was permitted shortly before his passing to have a glimpse into the hereafter, and to learn where he would soon be at work. He was a preacher of righteousness on earth, he is a preacher of righteousness today. He was a missionary from his boyhood up, and he is a missionary today amongst those who have not yet heard the gospel, though they have passed from mortality into the spirit world. I cannot conceive of him as otherwise than busily engaged in the work of the Master."[33]

Conclusion

The Lord loves all of his children and desires that every soul have the privilege of participating in the principles and ordinances of the gospel of Jesus Christ. Three grand revelations recorded in the Doctrine and Covenants teach us plainly of man's precious possibilities. The vision of the glories represented a page from man's book of eternal possibilities, and provided inspired commentary upon the Savior's words "In my Father's house are many mansions" (John 14:2). Joseph Smith's vision of the celestial kingdom opens us to the reality of an omniscient and omni-loving God. Joseph F. Smith's Vision of the Redemption of the Dead sets forth with remarkable clarity the manner in which the Savior "declared liberty to the captives" in the meridian of time, and also unfolds the pattern by which the doctrines of salvation continue to be made known in the world beyond the grave. And so it is that the work of redemption goes forward on both sides of the veil. "Because of this," Peter taught the Saints, "is the gospel preached to them who are dead, that they might be judged according to men in the flesh, but live in the spirit according to the will of God" (JST, 1 Peter 4:6).

Notes

1. *History of The Church of Jesus Christ of Latter-day Saints*, 7 vols., ed. B. H. Roberts (Salt Lake City: Deseret Book Co., 1957), 1:252–53.

2. *History of the Church*, 2:378–80.

3. See *History of the Church*, 5:126.

4. Ibid., p. 247.

5. Lucy Mack Smith, *History of Joseph Smith*, ed. Preston Nibley, (Salt Lake City: Bookcraft, 1958), pp. 86–87.

6. Ibid., p. 88.

7. *History of the Church,* 5:126–27.

8. See interview with William Smith by E. C. Briggs and J. W. Peterson, published in the *Deseret News* (Salt Lake City), 20 Jan. 1894.

9. Joseph Smith, *Teachings of the Prophet Joseph Smith,* comp. Joseph Fielding Smith (Salt Lake City: Deseret Book Co., 1976), pp. 196–97.

10. Bruce R. McConkie, expressing the sentiments of President Joseph Fielding Smith, in "The Salvation of Little Children," *Ensign,* Apr. 1977, p. 6.

11. *Teachings of the Prophet Joseph Smith,* pp. 199–200.

12. McConkie, "The Salvation of Little Children," pp. 5–6; see also Joseph Fielding Smith, *Doctrines of Salvation,* 3 vols. (Salt Lake City: Bookcraft, 1954–56), 2:54–57.

13. A report by Simon Baker in *Journal History,* under date of 15 August 1840, LDS Church Archives; also in Andrew F. Ehat and Lyndon W. Cook, *The Words of Joseph Smith* (Provo, Utah: Religious Studies Center, Brigham Young University, 1980), p. 49; see also *History of the Church,* 4:231.

14. "Nauvoo Baptisms for the Dead," Book A, Church Genealogical Society Archives, pp. 145, 149.

15. From Joseph Smith, Sr., Family Group Sheet, Church Genealogical Society Archives.

16. In Conference Report, Oct. 1918, p. 2.

17. Joseph Fielding Smith, *The Life of Joseph F. Smith* (Salt Lake City: Deseret Book Co., 1969), p. 466.

18. Ibid., p. 455.

19. Ibid., p. 474.

20. Ibid.

21. In Conference Report, Apr. 1916, p. 2.

22. *Improvement Era,* May 1918, pp. 567–74; Clark, *Messages of the First Presidency,* 5:90–98.

23. *Improvement Era,* November 1919, pp. 16–17; Clark, *Messages of the First Presidency,* 5:99–101; Smith, *Life of Joseph F. Smith,* pp. 445–47.

24. *Journal of Discourses,* 9:288.

25. *Teachings of the Prophet Joseph Smith,* p. 310.

26. Bruce R. McConkie, "A New Commandment: Save Thyself and Thy Kindred," *Ensign,* Aug. 1976, p. 11.

27. See Joseph F. Smith, *Young Women's Journal* 23 (1911): 128–32; *Gospel Doctrine* (Salt Lake City: Deseret Book Co., 1971), p. 461.

28. Ehat and Cook, *The Words of Joseph Smith,* p. 370, spelling and punctuation have been modernized.

29. See *Gospel Doctrine,* pp. 134–35, 460–61.

30. Bruce R. McConkie, "A New Commandment? Save Thyself and Thy Kindred," *Ensign*, Aug. 1976, p. 11.

31. Anthon H. Lund Journal, 31 October 1918, LDS Chuch Archives, Salt Lake City.

32. James E. Talmage Journal, 31 October 1918, LDS Church Archives, Salt Lake City.

33. In Conference Report, June 1919, p. 60.

13

"Save Jesus Only": The Greatness of Joseph Smith

H. Dean Garrett

There is not so great a man as Joseph standing in this generation. The gentiles look upon him and he is like a bed of gold concealed from human view. They know not his principles, his spirit, his wisdom, his virtues, his philanthropy, nor his calling. His mind, like Enoch's expands as eternity, and only God can comprehend his soul."[1] This assessment of Joseph Smith reflects upon the position and calling given to him to assist in the salvation of mankind. Joseph Smith's role was that of legal administrator of the dispensation of the fulness of times and revealer of truth for that dispensation. His work would have an impact on all mankind in every age of this earth. Thus it was said of him: "Joseph Smith, the Prophet and Seer of the Lord, has done more, save Jesus only, for the salvation of men in this world, than any other man that ever lived in it" (D&C 135:3).

H. Dean Garrett is Assistant Professor of Church History and Doctrine at Brigham Young University.

This bold statement could raise some concern when one considers the works of such great prophets as Adam, Enoch, Noah, Abraham, Moses, or Peter. However, a careful examination of the mission and accomplishments of Joseph Smith justifies such a declaration.

Legal Administrator

Joseph Smith's role in the salvation of mankind was defined before he ever came to this earth. He was one of the noble and great ones who, in the pre-earth councils, was chosen to be a noted leader in mortality. In speaking of those called from the foundation of the world, Joseph said: "Every man who has a calling to minister to the inhabitants of the world was ordained to that very purpose in the Grand Council of heaven before this world was. I suppose I was ordained to this very office in that Grand Council."[2]

Joseph's foreordination was due to his "exceeding faith and good works" in that premortal world (Alma 13:3). Because of this and the callings that were to come to him in mortality, his great forebear, Joseph of Egypt, was told by the Lord that "a choice seer will I raise up out of the fruit of thy loins; and he shall be esteemed highly among the fruit of thy loins. . . . And I will give unto him a commandment that he shall do none other work save the work which I shall command him, and I will make him great in mine eyes; for he shall do my work. And he shall be great like unto Moses." (2 Nephi 3:7–9.) Joseph also learned of this future seer that "out of weakness he shall be made strong, in that day when my work shall commence among all my people" (2 Nephi 3:13). The Lord's great work was to commence in the last days when the dispensation of the fulness of times would be ushered in with the Prophet Joseph Smith at its head.

A dispensation is a period in the history of the earth when the plan of salvation is given to man. It is a time "when the Lord, through one man, gives his word to the whole world and makes all the prophets, and all the seers, and all the administrators, and all the apostles of that period subject to, and exponents of, what came through that individual. What this means is that the head of a gospel dispensation, a dispensation of the sort that we are now mentioning, stands as one of the 10 or 20 greatest spirits who have so far been born on earth."[3]

Joseph Smith came to this earth as he was foreordained to do, and as it was prophesied that he should, reflecting the magnitude of the work he was to perform. His labors were to be accomplished in an era when the Lord would begin to "gather together in one all things in Christ" (Ephesians 1:10).

Joseph Smith was told by the Angel Moroni that "God had a work for me to do; and that my name should be had for good and evil among all nations, kindreds, and tongues, or that it should be both good and evil spoken of among all people" (Joseph Smith—History 1:33). This prophetic statement was fulfilled in many ways during and since his lifetime. This is one of the reasons the statement, "has done more, save Jesus only, for the salvation of men" (D&C 135:3), has meaning, for it was during this final crowning dispensation that the gospel of Jesus Christ would be taken to every nation, kindred, tongue, and people. Prophets in earlier dispensations had done their work among certain segments of the house of Israel, but Joseph's task was to take the gospel to all Israelites scattered throughout all gentile nations of the earth. During this final dispensation, the children of Israel would be invited to come out of Babylon and become covenant followers of Christ. The gentile nations would be invited to join them, if they would but repent and accept the covenants of Christ. The magnitude and significance of this work cannot be overemphasized. Also, during this final dispensation, the ordinances necessary for exaltation are offered to those who have died and are waiting in the spirit world. The keys received through Joseph Smith opened the door and made baptism, priesthood, and temple ordinances available to billions who lived on this earth without the blessing of such ordinances. This great work is of such magnitude that those who respond to the message of the gospel cannot be saved without their worthy ancestors.[4] Thus, for the first time ever in earth's history, all men and women who ever lived can anticipate the realization of their hopes that "the promises made to the fathers" (D&C 2:2) will be fulfilled.

Visitations of Heavenly Messengers

Joseph Smith's prophetic call was issued in conjunction with one of the greatest of all events in human history, when God himself and his son, Jesus Christ, appeared in a grove of trees to answer the urgent petition of a fourteen-year-old boy. The message given him by these exalted beings came as an initial ray of light following a long night of darkness; the dramatic events to be known as the dispensation of the fullness of times were ushered in.

In order that his critical mission might be successfully accomplished, it was necessary that Joseph be visited by many of the former prophets who had once lived on the earth. The first to appear was Moroni who enlightened him with knowledge concerning an ancient record that Joseph was to translate and publish as the Book of Mormon. In due time, John the Baptist restored the Aaronic Priesthood followed by Peter, James, and John who restored the Melchizedek Priesthood. The keys of the gathering of Israel were restored by Moses; the power to grant the blessings of Abraham was brought back by Elias; the sealing keys were given by Elijah. Others such as Michael, Gabriel, Raphael, and "divers angels, from Michael or Adam down to the present time" appeared to Joseph conferring upon him priesthood powers and keys that equipped him to successfully perform his labors (see D&C 128:20−21). Each one of these visitors obtained greatness in his own right and fulfilled his mission with faithfulness. The cumulative greatness of each is now focused on this one prophet, Joseph Smith, and the dispensation which he heads. The efforts of these former servants of God have or will come to fruition through the accomplishments of Joseph Smith and his successors.

Revealer of Truth

The greatness of the Prophet Joseph was particularly manifest in his ability to comprehend and clarify the doctrines of the gospel. The Lord told the Prophet that "this generation shall have my word through you'' (D&C 5:10). To a world that was steeped in spiritual darkness, the Lord, through the Prophet Joseph Smith, revealed the all-important concept of Deity. He restored to man in clarity the understanding that God was once as man now is and that God is now an exalted being. The Prophet thereby learned that the resurrection is a literal event, that the bodies we now have will be ours throughout eternity, and that as a product of righteous living, many may become as God is. God is not some mystical force, inattentive to man; nor is he some incomprehensible entity that is large enough to fill the immensity of space and small enough to dwell in one's heart. Rather, he is a kind, loving Father in Heaven who has concern for each of his children and has revealed a plan that will allow each of them the opportunity to receive all he has.

With this understanding of God came also an understanding of man. The Prophet taught that ''there are but a very few beings in the world who understand rightly the character of God. . . . If men do not comprehend the character of God, they do not comprehend themselves.''[5] The nature of God is inextricably tied to the nature of man. Man is of the same species with God, the spirit offspring of Deity. The fall of Adam was a fortunate event—not a tragedy, but rather a great act of love and compassion. The experiences of life can be positive and uplifting. The conditions on this earth, the role of Satan, the struggles and suffering of life can all be placed in their proper perspective due to the knowledge gained through the revelations and teachings delivered through a modern prophet.

It is also through the revelations received by Joseph Smith that a correct understanding of Jesus Christ and his atoning sacrifice has been gained. No greater witness of the power and importance of the Atonement can be found than in the revelations and translations that came through Joseph Smith. The Prophet made it possible for us to more fully understand Christ's suffering in Gethsemane and on Calvary and his atonement for all the sins of mankind, which made it possible for mercy to meet and fully satisfy the demands of justice for those who repent and strive to be as he is. Though these great messages are taught and believed by other Christian advocates, they are not presented with the clarity nor the power that characterized the words and writings of the Prophet Joseph.

As Elder Bruce R. McConkie said: "Every prophet is a witness of Christ; every dispensation head is a revealer of Christ for his day; and every other prophet or apostle who comes is a reflection and an echo and an exponent of the dispensation head. All such come to echo to the world and to expound and unfold what God has revealed through the man who was appointed for that era to give his eternal word to the world. Such is the dispensation concept."[6]

No other prophet of God has brought forth more scripture than has Joseph Smith. Through him the Lord revealed to the world the Book of Mormon; the writings of Moses, Enoch, and Abraham, as found in the Pearl of Great Price; the Doctrine and Covenants; an Inspired Translation of the Bible; and many other inspired statements found among his recorded sermons and personal history. Joseph Smith not only received and understood the teachings of other prophets, but he knew the prophets personally and could, therefore, describe clearly the meaning and intent of their writings. Through Joseph Smith the world has been given the great teachings of former dispensations, as well as further illuminating doctrines necessary for this last and most important dispensation.

Conclusion

One well-versed writer said of Joseph Smith: "He was beyond my comprehension."[7] A biographer and an acquaintance of Joseph Smith, George Q. Cannon wrote: "The Saints could not comprehend Joseph Smith; the Elders could not; the Apostles could not. They did do a little toward the close of his life; but his knowledge was so extensive and his comprehension so great that they could not rise to it."[8] Joseph's understanding was far beyond that of most mortals. The principles of eternity and the purposes of God were made known to him:

He understood things that were past, and comprehended the various dispensations and the designs of those dispensations. He not only had the principles developed, but he was conversant with the parties who officiated as the leading men of those dispensations, and from a number of them he received authority and keys and priesthood and power for the carrying out of the great purposes of the Lord in the last days, who were sent and commissioned specially by the Almighty to confer upon him those keys and this authority, and hence he introduced what was spoken of by all the prophets since the world was; the dispensation in which we live which differs from all other dispensations in that it is the dispensation of the fulness of times, embracing all other dispensations, all other powers, all other keys and all other privileges and immunities that ever existed upon the face of the earth.[9]

Surely when so viewed, Joseph Smith, Jr., accomplished more than any other mortal in offering salvation for every willing and repentant individual who ever lives on this earth. Undoubtedly, all those who preceded the Prophet Joseph in this great work would applaud such a conclusion and would confirm that their own efforts looked to this day and this dispensation for their ultimate expression and validation.

Notes

1. Wilford Woodruff, in *Journal History*, 9 April 1837.

2. Joseph Smith, *Teachings of the Prophet Joseph Smith,* comp. Joseph Fielding Smith (Salt Lake City: Deseret Book Co., 1976), p. 365.

3. Bruce R. McConkie, "This Generation Shall Have My Word Through You," in *Hearken O Ye People* (Sandy, Utah: Randall Book Co., 1984), p. 4.

4. See Hebrews 11:40; D&C 128:15; *Teachings of the Prophet Joseph Smith,* p. 356.

5. *Teachings of the Prophet Joseph Smith,* p. 343.

6. McConkie, "This Generation Shall Have My Word Through You," pp. 4–5.

7. Emmeline B. Wells, in *Young Women's Journal*, vol. 16, p. 556.

8. *Millennial Star,* 61:629.

9. John Taylor, in *Journal of Discourses*, 20:174–75.

Subject Index

Scripture Index

PEARL OF GREAT PRICE